Africans and Britons in t of Empires, 1660–1980

Africans and Britons in the Age of Empires, 1660–1980 tells the stories of the intertwined lives of African and British peoples over more than three centuries. In seven chapters and an epilogue, Myles Osborne and Susan Kingsley Kent explore the characters that comprised the British presence in Africa: the slave traders and slaves, missionaries and explorers, imperialists and miners, farmers, settlers, lawyers, chiefs, prophets, intellectuals, politicians, and soldiers of all colors.

The authors show how the oft-told narrative of a monolithic imperial power ruling inexorably over passive African victims has little basis in reality; rather, at every turn, Africans and Britons interacted with one another in a complex set of relationships that involved as much cooperation and negotiation as resistance and force, whether during the era of the slave trade, the world wars, or the period of decolonization. The British presence provoked a wide range of responses, reactions, and transformations in various aspects of African life; but at the same time, the experience of empire in Africa – and its ultimate collapse – also compelled the British to view themselves and their empire in new ways.

Written by an Africanist and a historian of imperial Britain and illustrated with maps and photographs, *Africans and Britons in the Age of Empires, 1660–1980* provides a uniquely rich perspective for understanding both African and British history.

Myles Osborne is Associate Professor of History at the University of Colorado Boulder. He received his PhD from Harvard University in 2008 and is the author of *Ethnicity and Empire in Kenya: Loyalty and Martial Race among the Kamba,* c. *1800 to the Present* (2014). He also recently edited *The Life and Times of General China: Mau Mau and the End of Empire in Kenya* (2015), and has published articles in a variety of journals including the *Journal of African History.*

Susan Kingsley Kent is Professor of History at the University of Colorado Boulder. Her publications include *Sex and Suffrage in Britain, 1860–1914*; *Making Peace: The Reconstruction of Gender in Interwar Britain*; *Gender and Power in Britain, 1640–1990*; *Aftershocks: Politics and Trauma in Interwar Britain*; *The Women's War of 1929: Gender and Violence in Colonial Nigeria*, with Misty Bastian and Marc Matera; *Gender and History*; and *Queen Victoria: Gender and Empire.*

Africans and Britons in the Age of Empires, 1660–1980

Myles Osborne and
Susan Kingsley Kent

Routledge
Taylor & Francis Group
LONDON AND NEW YORK

First published 2015
by Routledge
2 Park Square, Milton Park, Abingdon, Oxon OX14 4RN

and by Routledge
711 Third Avenue, New York, NY 10017

Routledge is an imprint of the Taylor & Francis Group, an informa business

British Library Cataloguing-in-Publication Data
A catalogue record for this book is available from the British Library

Library of Congress Cataloging-in-Publication Data
Osborne, Myles.
Africans and Britons in the age of empires, 1660–1980 / Myles Osborne and Susan Kingsley Kent.
pages cm
Includes bibliographical references and index.
1. Africa—Relations—Great Britain. 2. Great Britain—Relations—Africa. 3. British—Africa—History. 4. Africa—Colonial influence—History. 5. Great Britain—Colonies—Africa—History. I. Kent, Susan Kingsley, 1952 May 9– II. Title.
DT32.O83 2015
960.00421—dc23
2014039878

ISBN: 978-0-415-73752-4 (hbk)
ISBN: 978-0-415-73753-1 (pbk)
ISBN: 978-1-315-71904-7 (ebk)

Typeset in Sabon
by Apex CoVantage, LLC

MIX
Paper from responsible sources
FSC www.fsc.org FSC® C013604

Printed and bound by CPI Group (UK) Ltd, Croydon, CR0 4YY

For Anne and Jess

Contents

Figures

Maps

Acknowledgments

Myles Osborne: In 2009, as the newest hire in the History Department here in Boulder, I decided that volunteering to teach the senior capstone class with the department chair was a sensible diplomatic move. Little did I realize that Susan and I would end up teaching "The British Empire in Africa" four additional times in the four years that followed. Given our different perspectives – my own as an Africanist, and Susan's as a historian of imperial Britain – the course quickly took on a life of its own: it was challenging and fascinating, with a healthy dose of humor and friendly banter sprinkled over the top.

Perhaps our greatest challenge, however, was finding a text that spoke to both the experiences of the Africans and Britons that comprised our cast of characters; there was simply nothing out there that did justice to the rich subject matter. Consequently, as early as 2010, we were discussing ways to write a suitable book for the course, and moreover, one that described our own views of the interplay between Africans and Britons over this long period. The book quickly took on a life of its own as we lectured together, debated, and discussed our topics over a number of years, and we came to conclude that it also provided an opportunity to create a broader work of scholarship that – given its unique perspective – would hopefully provide Africanists with new insights about the British presence in Africa, and historians of Britain with similar understandings of Africa.

First and foremost, therefore, I am grateful to Susan Kent for her erudite research, good humor, and friendship that made co-teaching – and the writing of this book – a tremendously enjoyable experience, probably far more so than writing any book should be. Second, the students from all five years of our course have helped us to question our views in new ways; their contributions are embedded here too. And finally, I am especially grateful to friends and colleagues who took time away from their own work to read and offer comments and suggestions on the chapters that follow: they include Matt Carotenuto, Andy DeRoche, Meghan Healy-Clancy, Matt Heaton, Neil Kodesh, Paul Ocobock, Harmony O'Rourke, Ed Steinhart, and Bill Worger. Emmanuel Akyeampong offered his thoughts on the first chapter, and then both he and Antoinette Burton graciously agreed to read the entire manuscript and offer their views, in spite of other pressing commitments.

Susan Kent: In the years spent teaching and writing with Myles, I have learned a great deal. About Africa, certainly, but more importantly, I have come to know this Everest-climbing, Antarctic-marathon-running, irrepressible world traveler to be a kind, considerate, deeply moral individual whose humor, intelligence, and grace have made this book project a delight. He is a scrupulous scholar, an exciting teacher, a wonderful colleague, and an even better friend.

A number of people have given their time and expertise to help bring this book to fruition. I wish to thank Aaron Windel for his support and encouragement. Marc Matera steered me toward a number of issues and the sources with which to address them; our conversations made me think differently. Bonnie Smith gave us the benefit of her erudition, experience, and wide-ranging knowledge of history; she caught my mistakes, offered alternative interpretations, and made this a far better book. We are in their debt.

Together we wish to acknowledge the invaluable contributions of our editors at Routledge, who have provided welcome direction, advice, and assistance. We would like to thank Eve Setch for her help in the initial stages of the project and Amy Welmers for her continual and ongoing oversight. She never took her eye off the ball and the combination of her warmth and professionalism kept us on task. We also extend our appreciation to our copyeditor, Lana Arndt, and our project manager, Renata Corbani, for their careful work on our behalf. The anonymous reviewers of our manuscript offered useful critiques, for which we are grateful, and Glynis Osborne and Linda Woods kindly read the page proofs, saving us from several errors. We also greatly appreciate an award from the Eugene M. Kayden Fund at the University of Colorado, which enabled us to provide the maps and images included here.

Finally, our respective partners, Jess Leigh and Anne Davidson, made it possible for us to devote the time and energy necessary to write *Africans and Britons* in a relatively short period of time. We thank them for variously tolerating our antisocial discussions about the British empire at dinnertimes, removing wild Great Danes from our writing spaces, taking extra shifts at the barn, and generously agreeing to take responsibility for any and all errors that appear in the text. We dedicate this book to them.

The publishers would like to thank Corbis Images and Bridgeman Images for permission to reproduce the images in this book, and Hugh Masekela and Semopa Entertainment for permission to reproduce lyrics from the song "Stimela."

Introduction

Africans and Britons

In 1890, a Kikuyu leader named Waiyaki wa Hinga provided shelter and provisions to an appreciative Captain Frederick Lugard. Waiyaki was a prominent and wealthy landowning warrior, trader, and elder; Lugard, the leader of a caravan of British adventurers in the employ of the Imperial British East Africa Company (IBEAC), making its precarious and arduous way through Kenya to Uganda. Lugard had arrived in East Africa with instructions to build a fort and administrative center where other caravans headed for Uganda could stop to replenish their supplies. Waiyaki provided the site at Dagoretti, located on the edge of his cultivated lands and his village, and assisted in the building of the fort. Lugard found Waiyaki to be "extremely intelligent, good-mannered, and most friendly," and he cemented their friendship in a ceremony that made them blood-brothers.[1] The thin, mustachioed graduate of the Royal Military College at Sandhurst made peace treaties with several other local leaders too. It bode well for British-Kikuyu relations.

Just two years later, after a series of attacks by IBEAC forces on Kikuyu clans had left nearly a thousand people dead and numerous villages destroyed, an inebriated Waiyaki drew his sword against a young colonial official named W. P. Purkiss. Purkiss was in charge of Kikuyu Province – a newly created British administrative territory – and had tried to turn Waiyaki out of his office at Fort Smith, the company's new fort a few miles from Dagoretti. In his intoxicated state, Waiyaki was little match for Purkiss, who disarmed him and delivered a blow to Waiyaki's head. Waiyaki spent the night in the fort's square "handcuffed to the flagstaff with a chain around his neck as an additional safeguard," and he was tried the next day for assault.[2] Found guilty, he was marched in chains under heavy guard toward the coastal city of Mombasa for deportation, but never made it. He died from his injuries en route. Waiyaki's death symbolized the deterioration of British–Kikuyu relations, from a mutually beneficial agreement based on trade to one marred by hostility and enmity. Waiyaki had pressed other Kikuyu elders to work with Lugard and his colleagues, despite their misgivings. Now, it seemed, they had been right.

In the interactions of Waiyaki wa Hinga and Frederick Lugard we have a window into the dynamics that characterized the dealings between Africans and Britons between 1660 and 1980. They shifted constantly: beneficial relationships of trade morphed into war, and war gave way to commerce, sometimes on equal terms, at others, less so. At times, British colonialism inspired rivalries among various African groups, whereas at others, they joined forces to meet the new challenges. British systems of law and order threatened the autonomy of certain peoples, while providing new protections for others. Some prospered economically from the new foreign presence, building wealth and power, while others fared poorly. In some instances, the British presence was tangential to shifting dynamics of social and political ordering among African peoples. All of these encounters took place in an environment frequently marked by misunderstanding, confusion, and arrogance.

A deeper look into the lives of Waiyaki and Lugard reveals some of the misconceptions that typified relations between Africans and Britons during the period under study. A man involved in all three phases of the British presence in Africa – exploration, annexation, and administration – Lugard was regarded as "the chief agent of British rule in that continent in his generation."[3] He chased slavers in Nyasaland in 1888, claimed Uganda for Britain in 1890, and ended his career as the governor-general of Nigeria. Like most Britons at the time, Lugard believed that Africans lived in neat, discrete "tribes" run by "chiefs," and he therefore viewed Waiyaki as the leader of a vast horde of Kikuyu over whom he possessed complete political authority.

But Lugard was wrong on two scores. First, Waiyaki's father – Hinga – was born to Maasai parents; Waiyaki and his mother had fled to a Kikuyu village during a time of famine and "become Kikuyu." Waiyaki's adoption into a Kikuyu clan was a common experience in nineteenth-century Africa: what the British saw as hard and fast "tribes" were in actuality flexible groupings into which one might move depending on economic or environmental needs. Nor was Waiyaki a "chief," as Lugard thought. Waiyaki's ownership of property and his relationships with Swahili and Arab traders in the region had enabled him to amass a substantial estate on which a large number of landless people worked and lived. Property and wealth permitted him to become powerful and win respect and to earn the title of *muthamaki*, or leader. But he was no "chief" with widespread authority; instead, he led a relatively small group of Kikuyu living in and around his home. Thus when Kikuyu raiders from other villages harassed or stole from British caravans, company officials blamed Waiyaki. They held him responsible for the actions of men far beyond his remit.

In Lugard's career, we find a microcosm of the progress of the British in Africa. From adventurer and soldier of fortune to military commander and administrator, Lugard's path paralleled that of Britain as a nation as it ventured – at first tentatively and grudgingly, and then confidently and aggressively – into Africa, transforming commercial outposts and tiny pockets of close control into full-blown colonies. At every point – as Waiyaki's story shows – colonial agents depended upon the cooperation of Africans to accomplish their ends. African peoples often exploited the colonial presence to negotiate better conditions for themselves, often to the dismay or annoyance of British administrators.

In the following chapters we explore the complex relationships between Africans and Britons in all kinds of roles and settings. We treat slave traders and the men and women engaged in "legitimate" commerce; missionaries and their converts; British officers and African soldiers; judges and the accused; settlers and farm laborers; mine owners and mine workers; British "men on the spot" – like Lugard – and the indigenous men they established as their indirect rulers. We also consider the interactions between Africans in which British personnel did not directly appear: government-appointed chiefs and those they tried to force into compulsory labor; "collaborators" and "loyalists"; husbands and wives; elders and young men. These diverse groups often disagreed with one another; they struggled over such issues as the imposition of Christianity or Islam, land alienation, customary law, appropriate gender roles, race, and imperial control. The narrative we present below belies any simplistic treatment of Britain as the implacable aggressor ruling over hapless, benighted African subjects. The story is far more complicated than that.

Africa before Britain

Africa was, of course, no blank slate patiently awaiting the arrival of British visitors (though several respected historians writing as late as the 1960s seemed to believe just that). The continent played host to an extraordinarily diverse human population – both linguistically and phenotypically – which participated in a patchwork of political and social institutions that often bewildered (or simply escaped the notice of) the British.

Explorers and missionaries were intimidated by Africa's linguistic diversity. Africans spoke around 1500 different languages in 1900, approximately one-quarter of the world's total. All, however, belonged to one of only four language families: Afro-Asiatic, Nilo-Saharan, Khoisan, and Niger-Congo, with the majority of peoples living in central and southern Africa speaking only one sub-group of the Niger-Congo languages, called Bantu.[4] Historically, this enabled peoples living medium and long distances away from one another to communicate, an advantage in activities like trading. But more importantly, it meant that families who were forced to migrate due to famine or drought could quickly integrate into new communities. It was reasonably easy to pick up unfamiliar languages when they had similar verb and noun structures. European visitors were frustrated by the fact that African languages featured little of the consistency or stability brought by the written vocabularies, dictionaries, and grammar books with which they had grown up. Moreover, they viewed the fact that the majority of peoples did not use the written word as a mode of expression – preferring to record their histories in oral narratives – as a sign of Africa's "backwardness."

Physically, Africans exhibited (as today) a far greater diversity of appearance than their British visitors. The San (or pejoratively – but commonly – "Bushmen") living in the desert margins of southern Africa were slightly built with yellowish skin. Far to the north, many speakers of Afro-Asiatic languages living in the Saharan littoral were white. In the central African forests, pygmoid peoples were short and stocky, with skin tinged red, while many Bantu speakers in West and East Africa were closer to the stereotypical "black" African color. The explanation for this phenotypic breadth derives from the history of *Homo sapiens*: because modern humans have lived in Africa for approximately 150,000 years longer than in Europe, we have had longer to diverge from our ancestors here. The picture is further complicated by those whose appearance reflects Melanesian genes (like the inhabitants of Madagascar) or Indian genes (like the Asian inhabitants of East or South Africa).

African peoples organized themselves in a variety of different sorts of political groupings, which ranged from vast, bureaucratic empires in West Africa to tiny bands of nomadic hunters and gatherers in the deserts of the south. We know much about Africa's great empires (like Mali, Bornu, Oyo, or Asante – see Chapter 1) because they received detailed description in the words of Arab travelers like Ibn Battuta or Ibn Khaldun, who were a constant presence in West Africa from the eighth century onward. These empires boasted phenomenal wealth and dominant armies and left monuments to their success. Hunter-gatherers, too – like the Sandawe of Tanzania, or San of southern Africa – have long fascinated western scholars and observers. But the majority of peoples on the continent lived in smaller-scale societies. Most were organized around the extended family, or village, or clan, with wider networks only present in common consciousness through semi-annual events like dances (perhaps with neighboring villages) or through hunting or trading.

The core organizing principle in these small-scale societies was "wealth in people." Before the twentieth century – with exceptions such as the states of Buganda and Bunyoro in Uganda, or polities in the Nile valley – land had little value in Africa because it was in practically limitless supply in most areas. People, on the other hand, *were* valuable because of their labor power, which was so necessary for survival. Historically, societies such as these were polygynous: a man married to four women might produce 20 children in a decade, whereas one wife might bear only five, hence limiting the speed of population growth. But there are also examples of polyandry from sub-Saharan African history. In the eighteenth century, when faced with a need to clear the thick forests of West Africa's interior, Akan women married male slaves, who were purchased to do the hard work; but the slaves were denied community rights.

It is impossible to understand the centrality of labor for most societies throughout African history without taking the environment into account. Farmers in Africa face a series of challenges from which their colleagues in

France or Kansas are exempt. These include, most prominently, the vagaries of rainfall. Though the extreme northern and southern ends of the African continent have a Mediterranean climate, the majority is "tropical" – lying between the tropics of Capricorn and Cancer – where seasons are determined by the presence or absence of precipitation. From Nigeria to Zimbabwe, the rain comes in either one or two seasons (one in locations near the tropic lines and two nearer the equator) as a result of shifting pressure zones and climatic phenomena on and beyond the African continent. The only areas that do not experience these patterns are those of sufficiently high altitude, which trumps latitude in places like central Kenya's highlands. These rainy seasons last for two to three months, during which time thunderstorms produce rain almost every day. The rain is both a blessing and a curse: in the right amounts – at the right times – it can produce a bounty of crops. But if too little rain comes the crops do not have a chance to grow; too much, and the soil becomes waterlogged and erosion is a problem. In addition, large volumes of rain drag nutrients from the topsoil too far down into the earth to be useful for plants (a process known as "leaching").

Once the rains end difficulties persist: the sun will soon bake the soil to the consistency of concrete. Unless this "pan" is broken up the following season's planting cannot take place. Africans have typically undertaken this physically demanding task by hand rather than use horse-, donkey-, or oxen-drawn plows because of a disease called trypanosomiasis. Manifesting in humans as "sleeping sickness," this disease appears in many parts of Africa and is fatal to beasts of burden. As a result of these limitations, human labor was vital for survival in small-scale societies, and still is today in many countries.

Further difficulties compound those of erratic rainfall and disease, meaning that much of the African continent is poorly equipped for growing crops. Large swathes of Africa are covered by desert: these include, famously, the Sahara in the north and the Kalahari in the south, but arid conditions exist in areas such as northern Kenya as well, with the result that the region is practically uninhabited. Rainforests too – such as the band stretching from the Gambia river in West Africa across to the Great Lakes in the east-central highlands – can be extremely barren ecologically. In addition, soil across the continent often lacks sufficient humus content to render it fertile (humus is decaying organic matter that releases nutrients into the soil). In Iowa's best farms, for example, humus content can reach as much as 16 percent, and 10 to 12 percent is common in the central United States. In tropical Africa, however, it typically falls below 2 percent.[5] Historically, African peoples have negotiated these limitations by using techniques such as slash-and-burn agriculture, participating in livestock rearing, and/or growing different types of crops, but the only real solution for exhausted land is to let it lie fallow for a decade or more in order to regenerate – an impossible proposition in the twenty-first century given the need for food and recent population increases that have made good land scarce. Because of these environmental factors that have placed labor at a premium – and contrary to British

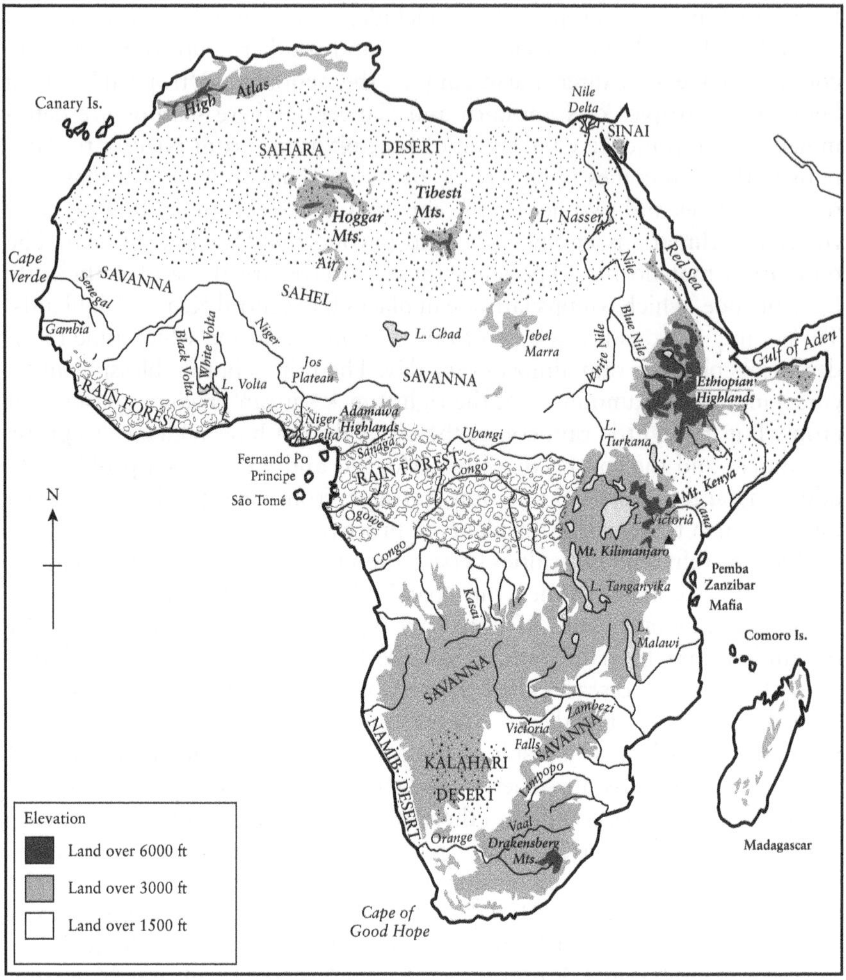

Map 0.1 Environmental and topographical zones of Africa

conceptions about African savagery and endemic violence – African peoples have historically *avoided* conflict as much as possible, preferring to mediate disputes peacefully and not risk their labor resources.

British explorers and missionaries had little intellectual foundation to help prepare them for their time in Africa. First – following popular ideas of Social Darwinism – they supposed that Africans had not yet reached the stage of "civilization" to develop "proper" political institutions. The British, after all, regarded the nation-state and its systems of government as the pinnacle of political development. Second, they viewed African societies as non-hierarchical and therefore lacking in proper leadership, because few men seemed to demonstrate greater trappings of wealth than others. Back home, of course, their country was run by prominent men whose positions of power were demonstrated by spotless suits, powdered wigs, and ornate carriages. Third, they assumed that Africans lived in discrete "tribes," a belief that originated in the Enlightenment desire to classify and organize the natural world.

As a result of these assumptions, explorers drastically misunderstood the ways African societies were in fact organized. First, European-style bureaucracies were unsuited and unnecessary for areas of low population density like sub-Saharan Africa, where they would have proved a waste of resources. Second, prominent community leaders did exist, but they did not distinguish themselves with material goods. Instead, they demonstrated their wealth and power through their ability to control large numbers of people, and therefore resources: the richest men were those who had vast extended families and enjoyed close bonds with peoples living some distance from them. In addition – and unlike in Europe at the time – women played a direct role in political organization. And third, neatly bounded "tribes" almost never existed in sub-Saharan Africa before 1900. Instead, people moved easily between groups as circumstances dictated and almost always found welcome wherever they went, owing to the value of their labor and the increased security greater numbers produced.

The qualities that male and female leaders were expected to exhibit varied widely across sub-Saharan Africa before 1900. Common to most was talent in passing judgment and reaching consensus, both essential skills in the councils of family, village, or clan that headed most societies. Some could predict or call the rain, an important attribute in marginal parts of the continent. Others demonstrated an ability to predict the future or communicate with dead ancestors. Among some still-existing hunter-gatherer societies, knowledge of hunting and pathways through the wilderness was important. Old age in itself did not necessarily bring respect, but was a strong indication that a man or woman was in some way favored: in the insecure world of early Africa, a person did not reach 50 or 60 years of age without the assent of the spirit world, and if they had produced many children, the respect they commanded was further heightened. Rarely did birthright hold weight; these societies could not afford the liability of a weak leader with a powerful father or mother who did not demonstrate that he or she could lead the community.

In many regions of higher altitude – such as east-central Africa's highlands or the Zimbabwe plateau – cattle played a central role in social organization, and the owner of a large herd was a person of authority. At higher elevations tsetse fly – the vector for trypanosomiasis – could not survive. Cattle were sometimes valuable as a source of food but this was rarely their primary function, and indeed many communities had prohibitions against slaughtering them except in emergencies or as part of a specific ritual practice (the Xhosa of southern Africa, for instance, consider a cow's bellow as it is slaughtered to be a form of communication with dead ancestors). The true value of the animals derived from their role in permitting the expansion of the kin group, usually via marriage.

In many communities marriage could not take place without the payment of bridewealth, a sum given by a young man to his prospective bride's family that was paid at least in part in cattle. Young men did not own herds of cattle and thus relied on their older (usually male) relatives or extended families to provide the beasts. Young men spent many sleepless nights worrying about this issue; without a wife, a man – irrespective of age – was forever a child, unable to achieve the honor or respect that came with adulthood. The mechanism also served to keep social order. Young men were unlikely to misbehave with this sword of Damocles hanging over their heads.

The many British travelers, explorers, missionaries, and administrators who poured onto the continent after the 1870s missed or ignored many of the instruments and systems of organization that characterized African societies. To be sure, British merchants and traders had been engaged in trade with West Africa for two centuries by that time; and in South Africa, British settlers had established stable communities in Natal and the Cape Colony. But with these exceptions, Africa was something of a blank slate. All of that changed abruptly starting in the 1870s, when a "scramble for Africa" took place among the major European powers. Over the next 30 years or so, Europeans eager to stake their claims over the lands and peoples of the continent gobbled up African territory. In 1870, Europeans held around 10 percent of Africa's territory; by 1900, they had carved up fully 90 percent of the continent. Britain took possession of the greatest share.

We use the term "British empire" as if it was a single authoritative entity that exercised hegemonic rule over its colonies; in fact, the empire possessed no geographical, administrative, political, or economic coherence. It was comprised of a bewildering array of colonies of occupation, colonies of settlement, protectorates, suzerainties, mandates, and trusteeships, and all of them posed challenges of their own. No two colonies were alike, and over time they might change from one kind to another, as, for instance, the British government formally claimed control over an area previously administered by a private trading company.

The actors of empire, moreover, demonstrated the same kind of diversity and impermanence of occupation that characterized the British colonies in Africa. A man might start out in Africa in one guise – as a soldier and adventurer working for a commercial operation, say – and over the space of 20 years gradually transform himself into a high-ranking colonial official. Explorers such as Richard Burton and missionaries like David Livingstone; commercial ventures such as the British South Africa Company led by Cecil Rhodes or the Royal Niger Company under George Goldie; military commanders, colonial administrators, and politicians (sometimes one and the same person, at least at some point over the course of their careers); anthropologists and historians like Margaret Green or Margery Perham; and characters of all stripes, good and bad – these were the men and women whose beliefs, thoughts, actions, personalities, temperaments, talents, skills, disabilities, interests, and power made the British empire in Africa what it was: a confusing agglomeration of missionizing, educating, exploiting, and frequent contradiction.

Just as "the British empire in Africa" was no single thing, the Africans it ruled and the Africans through whom it ruled must not be thought of as monolithic. The continent possesses such climatological, topographical, environmental, historical, ethnic, political, social, cultural, and economic diversity as to constitute a whole range of different worlds and different peoples who populate those worlds. Consequently, African responses to the British presence varied by age, gender, ethnicity, location, status, religion, and more. Nuance and variety characterized all of the relationships between Africans and Britons between 1660 and 1980, and nowhere was this more evident than in the interactions that followed the arrival of the first British ships on the West African coast in the middle of the seventeenth century.

Notes

1 Quoted in L.S.B. Leakey, *The Southern Kikuyu before 1903*, Vol. I (London: Academic Press, 1977), 73.
2 Quoted in Godfrey Muriuki, *A History of the Kikuyu, 1500–1900* (Nairobi: Oxford University Press, 1974), 149.
3 Margery Perham, "Introduction," in *The Diaries of Lord Lugard*, Vol. I, ed. Margery Perham (Evanston, IL: Northwestern University Press, 1959), 13.
4 If one takes into account the island of Madagascar, however, there is a fifth language family: the indigenous language of Malagasy is an Austronesian language, as a result of settlers from Borneo who landed on the island during the early first millennium.
5 Paul Bohannan and Philip Curtin, *Africa & Africans*, 4th edn. (Long Grove, IL: Waveland Press, 1995), 23.

Bibliography

Bohannan, Paul, and Philip Curtin. *Africa & Africans*, 4th edn. Long Grove, IL: Waveland Press, 1995.

Iliffe, John. *Africans: The History of a Continent*, 2nd edn. Cambridge: Cambridge University Press, 2007.

Leakey, L.S.B. *The Southern Kikuyu Before 1903*, Vol. I. London: Academic Press, 1977.

McCann, James. *Green Land, Brown Land, Black Land: An Environmental History of Africa, 1800–1990*. Portsmouth, NH: Heinemann, 1999.

Muriuki, Godfrey. *A History of the Kikuyu, 1500–1900*. Nairobi: Oxford University Press, 1974.

Perham, Margery. "Introduction." In *The Diaries of Lord Lugard*, Vol. I, edited by Margery Perham. Evanston, IL: Northwestern University Press, 1959.

1 The slave trade, abolition, and beyond, c. 1600–1840s

In the late 1780s, an Efik trader named Antera Duke followed an identical morning routine. From his bed in Duke Town, east of the Niger Delta, he arose between 3 and 5 AM (groggily, we imagine, given his almost constant use of alcohol) and walked down to the beach at Aqua Landing. From the beach Duke would scan the ships lying at anchor, all lined up and preparing to receive their human cargo for transport across the Atlantic to islands like Jamaica and Barbados. Many he could identify instantly by the outline of their masts and rigging. He knew their captains personally, having "broken book" – engaged in trading agreements – with them. It was his job to know these details; after all, slave trading was his business.

The slave trade had catapulted the small fishing village of Duke Town into a wealthy commercial center, an economic transformation that a number of villages in Old Calabar, a region in the eastern section of the Bight of Biafra in West Africa, experienced. The merchants of Duke Town, Old Town, and Creek Town – all situated close to one another in the Cross river estuary – competed with each other for larger stakes in the trade and with the bigger towns of Bonny and New Calabar in the western section of the Bight. In the mid-1780s the end of the American War of Independence (1776–1783), which had caused something of a recession in the slave trade, magnified the competition. Duke and his men had responded quickly by diversifying their goods beyond slaves to include large quantities of peppers and ivory.

Duke Town's leading men were on first-name terms with British slavers, who comprised the majority of those Europeans who arrived in Old Calabar. They spoke a form of trade English that permitted them intercourse with their British partners and they made sure that their sons received careful instruction in the English language (some even sent them to school in Britain for further studies). Their sons would eventually join the senior men of the families in a secret and much-feared order called Ekpe ("leopard").

Duke and his colleagues had gained power through profitable slave trading, and the trade itself underwrote their positions. They sold slaves in exchange for prestige goods that demonstrated their status and distributed these items widely to various groups of people to build bonds of personal allegiance. Slaves also played a central role in social ordering. For example, in July 1786 at the funeral of Duke Ephraim – the head of the family – Antera Duke and his men killed slaves to honor Ephraim's memory. They believed that the dead slaves (nine in this case) would accompany him into the afterlife. On another occasion, a similar kind of episode involved 50 slaves, and occasionally the severed heads were kicked about like soccer balls.[1]

Ultimately – inexorably – individuals, communities, and empires in West and west-central Africa found themselves drawn into the vortex of the trans-Atlantic slave trade. As with anything related to the human experience, motives were complex and wide-ranging. Beneath the greed, religious motives, desire for political gain or increased security, and other drivers that animated the commerce in human beings, there seemed to lie a commanding and unifying logic, as true for individuals as it was for empires: enslave, or be enslaved. Ummi Hammid – the granddaughter of the notorious Zanzibari slave trader Tippu Tip – perhaps put it best: "It was the trend of the time. . . . You either be a slave or a slaver."[2]

In many respects slavery served as the lynchpin of the British presence in Africa. The numbers are staggering: between 1556 and 1810, 3.2 million out of the total 12.5 million Africans who made their voyage west did so aboard British vessels.[3] Few returned. The trade brought Britons into intimate contact with African peoples and enriched a crucial segment of British society. But even as the abolitionist movement took hold during the late eighteenth century, it did little to reduce Britain's level of interaction with the continent. Efforts to rid Africa of the evil that was slavery compelled missionary societies to journey to the land about which they knew little but presumed much. And a variety of other "legitimate" trading expeditions soon followed the abolition of the slave trade in 1807, drawing Britons into ever-increasing levels of contact with the continent. By 1807, the British presence was felt keenly not just in West Africa, but also in South Africa, where the declaration of a colony in the western Cape after 1806 (the "Cape Colony") would have long-term repercussions for Africans, resulting in the spread of white dominance throughout the region by the mid-nineteenth century.

European-African relations before 1660

Given the horrors of the slave trade and the tempestuous history of colonialism that followed, we tend to focus our gaze exclusively on slave trading when we think of European-African relations before the scramble for Africa. There are a variety of dangers in this approach. First, we forget that for some years before 1660 Britons had relatively little interest in African slaves; second, we ignore the fact that other slave trades from the African continent existed beyond that in the Atlantic world; and third, we often assume that all relations between Europeans and Africans put the latter at a disadvantage, whereas in fact the opposite was often true. If we are to truly grasp the import of the slave trade we must place it within the wider chronology of European-African relations, which included not just the exchange of slaves but other material goods too, as well as ideas, languages, religious practices, and culture.

Contact between Africans and Europeans existed at a significant level before the era of the slave trade. Small numbers of Africans had appeared in Europe in various guises for two centuries by 1600; they ranged from Ethiopian diplomats serving in Lisbon to West African slaves in central Europe. And by the time British ships began arriving in West Africa in large numbers in the early eighteenth century, many coastal peoples had become familiar with the range of religious ideas, trading goods, and characteristics of these pale-skinned visitors. This was because Portuguese ships had plied trade with West Africa since the 1430s, and other European peoples had appeared in ever-increasing numbers during the following century.

The peoples of West Africa enjoyed a complex and extensive trading system that was in place long before the European arrival. The system was not oriented toward the coast but north toward the "inland sea" of the Sahara, and complemented by east-to-west movement through the lagoon systems near the coast. West Africa's distinctive geography – comprised of a series of shifting horizontal climatic bands running from east to west – catalyzed this trade. In the north, the Sahara (meaning "desert" in Arabic) is dry and rain is rare, but it contains excellent sources of salt. (Caravans had also brought goods from the Mediterranean world across the Sahara in significant quantities since the eighth century.) Below the Sahara, the sahel ("shore" in Arabic) receives enough rain to make it ideal for pasturing domesticated animals like cattle, goats, or sheep. Further south lies the savanna, where much of the Niger river runs. Here rainfall levels permit the growth of crops like rice, sorghum, cassava, millet, and maize (the latter brought to West Africa in Portuguese ships around 1500). Between the savanna and the coast thick forests dominate the landscape; here, much of the region's gold and kola nuts are found. Finally, the coastal areas yield bountiful supplies of salt and products like fish. This climatic diversity has meant, historically, that each part of West Africa produces something that its neighbors to the north or south do not, creating an extraordinary stimulus for trade that has underwritten polities ranging from the Almoravids of Morocco to the Songhay of the Niger Bend to the Hausa city states further to the east. At the coast this system was supported by the activities of skilled, Ewe-speaking mariners who operated canoes made from single tree trunks. They shifted goods east and west between modern-day southeastern Ghana and southwestern Nigeria, using the lagoon system. Their skills and networks would soon become useful in stimulating and assisting the slave trade.

Europeans had to try to fit into this well-established and vibrant system of commerce if they wished to engage in trade with African peoples. It required hard work. In some areas they paid taxes to the local elites in order to get permission to trade or construct buildings. In others European men married African women to take advantage of their family connections and the women's trading networks, both regional and long-range. European traders were frustrated to find that neither their cloth nor iron products were superior to those already in production on the continent and they often had to accept bottom-drawer prices to shift their cargoes. Africans were delighted to trade their gums, spices, ivory, peppers, and gold for the iron implements, ornate jewelry, cloth, pots, or alcohol that Europeans brought, but in truth, the foreign ships brought nothing Africans actually *needed* or could not live without.

The first British ships that arrived on the West African coast before 1641 were little interested in slaves (though the explorer John Hawkins gained notoriety as the first Englishman to transport slaves to the New World in 1562). They focused primarily on gold and on protecting any they might procure from the covetous hands of other European powers. For by the mid-sixteenth century, the Portuguese, French, Dutch, Danish, Swedish, and Spanish all competed for trade in West Africa. As a result, the first European buildings that appeared on West Africa's beaches – like Elmina and Cape Coast castles – were fortresses designed to secure gold. (The buildings were later used to store slaves for transport, earning them the still-used moniker "slave castles.") The majority of West African gold passed through the area roughly contiguous with contemporary Ghana, which inspired Europeans to label the region "Gold Coast," a name the British gave to their protectorate there after 1901.

European powers – especially the Portuguese – made periodic efforts to use physical force to compel trade and gain influence in Africa during the fifteenth and sixteenth centuries, but by and large these efforts were few and far between, as it became quickly apparent that friendly trading relations were far more efficient in generating profits. Two additional factors encouraged this approach. First, the armies of large empires like Asante, Oyo, or Dahomey (all in existence during the eighteenth century) could have obliterated any landing party of armed European sailors with ease. Second, the disease environment made it almost impossible for Europeans to sustain their health on the African coast, making any notions of a military campaign unthinkable. Approximately 50 percent of Europeans who set foot on the continent at this time died from "fever," usually malaria. Europeans believed that the swampy, humid air at the coast was responsible for their sickness, though the term *malaria* (from the Italian *mala aria,* meaning "bad air") was not used in the English language until 1740.

The slave trade

After 1680, slaves became the most important commodity traded between Africans and Europeans. The numbers peaked late in the eighteenth century. In the 1780s, Antera Duke and his band probably contributed several thousand of the 867,993 slaves that left Africa that decade for the Americas.

The trade's impact was greater on men than on women (approximately two-thirds of slaves were men) and on adults than children (60 percent of slaves were adults). Slaves were greatly desired as labor in the New World, especially on sugar plantations, but also on those producing coffee and tobacco, which sucked up an almost inexhaustible supply. The variety of trade goods exchanged between Africans and Europeans became far more simplified; Europeans predominantly sold firearms to Africans in exchange for slaves. Technological advancements in Britain meant that factories could produce large numbers of firearms rapidly and efficiently. In 1682 an African trader could expect to exchange a slave for two guns; in 1718 he might expect as many as 32 guns in return for a single slave.

The British expansion in slave trading from the late seventeenth century was in part due to the Spanish loss of its hold on the monopoly. With the culmination of the War of the Spanish Succession in 1713, Britain and Spain reached an agreement in the Treaty of Utrecht that granted Britain the exclusive possession of the *asiento*, the right to supply slaves to Spain's colonies in the Americas. In the years between 1700 and 1810 some 6.5 million African men and women were sold as slaves and carried across the Atlantic Ocean in the holds of slave ships. Until about 1750, by which time the natural increase amongst the slaves in North America could be counted upon to meet the demand for their labor, British slavers sold their human wares to colonists in North America and the West Indies. After 1750 the slave trade was largely confined to the West Indies and to Brazil, and despite the decline of North American markets for newly transported slaves the trade continued to flourish. Britons managed fully one-quarter of the world's slave trade up to 1791 and more than half of it between 1791 and 1806. Ships hailing from the port towns of Bristol, London, and Liverpool carried the majority of slaves to the Americas; their owners grew wealthy and powerful.

Life on the plantations was harsh. In the eighteenth century, the life expectancy of slave women reached only 25.5 years; men could expect to live only 23 years. Certainly, living conditions contributed to the heavy mortality of plantation life, but the greatest killer proved to be disease. Dysentery and malaria carried off perhaps one-third of newly arrived slaves. Unlike in North America, natural increase could not sustain slave populations in Brazil or the Caribbean islands; the great mortality rates of slaves in the West Indies ensured that the slave trade would only increase in volume.

The slave trade constituted one crucial leg of the triangular trade between Britain, Africa, and the Atlantic colonies. British ships carried between one-quarter and one-half of all African slaves sold in the Americas in the second half of the eighteenth century. Those same ships then carried cargoes of spices, tobacco, rum, molasses, but especially sugar to the North American colonies and to Britain, where demand for the sweetener had risen astronomically by 1775. Once in England, the ships took on cargoes of manufactured goods such as textiles, brass pans, copper rods, iron bars and bowls, beads, pots and pans, beer, and, increasingly, muskets and gunpowder, and sailed to West Africa, where agents traded them for slaves. African demand for manufactured items was considerable, accounting for about 25 percent of Britain's cotton exports in 1792. Exports of wrought-iron goods to Africa were second only to those to the American colonies at mid-century. Demand for these items in Africa played a large part in stimulating British manufacturing, as did the demand of the Caribbean colonists, who consumed some 12 percent of English manufactured goods between 1748 and 1776.

The use of slave labor in the West Indian and North American colonies made it possible for small populations of white colonists to exploit the resources – largely sugar and tobacco – of those areas profitably. Slavery therefore stood at the crossroads of foreign trade, colonization, and consumer demands – both domestic and foreign – that stimulated economic growth; it was central, in many ways, to the development of the British economy of the eighteenth century. Much imperial trade was driven by domestic demand for a small number of agricultural products: coffee, tea, chocolate, sugar, and tobacco. By 1700 or so Britain had become one of the chief consumers of coffee in Europe, but unlike the French and the Dutch, the British turned to tea by 1750 in consequence of the East India Company forcing it onto the market. By that time, the British were importing £40 million worth of tea each year. The consumption of sugar tended to follow the patterns established by coffee and tea. Although sugar constituted only a small portion of Britons' food budgets, it became an important and then necessary component of people's diets. Placed in tea it provided a vital source of calories to those involved in heavy labor and working long hours. Added to what Britons considered inferior grains – like oats or rice – sugar supplemented the food supply by rendering those grains more palatable. Exports of sugar from the British West Indies increased from 25,000 tons in 1700 to 97,000 tons in 1770. In 1700 Britons were consuming some four pounds of sugar per person each year; that number had risen to eight pounds a year by 1750 and to 18 pounds a year by the early nineteenth century.

Slavery produced great wealth. West Indian planters used slave labor to generate profits from the sale of sugar; slaves owned by the American colonists produced tobacco and cotton that were sold to manufacturers in England. With their profits colonists purchased commodities from Manchester, Birmingham, London, Sheffield, Glasgow, and Leeds, enriching the manufacturers of those items. The ships that carried African slaves to the Americas, raw materials to Britain, and manufactured goods to Africa and the American and West Indian colonies realized generous profits from their transport, as did the insurance companies that protected their cargoes and the banks that financed them. The great financiers – the bankers and insurers – built fortunes that made them attractive to Britain's landed elites, who sought appropriate marriage partners for their younger sons and daughters. The amalgamation of land – held by the gentlemen of the country – and capital – earned by the financial elites in the City of London – that resulted from such marriages produced a political elite that would govern Britain until the middle of the nineteenth century. This cadre of "gentlemanly capitalists," as they have been styled by two historians, played a crucial role in the economic and political decision-making that helped build the British empire across the globe, but especially in Africa.[4]

In West Africa during the eighteenth century large states like Dahomey, Oyo, and Asante came to undertake trading in slaves in order to procure firearms. Firearms were vital for their survival: any state without access to weapons could not hope to maintain its position in the face of better-armed neighbors. Firearms played a significant role in catalyzing large-scale conflict in many areas. War, after all, produced captives and captives might be sold into slavery. Many states came to own thousands of slaves.

The Yoruba-speaking state of Oyo in modern-day western Nigeria was one of the most powerful states in West Africa during the peak of the slave trade. Occupying territory stretching from the savanna south to the coast, Oyo's cavalry took advantage of a break in West Africa's forests to send expeditions deep into the interior to find slaves. The slaves were then transported south over the course of several weeks or months and sold to European traders at the ports of Badagry or Porto Novo. To the west of Oyo lay its perennial enemy, the Fon-speaking kingdom of Dahomey, with which it often fought (and to which in the following century it lost its primacy). Dahomey produced slaves in such great numbers that Europeans came to call the region the "Slave Coast." Perhaps one million slaves were sold from its main port at Ouidah alone.

Figure 1.1 West African slave market, eighteenth century
© Corbis

Dahomey serves as perhaps the quintessential example of a slaving state. The kingdom came to prominence at the same time as slave trading increased after 1680. Its center of power sat some 50 miles behind the coast at Abomey, but it came to control the coastal ports of Allada and Ouidah during the 1720s. From the beginning the Dahomey state was highly militarized, and gangs of slave raiders and gangsters patrolled the land, most bound to the center of power. As one historian puts it, "it is not easy to determine whether the bandit gang has turned itself into a state, or the state turned to banditry."[5] The entire economy of the state revolved around the production of slaves. Though the majority of them were marked for export, the kings of Dahomey also used thousands – mostly women – to work on plantations at the coast.

The positions of elites in Dahomey and a variety of other slave trading areas were entirely underwritten by the slave trade. Elites used profits from the trade to seize autocratic control of the political system. Their control of firearms permitted them to access and secure military and political power. But other goods from the trade in Dahomey and in the Niger Delta, close to where Antera Duke lived, also allowed the collection of supporters. Elites gathered products like alcohol – brandy in particular – which they distributed to their followers. These "prestige goods," freely dispersed, bound followers to elites by demonstrating their high status and cementing their authority. They and other rich men throughout West Africa could afford to take multiple wives with ease, given the lack of men who remained to marry.

Though tiny in size compared to Dahomey, Oyo, or Asante, the Gambia, situated just north and south of the river from which it derived its name, also engaged extensively in the slave trade. The rulers of the area earned income from the riverine commerce that flourished in the seventeenth and eighteenth centuries, in which local merchants and traders acted as intermediaries between European slavers and the inland providers of slaves and other commodities. Merchants paid taxes and tolls to ensure the continuation of their activities; British traders also paid annual customs duties to the local rulers, enriching the coffers of elites. Lower down the commercial scale, many Gambians earned their livings through small-scale trade or by servicing river-borne commerce as interpreters or providers of transportation along smaller watery byways. Many of the local merchants were women descended from unions between Portuguese traders and African women. Their wealth and the prominence they gained from it gave them a social position that women further upstream could not attain. In the 1730s several "senoras," as they were called, appeared in the account books of British traders, testimony to their mercantile activities and the riches they commanded.

The slave trade also infiltrated the religious and judicial systems of a variety of societies, especially in the Niger Delta. Here, the demand for slaves warped established mechanisms for social ordering. The central players in this aspect of the system were prominent traders called Aro, who traversed

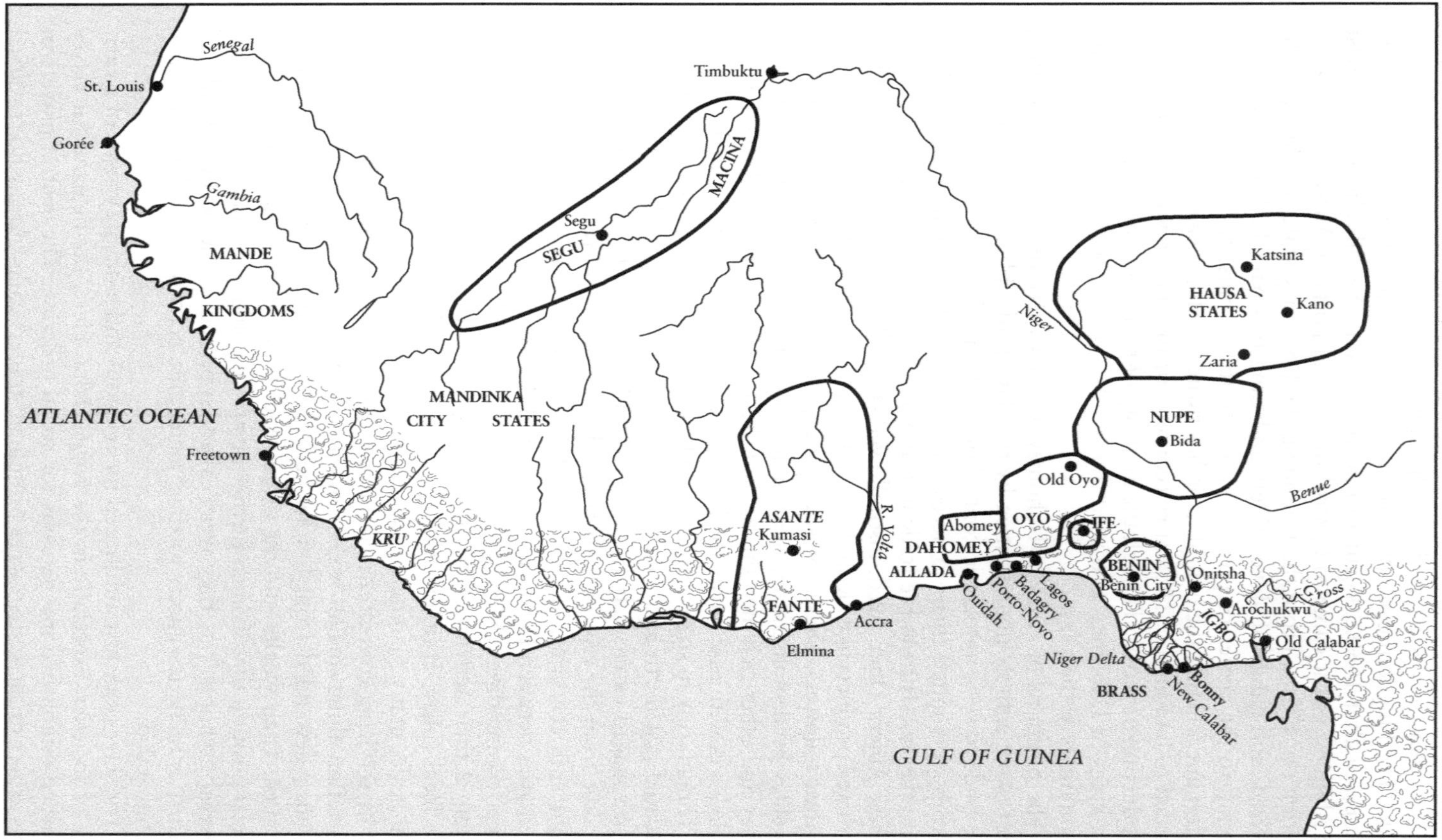

Map 1.1 West African kingdoms, c. 1800

the country far and wide hunting for slaves, going as far away as Cameroon. Aro traders had a close alliance with one of the major religious oracles in the region, called Arochukwu (described by Europeans at the time as "Long Juju" and destroyed by them in 1900). Because the Arochukwu oracle possessed immense power the Aro enjoyed great influence and authority through their connection with it.

The purpose of oracles in many communities in West Africa was to provide judgment in disputes and to determine punishment for crimes. Oracles helped to reduce conflict by placing the burden of judgment on priests associated with the oracle, people whose decision-making was respected because it was inspired by the supernatural world. They lived separately from the common people and were thus absent and remote. At the peak of the slave trade, the oracle demanded "fines" for perceived offences and demanded that they be paid in slaves. The oracle would then "eat" the slaves: slaves were brought to the entrance of the cave where the oracle and its priests were located and were then sold through Old Calabar to European slavers. Because Arochukwu was so highly esteemed, people obeyed its decrees; thus these "priest-slavers" – in the words of one of Africa's most highly respected historians – profited in a different way from the trade in slaves.[6] The Aro traders themselves, who became wealthy from their connection with the oracle, made little attempt to disguise the fact that the entire thing was a cunning manipulation of the peoples and customs of their home areas.

At the risk of generalizing, it is perhaps fair to say that those most at risk during the Atlantic slave-trading years were individuals who were "poor in people." Those living in areas behind the coast without larger communities to protect them or without the family connections to insulate themselves in areas around the Niger Delta felt its impact most keenly. Many families and communities in the interior experienced the threat of violence on an almost daily basis: they feared the well-armed militias and armies of the coastal kingdoms as well as the slave raiders who operated in the interior.

This insecurity is perhaps best illustrated by the story of a former slave called Olaudah Equiano, who later became a famous abolitionist and author. In 1789 Equaino wrote a best-selling narrative of his life, purportedly from the time of his capture in West Africa to his arrival in Plymouth in Britain as a free man in 1777. Scholars believe that Equiano's story, while true, is likely a composite testimonial based on what he knew about the Atlantic slave trade. His depictions of his childhood in West Africa before his capture have a particularly distinct ring of truth to them:

> When the grown people in the neighbourhood were gone far in the fields to labour, the children assembled . . . to play, and commonly some of us used to get up a tree to look out for any assailant or kidnapper that might come upon us, for they sometimes took these opportunities of our parents' absence to . . . carry off as many as they could seize.[7]

Some time later, two men and a woman climbed over the wall into Equiano's compound and captured him and his sister, dragging them off into the forest. The experience of Mohammed Baquaqua similarly reflects the all-encompassing danger of the slave trade. Baquaqua was tricked into drinking strong alcohol; when he awoke, he discovered he had been sold into slavery.

Throughout this process, many communities in West Africa were drawn into the orbit of the slave trade. But one of the difficulties in popular histories of the period – and indeed some academic works – is that people have viewed it as an example of Europeans simplistically taking advantage of helpless and hapless Africans. This view reached perhaps its most powerful expression in Walter Rodney's famous *How Europe Underdeveloped Africa*. Drawing on evidence from the Upper Guinea coast, Rodney laid the blame for the slave trade firmly at the feet of Europeans. He further argued that the roots of Africa's post-colonial economic problems could be traced directly to the slave trade.

The historical evidence makes it difficult to sustain Rodney's view. The ever-increasing numbers of European ships arriving at the coast in fact acted to stimulate trade in many areas. Between 1820 and 1850, for instance, as the slave trade began to wind down, the volume of cloth purchased from European traders in West Africa rose from 350,000 to 17 million yards of material. Domestic trade, too, increased. The years of the slave trade produced an overall increase in the monetization of West Africa's economies, as Europeans paid for the slaves they purchased in the currency of cowry shells. Commerce in all kinds of goods and services flourished.

One popular misconception has Europeans arriving on the African coast, ships bristling with guns, and landing troops for inland raids. In fact Europeans almost never procured African slaves themselves. Afraid of disease, European captains typically anchored their ships a mile off the West African coast, and traders like Antera Duke visited them in canoes to engage in business negotiations. This reflected the organization of the slave trade in the eighteenth century: it was a formalized affair, with established practices and rules of the game well known to both sides. Few Africans showed any more remorse over their occupations than did European purchasers.

Africans were far from being the unwitting victims of European financial dealings; they were highly skilled in negotiating prices and deals with Europeans and many spoke excellent English by the eighteenth century. The days of Africans being unaware of the quality of European metals or gold were long gone. European testimonies recount the frustrations they felt at their inability to cut profitable deals with their African partners on a regular basis. African traders knew full well that remaining long at the coast might prove disastrous for European companies. A day in port was a day wasted in moving cargo, but extra time also allowed diseases like typhoid or dysentery to spread among captives held at the coast or in the holds of ships. Europeans also had to contend with the kings or rulers of the areas in which they wished to trade. When one ship arrived at the mouth of the Benin river in 1778, its captain had to pay the value of 150 slaves simply for the privilege of dropping anchor and gaining permission to negotiate for trade.

It is also vital to remember that "slave trading" did not only encompass the trans-Atlantic commerce (an easy slip to make in the United States, where slaves have played such a foundational role in African-American history). In actuality, the trans-Atlantic trade encompassed only two-thirds of the slaves departing from the African continent between 1500 and 1890. The remaining third, around seven million people, journeyed across the Sahara to North Africa and from the East African coast into the Indian Ocean world.

Historically, the trans-Saharan trade differed dramatically from its trans-Atlantic counterpart. At a basic level its impact was felt far less suddenly by the communities from which the slaves departed, because their removal was spread across more than a millennium. Between 800 and 1900 CE some four million slaves crossed the Sahara to be sold in the Islamic societies of North Africa and the Middle East, and another two million traveled north along the Nile corridor from Ethiopia and Sudan. Most were women – unlike in the trans-Atlantic trade – and the bulk of them served in the homes of middle- and upper-class Muslims in cities of the region; others worked for caravans, in mines, on farms, or in the armies of military leaders. Many became highly respected for their achievements and won positions of authority in households or the state system; levels of manumission were high. One of the foremost experts on the trans-Saharan trade in human beings concludes that they had "far greater opportunities for integration into mainstream society than Africans transported to the Americas."[8]

Another four million slaves traveled into the Indian Ocean world and the Middle East from the East African coast and via the Red Sea corridor during the same period. They held occupations similar to those who crossed the Sahara. This trade was even older than the trans-Saharan and it expanded in scope during the eighteenth and nineteenth centuries, dramatically so once Britain abolished slave trading in 1807. When the embargo against slaving made it more difficult to move slaves from West Africa, slavers moved to East African ports to obtain their human wares. At the coast Arab peoples from Oman or Swahili peoples claiming Arab descent controlled the export markets. The greatest of these was at Zanzibar, where the Omani sultan Seyyid Said had moved his capital in 1840. Africans in the interior, especially the Nyamwezi and Kamba, came to dominate trade, though Arabs ultimately played a more powerful and eventually determinative role. During the mid- to late-nineteenth century trading reached its zenith under the notorious Zanzibari merchant, Tippu Tip. This slaver reputedly owned 10,000 slaves, burying some in the foundations of his house in Zanzibar to give it strength. The moral imperative to snuff out the slave trade would give the British the perfect justification to colonize East Africa at the end of the nineteenth century.

Abolition

Britain's long engagement in the slave trade and in slavery itself inspired few voices critical of its complicity in the unsavory practices inherent within the traffic in human beings. In the 1770s, however, things changed. The campaign to outlaw British involvement in the slave trade began at the initiative of John Hylas, an Afro-Caribbean slave brought to England by his owner in 1754. In 1758, with the permission of their respective owners, Hylas married a slave named Mary, who had been brought to England from Barbados in 1754 by a family named Newton. John Hylas received his freedom and for eight years he and Mary lived together as husband and wife. In 1766, however, the Newtons ordered the kidnapping and transportation of Mary back to the West Indies, where she was to be sold as a slave.

Hylas appealed for help to Granville Sharp, a clerk in the Ordnance Department who had a history of success in advocating for slaves' rights. The previous year Sharp had managed to secure the release of a former slave from jail, where he was awaiting transportation back into slavery in Jamaica. Sharp helped Hylas successfully sue for Mary's freedom from the Newtons, who were ordered by the court to return her on the first ship heading for England. Then in 1772 Lord Chief Justice Mansfield ruled in the Somerset case that slave owners in England could not force their slaves to go out of England. The Somerset ruling did not constitute the end of slavery in England (though in Scotland, by the 1778 ruling in *Knight v. Wedderburn*, slavery was condemned as contrary to the laws of the country) nor even the forced deportations of blacks, which continued at least until 1792. But it did publicize the plight of slaves and galvanized many Britons into action and formal association for the abolition of the slave trade.

Anti-slavery activists came to their beliefs from a variety of philosophic positions. Some radical men and women took a political stand on slavery, seeing it as a violation of fundamental rights to freedom that all persons enjoyed, regardless of class, race, or gender. But after the outbreak of the French Revolution and the revolt of slaves in San Domingue (modern-day Haiti) in 1791 this particular strand of anti-slavery belief lost popularity, certainly among middle- and upper-class white men and women. Political economists such as Harriet Martineau came to see in slavery an inefficient use of labor that stood in opposition to principles of *laissez-faire* and unnecessarily drove up the cost of commodities. John Stuart Mill, the preeminent spokesman for classical liberal thought, objected to slavery on the grounds of justice; he believed that education could render all men and – unusually for his time, women – capable of the reasoning necessary for the exercise of personal freedom. At different times differing perspectives on anti-slavery came to the fore, but the single most dominant strand of thought derived from evangelical religion. Slavery was sinful, believed evangelicals of every stripe, a crime against God's law, and on moral and spiritual grounds had to be extirpated. Humanitarian sentiments about the cruel fates experienced by others of God's creatures often prevailed over more abstract liberal notions of utility, reason, or justice, though many abolitionists combined their humanitarian ethos with a liberal economic rhetoric of free trade.

The anti-slavery cause received impetus from the successful breaking away of the American colonies. When British troops marched out of New York City on Evacuation Day in late November 1783, marking the official end of the British presence in the United States, some 5000 formerly enslaved African-Americans who had responded to the British appeal for support in return for their freedom faced serious difficulties. For many, the best option seemed to be to travel to Britain, where they found themselves in an alien land of people not necessarily well disposed toward them. They found life in their new home stressful and difficult. Dreary weather, crowded cities, and the fast-paced bustle of urban life among strangers proved disconcerting. Making ends meet was impossible without the assistance of poor relief. Soup kitchens could do little to stem the unemployment and poverty exacerbated by postwar depression. The highly visible presence of ex-slaves on the streets of London who had served as sailors, soldiers, or laborers during the war excited much adverse comment, some of it verging on racist hatred.

But another, more generous, response emerged as well. The Committee for the Relief of the Black Poor, established initially to offer material support at home, soon began to hear appeals from the black poor themselves to help them settle in Africa instead, a proposition taken up and advanced by abolitionists Granville Sharp and Henry Smeathman. Smeathman especially urged the colonization of Sierra Leone, where a deep harbor promised greater possibilities of success; more pointedly, Bunce Island, one of Britain's largest slaving stations, lay in the harbor at Sierra Leone. What better method for advancing the cause of anti-slavery could exist than planting a colony of freed slaves on that very spot? Smeathman convinced the committee to join in on the plan and by 1786, under the leadership of Sharp, it had persuaded the British government to provide ships and supplies with which to transport and settle 300 blacks in Sierra Leone.

After months of wrangling and delays, during which time 50 colonists died from fever on board ships that sat in harbor waiting for orders to depart, the small fleet of black emigrants set sail in 1787. They landed on the coast of Africa at an inauspicious time – the rainy season was underway, and its torrential downpours destroyed crops, turned the land to mud, and fostered the explosion of disease-bearing insects. By the time the colonists had negotiated a treaty with the local King Naimbana for the land on which they established Granville Town, a quarter of their number had died. Hungry, sick, and lacking adequate shelter, many others abandoned their settlement to join the slavers at Bunce Island, where they could at least find food. The slavers, eager to undermine the entire abolitionist purpose of the colony, conspired with a local subchief, King Jimmy, who ordered the remaining residents of Granville Town to leave. Then he burned down their houses. The initial effort to colonize Sierra Leone with free blacks had proved a disaster.

But abolitionists, driven by a variety of motives, refused to let this setback divert their efforts. They continued on a wildly effective propaganda campaign that offered up gruesome descriptions of the inhumane and brutal treatment of enslaved Africans as they huddled chained in shipholds or worked the plantations of the Caribbean and the American south. Heart-rending stories about the breakup of families through the sale of individual members, usually children, and lurid tales of physical and sexual violence against slave women served as some of the most effective means of gaining support from the general public, the popular press, and ultimately from members of parliament. In 1788, Hannah More, a prominent evangelical, published *Slavery, A Poem*, contriving to ensure that its appearance coincided with a scheduled parliamentary debate on abolition. Though her entreaties against slavery constituted an incursion into the public realm of politics and commerce, she was careful to argue her case in exclusively sentimental terms. "See the dire victim torn from social life," she wrote,

> The shrieking babe, the agonizing wife!
> She, wretch forlorn! is dragg'd by hostile hands,
> To distant tyrants sold, in distant lands! . . .
> By felon hands, by one relentless stroke,
> See the fond links of feeling Nature broke!
> The fibres twisting round a parent's heart,
> Torn from their grasp, and bleeding as they part.[9]

Public opinion did an abrupt about-face. Newspaper editors, clergymen, politicians, and regular folks joined in an impassioned, collective cry for ending the trans-Atlantic slave trade, and their pressures created a political groundswell that was impossible to ignore. William Pitt, the prime minister, promised in 1788 that parliament would debate the issue during the next session; the following year William Wilberforce, the great parliamentary champion of abolition for the next 25 years, introduced the first abolition bill taken up by Westminster. It would, alas, find no traction, for before it could be seriously debated the French Revolution broke out, commanding the attention of parliament for the foreseeable future.

The anti-slavery movement largely fell dormant during the years of the French Revolution and the succeeding wars against France, but Sharp and Wilberforce continued to believe that Sierra Leone could be a powerful weapon in the anti-slavery struggle. In 1791 Sharp established the Sierra Leone Company and sent agents to the West African territory to create the colony anew. Having successfully renegotiated the necessary land deals with local chiefs there, the company now needed to find people to settle the colony. This time they would come not from the freed black slaves who had emigrated to London following the American Revolution, but from those who had moved to Nova Scotia and New Brunswick following the conflict, and who had found the climate there – social and political as well as meteorological – inhospitable.

On January 15, 1792, some 1700 free blacks set sail from Halifax, Nova Scotia, on a seven-week voyage. After a difficult and dangerous passage, the emigrants landed at what had once been Granville Town, now overgrown after five years' abandonment. They set to work cutting down trees and raising up a church, houses, and buildings in what they would name Freetown. But some of the problems they had faced in Nova Scotia re-emerged in West Africa, particularly the issue of allocating land to settlers. Company officials had their own ideas about how the process would take place, putting them at odds with the settlers. Part of the problem resided in the individual company officials charged with carrying out company policies. One, William Dawes, had been transferred to Freetown from the prison colony at Botany Bay in Australia, where he served as an officer; his successor, Zachary Macaulay, had spent five years overseeing a sugar plantation in Jamaica. Black settlers seeking justice and respite after years of slavery and abuse could hardly have found a more unsuitable pair of governors. Their grievances festered as years of dissatisfaction passed with no relief. When Macaulay left his post in 1799, a number of settlers seized the opportunity to insist that the company give them greater freedom to determine their own governance. The company refused, and a group of settlers rebelled, declaring a new government headed by Governor Isaac Anderson. They took up arms and, commanding the support of perhaps half of the black colonists, prepared to defend their liberties and their rights. But at just that moment, another group of free blacks called Maroons entered the scene, and under orders from the Sierra Leone Company helped put down the rebellion.

The Maroons had been transported from their lands in the Cockpit Country of Jamaica to Nova Scotia in 1796 following a series of clashes with the colonial government. Maroons, like other once-enslaved peoples across the colonial world, had escaped their former situations (or their ancestors had) and lived freely in the mountains of Jamaica, enjoying autonomy and land ownership in return for their agreement to help track down and return runaway slaves on the island. In 1795, a particular group of them living in Trelawny Town remonstrated against indignities they felt the colonial government had unfairly imposed upon them, demanding an apology and the dismissal of a local official. In this situation of tension, heightened by the Haitian Revolution and the wars with republican France, the new Jamaican governor, the Earl of Balcarres, determined to use the moment to demonstrate his firm anti-revolutionary principles. He declared the Trelawny Town Maroons to be in a state of rebellion and sent troops against them. Fighting convulsed the island in August and September 1795, destroying lives and property and leading ultimately to a stalemate by October. Balcarres promised that if they laid down their arms, the Trelawney Town Maroons could stay in Jamaica, an undertaking they accepted. Then, to the dismay of many of his officers and subordinates in the colonial government, Balcarres reneged on his promise, exiling the Maroons to Nova Scotia instead.

The Trelawny Maroons suffered terribly in the cold of British North America. When one of their many petitions to be relocated reached the ears of officials of the Sierra Leone Company, it found immediate approbation. Eager to continue to populate the West African colony, and mindful of the services long given to Jamaican authorities in their efforts to track down escaped slaves, the company jumped at the chance to bring the Maroons to Freetown. Their numbers, officials hoped, would act to temper the rebellious nature of the colony's inhabitants. In August 1800, 550 Maroons boarded the transport ship *Asia*, arriving in Freetown just in time to help put down the revolt there. With their assistance, company officials hunted down those rebels it did not kill or capture, hanged the putative governor, Isaac Anderson, and banished the other leaders of the rising, among them Harry Washington, the slave who had run away from George Washington's plantation 20 years earlier during the American Revolution.

Against the odds, Sierra Leone survived. In 1807, Great Britain outlawed the slave trade, the enforcement of which required it to send the Royal Navy to intercept slave ships that defied its ban. The slaves set free by these actions were settled in Sierra Leone, augmenting the numbers of freed blacks from Nova Scotia and Jamaica (via Nova Scotia) and contributing to the growth and development of the colony. Known as "liberated Africans," they also settled along the Gambia river, at the mouth of which Britain established a formal outpost on Banjul Island. They renamed it Bathurst, and from that vantage point set about establishing the terms of "legitimate" trade that would soon come to supplant the commerce in human beings.

The anti-slavery act made it illegal for any British captain to trade in slaves from Africa and authorized British naval officers to capture and hold "pirates" who sought to do so. The act included in its remit ships whose papers were deemed to be false, enabling British captains to seize Portuguese, Spanish, and French vessels and their slave cargo. The British government charged a new West African Squadron with enforcing the law, and set up a court in Freetown where offenders would be tried. Given the size of the squadron, however – only three ships – and the scope of its jurisdiction – 3000 miles of African coast – suppression proved lamentably ineffective. In the 1830s, slavers – some British, but largely French, Spanish, and Portuguese – still exported 20,000 Africans from the Gulf of Guinea each year, and the slave trade continued to flourish before the 1840s. The Atlantic commerce in human beings only began to wane when Britain established a naval base on Fernando Po, an island just off the Niger Delta; entered into treaties with both European and African leaders to end the trade; and engaged in the widespread purchase of palm oil that would lubricate the machines of the industrial revolution. These actions meant that the numbers of slaves traded dropped to 10,000 in the 1840s and to 3000 by the 1850s. By the 1860s, the shipment of African slaves across the Atlantic on British ships had virtually ceased.

Outlawing the slave trade did not end the institution of slavery itself. It did, however, cut the continual resupply of slaves to the West Indies, which, paradoxically, compelled Jamaican planters to redouble the harshness of their treatment of their unfree labor force. In 1823, the cabinet issued Orders in Council "requiring West Indian legislatures to ameliorate the conditions of slave labour," a command that fell on deaf ears. That same year, a slave revolt broke out in Demerara in British Guiana, supported by a white missionary by the name of John Smith. Following his trial and sentencing to death, Smith died in prison of consumption, an event that revived the anti-slavery movement at home and turned it into a significant political force. Its leader in parliament, Thomas Fowell Buxton, wanted to move slowly, bringing about emancipation gradually and in a series of remedial steps, but his caution was soon overcome by the demands of the women in the movement who supported full and immediate abolition.

Under pressure from a huge constituency of Britons who would no longer tolerate the practice, parliament abolished slavery in 1833. For a brief period in the 1820s, 1830s, and 1840s, eighteenth-century notions of racial difference were driven underground by liberal and humanitarian sentiments expressed through the anti-slavery movement. Britons found slavery incompatible with their sense of rightness and their sense of themselves. To be "British" in the 1830s and 1840s entailed holding an abolitionist position, whether for political, economic, or sentimental reasons. For British women, anti-slavery sentiments dovetailed precisely with their purported greater sensitivity to cruelties and injustices, their greater morality, and higher spiritual natures. For British men, devotion to Christian precepts as much as to liberal principles of justice and legal equality meant that no respectable middle-class male could turn a blind eye to the brutalities of slavery. Notions of manliness contained a strong element of abolitionism, of ending the oppression of African men, women, and children at the hands of British planters and overlords.

True to its adherence to property rights and, more crucially, cognizant of the need to placate the interests of the empire in which Britain had an enormous stake, the government handsomely compensated those who were financially hit by their measures. West Indian planters extorted a policy of apprenticeship and £20 million from parliament upon the manumission of their slaves in 1834 (the year parliament's decision was implemented), a figure that amounted to half of all the tax revenues Britain took in that year. Apprenticeship virtually ensured that slavery by another name would prevail. "Former" slaves owed their masters 40 hours of work each week, for which they earned no wages. If they worked beyond the 40 hours, they received whatever wages they could negotiate from their employers as if they were free laborers; alternatively, they might work for themselves or for another employer. The planters won these concessions by threatening increased unrest in the West Indies that would interrupt the flow of raw materials from the islands to the industrial and commercial centers of Great Britain. Evangelical missionaries and former abolitionists continued to work to end the system of apprenticeship, a system under which little had appreciably changed for "formerly" enslaved people.

Ironically, the abolition of slavery led Britons to draw firmer lines between black and white peoples so that hierarchical relations of power could be sustained in the absence of legal differentiation based on race. Moreover, the end of slavery helped to further the imperial project. Once Britons could no longer be regarded as responsible for slavery in their own territories, blame for the continuation of the institution could be shifted onto others. This included Americans, in particular, and increasingly Africans, who – moralists asserted – relied on the slave trade to sustain their economies. In 1841, combining missionary zeal with political economy, Buxton, with the approval and financial backing of the British government, launched an expedition to the Niger to end slavery and establish "proper" commercial undertakings there. As depicted by Buxton's campaign literature and publicity, Africa was a place of darkness and barbarism. "Bound in the chains of the grossest ignorance," he wrote, its people were "prey to the most savage superstition."[10] Slavery, torture, butchery, human sacrifice, cannibalism, dismemberment, infanticide – these practices could be ended and African peoples redeemed if Britons could show Africans alternative methods of using their material resources, help establish commercial ventures in agriculture and trade in commodities, and assist in setting up schools and missions, thereby bringing the "light" of European and Christian ways to the "dark" continent.

The Niger expedition failed spectacularly. Of the 150 white Britons who departed their homeland to stamp out slavery at its source in the hinterlands of West Africa, 44 died of malaria. The remaining Britons, themselves ill with fever, withdrew from a model farm they had established with 150 Africans from the coast, leaving the African members of the expedition in control of the enterprise. When Britons returned the next year to bring relief to the settlers, they found the farm in disarray and barren fields where they had planted cotton and maize. Warfare in the area had produced refugees looking to escape the bloodshed, and the African settlers had put them to work. Lieutenant Webb, the head of the relief expedition, reported that the settlers would do no work themselves. "I found them indolent and lazy," he wrote, "not one willing or even disposed to manual labour, but ready enough to exercize authority over the negroes they hired." Reports circulated about settlers molesting the refugee women, as did a story about the settlers using whips "apparently for the purpose of urging the natives to greater exertion." What had begun as a great moral undertaking to bring salvation and enlightenment to the "savage" peoples of Africa had turned into a debacle. Not only had the trade in slaves not been abolished, but the settlers charged with establishing alternative forms of commerce had apparently resorted to slavery themselves. As *The Times* put it scathingly upon hearing the accounts of Webb and others, "the Niger ANTI-Slavery Expedition has . . . planted a *very* 'model' of the most cruel and iniquitous SLAVERY, and that in a spot where such, as at least such systematic scourge-bearing slavery, was probably unknown before."[11]

The disaster of the Niger expedition, combined with other developments, helped transform British racial thought after 1850. Charles Dickens sounded one of the first blasts against the prevailing liberal view – that all races were equal in capacity and could be raised up to European levels – in his excoriation of the anti-slavery campaigners in an 1848 article entitled "The Niger Expedition." "Between the civilized European and the barbarous African," he insisted, "there is a great gulf set. . . . To change the customs even of civilized . . . men . . . is . . . a most difficult and slow proceeding; but to do this by ignorant and savage races, is a work which, like the progressive changes of the globe itself, requires a stretch of years that dazzles in the looking at." Only fools could expect to "railroad" savages into Christianity and civilization, he asserted, and they should not waste their efforts in a land as dark and benighted as Africa.[12]

For the time being, the British government abandoned efforts to intervene in the African hinterland to suppress the slave trade. Stymied by recalcitrant and sometimes hostile African kings and merchant princes, overwhelmed by disease, and discouraged by behaviors regarded as antithetical to free trade and progress, British officials saw little reason to continue their involvement in African affairs. The Church Missionary Society, on the other hand, two of whose members had accompanied the expedition up the Niger, took more positive lessons from the journey, and determined to follow it up with further missionary trips. British initiatives in what would much later become the colony of Nigeria thus passed from the government to missionary societies. Their activities over the next six decades had a powerful impact on African communities and polities across the continent, as we will see in the next chapter.

More immediately, abolition had profound effects on those people involved in both the trade and the institution of slavery. West African and British merchants, brokers, and distributors found their commerce in human beings halted, though they soon found other commodities to replace them. Plantation economies in the West Indies suffered dramatically, especially after the system of apprenticeship came to an end in 1838. Abolition also produced deep discontent in South Africa, where the descendants of early Dutch traders and farmers (soon known as "Boers" and later "Afrikaners") utilized slave labor extensively, a story we now take up.

The Cape Colony

In the southwestern corner of South Africa, far beyond the reach of the trans-Atlantic or East African slave trades, lay a territory that would become the British-controlled Cape Colony. Acquired first during the Napoleonic Wars in 1795, it was returned to the Dutch in 1803 after the Peace of Amiens, and re-acquired by Britain in 1806. Its mild Mediterranean climate and regular rains had long proved attractive to European visitors, who faced none of the malaria, trypanosomiasis, or extreme weather of tropical Africa here. This was one of the oldest European settlements in Africa: the Dutchman Jan van Riebeeck, an employee of the Dutch East India Company (Vereenigde Oost-Indische Compagnie, or VOC), had landed three ships and set up a permanent station in what became Cape Town in 1652. A century-and-a-half later, during the Napoleonic Wars in which France had overrun the Netherlands, Britain took control of the "Cape Colony." Excellent conditions for producing wine provided scant consolation for the British government, which viewed the Cape as little more than an irritation. Though it was a useful refueling station and port city, it produced nothing, and at 6000 miles from London, proved difficult to communicate with. In 1793 its population consisted of 13,000 white settlers whose seeming aim was to create administrative difficulties for the British. The history of these settlers and their interactions with Africans had a profound impact on the ability of Britain to govern the Cape from the moment its administrators arrived and for many years after.

Who were these settlers? They were descendants of French and Dutch immigrants who had arrived in southern Africa during the second half of the seventeenth century. While some had established themselves in the rapidly expanding Cape Town, others had moved eastward from the city. There, on lands in the dry Karoo desert and its margins, they set themselves up as ranchers, eking out a living selling hides or wool. Genuine pioneers, they traveled by wagon and on horseback, professed a fervent Calvinism, and disdained education. As they moved east during the course of the eighteenth century, they became physically and culturally separate from those they left behind in Cape Town: it took three months, after all, to travel in an ox-wagon from Graaff-Reinet to Cape Town. The settlers even developed a new language – later known as Afrikaans – that was based on Dutch but included a series of loan words in Malay, French, English, and a variety of African languages.

Before the 1760s, the passage eastward of these "trekboers" (the term "Boer" means "farmer") had proceeded in relatively simple fashion, for the land was almost empty. Apartheid-era historians would later argue that the vacant land justified white settlement in South Africa. But their pronouncements usually neglected to explain why the land was unoccupied, for this was, in fact, a recent phenomenon. The original inhabitants – Khoikhoi pastoralists known to the Dutch as "Hottentots" – had ceased to possess any sort of social or political independence; they had fallen prey to a series of VOC-sanctioned cattle raids by Dutch farmers and ranchers who insisted that they needed the stock and the land to establish themselves and survive. Raids by other Khoikhoi groups who seized upon the weak and by San "hunter-robbers" who carried off many thousands of beasts in the late seventeenth century compounded the disaster, making it impossible for the Khoikhoi to continue their centuries-old practices. Many sold their sheep and cattle to the company or to the settler farmers, who after 1700 had few limits on their activities from the company.

Khoikhoi society at the Cape had gone through cycles of prosperity and decline in the past, but now the presence of the Dutch settlers prevented regeneration. Many men went to work for the settlers, their opportunities to participate in the renewal of Khoikhoi society now closed off. They earned wages paid not in beasts, which would have allowed them to rebuild their herds, but in food, a place to live, and goods. The final straw came in 1713 when a smallpox epidemic swept through the Khoikhoi population. They enjoyed no immunity to the disease, and perhaps 90 percent of them died. Those who remained often took on jobs as servants for the trekboer pioneers, for few other options existed.

By the 1760s the trekboers on the frontier had come into extended contact with a larger and more resilient population of Africans, the Xhosa. Black-skinned, part-agriculturalist, part-pastoralist people, the Xhosa lived in a series of loosely knit chiefdoms extending from the environs of the Fish river eastward. Roughly speaking, the land beyond the Kei river was inhabited by the Gcaleka sub-group; between the Fish and Kei rivers, the Ngqika; and the Ndlambe lived to the west of the Fish river.

The trekboers first encountered the Ndlambe in a region known as the Zuurveld, which provided excellent conditions for pastoralism. Both Xhosa and Boer grazed their cattle there seasonally. The two groups shared similar modes of life and their initial interactions were positive. Boer pastors traveled unmolested into Xhosa lands to preach the gospel; both sides traded with one another; and intermarriage took place as well. But by the following decade the benevolent interactions had devolved into a series of often-violent conflicts. Though the Xhosa possessed greater numbers, the trekboers had more modern firearms. They had also perfected a highly effective defensive strategy in which they circled their wagons into a *laager*, placed their animals in the center, lashed the wagons together, and fired outward from the gaps in between. Neither side could achieve dominance and thus a protracted stalemate ensued. These so-called "Frontier Wars" broke out periodically over the following century.

When the British arrived at the Cape in 1795, they viewed the disorder at the frontier as problematic. Initially they did little to address the situation, believing that they would hold the Cape only temporarily while the Napoleonic Wars played out. But in the years after 1806, British authorities acted. From an imperial perspective, the strategy was simple: keep the peace at as low a cost as possible. In 1811 and 1812, in an effort to resolve the problem once and for all with overwhelming force, Governor Sir John Cradock ordered British troops to "close" the frontier by forcibly removing Xhosa and creating a buffer zone between them and the Boer farmers. As Cradock put it, "I am happy . . . that in the course of this service there has not been shed more Kaffir [a derogatory term equivalent to "nigger"] blood than would seem to be necessary to impress on the minds of these savages a proper degree of terror and respect."[13]

Xhosa society came under progressively more stress after the British arrival. The Xhosa example, indeed, encapsulates the experience of many peoples in their first interactions with the British. In the 1811 and 1812 campaigns, the

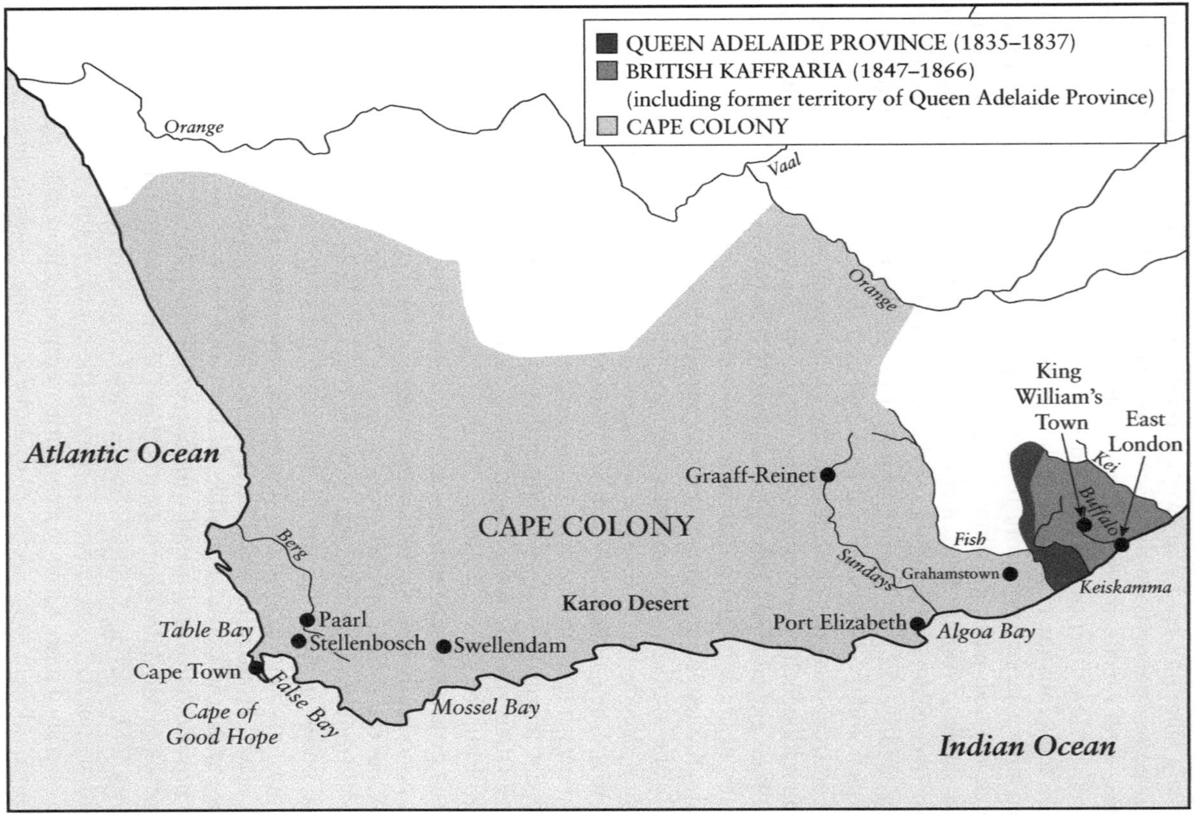

Map 1.2 The British in southern Africa, c. 1835

British drove all Xhosa living to the west of the Fish river from their land, and government soldiers burned their crops and settlements, confiscating thousands of cattle. The British presence caused a rupture in Xhosa political ordering. The government made a temporary alliance with the Ngqika chief, elevating him to the highest status among Xhosa chiefs. Under Xhosa custom, that honor should have been accorded to the chief of the Gcaleka. The snub led the Gcaleka and Ndlambe to join together to attack and defeat the Ngqika in 1818. The following year, the two joined forces again to attack the British settlement of Grahamstown in the Zuurveld. British reprisals were severe.

Conflict increased over the following decades. In 1820, 5000 men, women, and children arrived from Britain to settle the land from which Cradock had forced the Xhosa. These new arrivals enjoyed the full backing of the government and a free hand to establish themselves in trade at the expense of the Xhosa and the Boers. Together these developments brought about an economic collapse in Xhosa society. In 1834 the desperate Xhosa attacked the settlers in the eastern reaches of the Cape Colony. The main chief, Hintsa, was captured and executed, with one British official reportedly making off with his ears. In 1835 the British temporarily declared all the land to the west of the Kei river the province of Queen Adelaide, placing it under the governorship of Sir Harry Smith, Hintsa's vanquisher.

Smith is one of the more colorful characters in British imperial history. A skilled horseman, dashing military leader, and favorite of Queen Victoria, he had won success in India before his arrival in the Cape Colony. A darker and harsher side, however, accompanied his daring qualities. In 1847 Smith reestablished and then took charge of the short-lived province of Queen Adelaide, designating it British Kaffraria. He humiliated high-ranking Xhosa chiefs by publicly forcing them to kiss his boots. He also meddled in Xhosa political life, removing the paramount chief among the Ngqika, Sandile, and appointing British magistrates to oversee all decisions made by Xhosa chiefs. Smith's actions, predictably, produced another round of fighting (the War of Mlanjeni, 1850–1853), which brought Xhosa society to the brink of destruction as British settlers continued their march eastward.

The final obliteration of the Xhosa was completed in a series of events circulating around a 16-year-old girl named Nongqawase in 1856 and 1857. At the end of the War of Mlanjeni, the fragile Xhosa political economy had come under further assault by an epidemic of bovine pleuropneumonia, a bacterial disease that swept through the country. From the perspective of senior Xhosa men, the previous 70 years of contact with Europeans had ruined their society. Even British missionaries seemed to be seducing their people away from long-held beliefs. In response more and more of the population came to put their trust in a series of visions Nongqawase claimed she had experienced. In these visions long-dead ancestors visited her and prophesied that the only way to purify the land and redeem the fortunes of the Xhosa was to slaughter their cattle; their deaths would pave the way for a renewal of the Xhosa world. At first many Xhosa people doubted the veracity of her message, but as 1856 turned into 1857 more and more came to believe the prophecy. Ultimately, the Xhosa slaughtered perhaps 400,000 of their cattle; 40,000 men, women, and children died of starvation.

The British reaction to these events helped determine the final outcome for the Xhosa people. The governor-general of the Cape Colony, Sir George Grey, claimed that the chiefs had concocted the cattle killing to inspire their people to a final massive effort to drive out the colonizers with the help of the Sotho king, Moshoeshoe (see Chapter 2). This so-called "Chiefs' Plot" was barely credible for a number of reasons, not least because starving people make poor soldiers. Many Xhosa genuinely believed the prophecies and chiefs could not manipulate those who didn't like puppet masters. Moreover, the British presence was somewhat tangential to the cattle killing, which sought to renew *Xhosa* society. But Grey chose to believe in the plot. He refused to stop the killing when he had opportunities to do so and rejected the entreaties of Xhosa chiefs who pleaded with him in 1857 for food as thousands of their people starved. Grey's inaction resulted from a specific agenda. He believed that the entire region of British Kaffraria would be a better place without Xhosa living in it and that white settlers should inhabit the whole area. As the Xhosa collapsed he set about implementing his vision for the land.

The other whites in the interior – the trekboers – had initially assumed that the British would side with them in their conflicts against the Xhosa, purely on racial grounds. But the British had little more regard or sympathy for them than for African peoples. When the British had arrived in 1795 an incipient rebellion was underway in Graaff-Reinet and Swellendam. Calling themselves the "Patriots," the rebels had risen up against VOC regulations. The British quickly stepped in and crushed the rising, hanging the ringleaders. Periodic discontent continued during the following two decades, culminating in the Slagtersnek rebellion of 1815. Its inspiration was significant: a farmer named Frederick Bezuidenhout had ignored a summons from a colonial magistrate to answer charges that he had mistreated one of his workers. Troops were sent to arrest Bezuidenhout, who was killed in the ensuing firefight on his farm. Bezuidenhout's brother, Hans, instigated the uprising against British authority but it didn't last long. The five leaders of the fledgling rebellion were quickly caught and hanged.

Bezuidenhout and his supporters – like the majority of the trekboers – believed that the British had no business telling them how they should treat their servants and employees. At the time, most trekboer families employed African servants, but of far more significance for the future of South Africa was their ownership of slaves. The issue of slavery stands at the heart of South African history, implicated in virtually every aspect of South African life, including the twentieth-century institution of apartheid. Slaves constituted a highly diverse population at the Cape. From the mid-seventeenth century onward, VOC ships had sold slaves from Dutch possessions in the

East Indies (modern-day Indonesia) at Cape Town as they made their way west. More slaves had come from Mauritius and Madagascar on orders from Van Riebeeck. Others arrived on ships from Angola or Mozambique (sometimes flying the Portuguese flag), and still more from India, Sri Lanka, Guinea, Cape Verde, China, East Africa, and other ports of the Indian Ocean world. Approximately one-quarter of the Cape's imported slave population came from Africa and the other three-quarters from Madagascar, India, and Indonesia respectively. Slaves had thus played a part in the colony's life from its earliest days: Van Riebeeck himself, after all, owned slaves. The majority, however, were owned by settlers. Over 63,000 slaves were imported between 1652 and 1808. In 1795, the year the British arrived in Cape Town, 21,474 slaves lived in the colony: 12,996 men, 5529 women, 1541 boys, and 1408 girls. Slaves had outnumbered white settlers ever since 1717.

Slavery institutionalized a racial hierarchy in South Africa's earliest years of interaction between Europeans and non-Europeans. No European could be a slave – based on common practice – and legally no indigenous person from the Cape could either, though they often found themselves in the positions of serfs or servants. The large proportion of European men at the Cape, however, meant that many offspring were produced from interracial unions. Because slave status passed through the mother's line, European men who fathered children with slave women had children who were legally slaves; free women who had children with slave men had free children. It was common at certain points in Cape history for householders to father children with their women slaves, thereby increasing the numbers of slaves they owned.

Overall, the treatment of slaves compared unfavorably with North American plantations. Those belonging to the VOC received baptism, could gain an education, and might eventually receive manumission after 25 years, but those slaves belonging to individual farmers beyond company control generally enjoyed a less secure existence. As in all slave populations with the exception of the American South, they did not naturally increase in numbers through biological reproduction owing to the poor conditions in which they worked. Some took risks and escaped, trying to make meaningful lives beyond the reach of white settlers in rough-and-ready frontier regions, but the going was difficult.

The arrival of the British presented difficulties for slave-owning settlers in the western Cape. The British had abolished the slave trade in 1807, a law that was applied to all colonies in 1808. It meant that no more slaves might be imported into the Cape Colony, though illegal trade continued until 1822. Many farmers greeted the news with horror because they depended on slave labor for their livelihoods.

The abolition of the slave trade was just one in a series of episodes that made the majority of the Boer population desperate to be free from the regulations of the Cape Colony. The British changed the colony's official language to English in 1826, effectively making Boers second-class citizens.

Figure 1.2 The Great Trek, c. 1835

(This policy entailed opening English-speaking schools and bringing in clergy from Scotland and England to preach in English.) British economic favoritism toward the 1820 settlers disadvantaged the Boers, who found it now more difficult than ever to procure legal title to land. Most importantly, British regulations against the ill treatment of servants, passed in Ordinance 50 of 1828, infuriated them. These policies were soon enshrined in "Cape liberalism," a subject we will take up in Chapter 2. When the British abolished slavery in all of their territories in 1834, the Boers had had enough. The following year the majority of Boers living in the Cape Colony climbed into their wagons and left.

The Great Trek, as their dramatic self-exile became known, forms one of the foundational moments in Boer (later "Afrikaner") history. Some 6000 Boers – known as voortrekkers – departed the Cape Colony for the interior, wishing to live under the "old Burgher regulations and duties" that had governed them in earlier days. At their head rode the men whose statues adorn three of the four corners of the imposing Voortrekker Monument outside Pretoria today: Piet Retief, Andries Pretorius, and Hendrik Potgeiter. They – and others – led the slow-moving parties to find new land to settle.

The parties dispersed in different directions. Retief headed toward the coast, where he attempted to make a pact with the Zulu king, Dingane, for land and protection for his people. Dingane, however, had come to view Retief as a threat. He lured Retief and his generals into an ostensible celebration unarmed and had them beaten to death, leaving their bodies for the hyenas. Those remaining in Retief's party warded off the Zulu attack that followed, and later that year, Pretorius avenged him. Boer forces numbering a mere 500 met 10,000 Zulu on the banks of the Ncome river. The Boers won handily, killing 3000 Zulu without the loss of a single man, woman, or child. The "battle of Blood River," as this clash became known, would later become a central moment in the narrative of Afrikaner history. Pretorius' victory paved the way for a short-lived settlement of voortrekkers in Natal, abandoned when the British arrived in 1841 and declared it a colony. Thousands more British settlers soon arrived, complementing those who had landed in 1820.

The voortrekkers had more success in the center of the country, between the Orange and Vaal rivers, where they established themselves on large farms. Others moved across the Vaal river: following an engagement with British forces at the battle of Boomplaats in 1848, Pretorius removed his followers here, establishing the Transvaal Republic. From the British perspective this was a workable solution: in areas apart from the Cape Colony and Natal's port city of Durban, they had little interest in becoming involved in conflict unless absolutely necessary. They therefore recognized the Boer-occupied Transvaal (soon renamed the South African Republic) as sovereign in 1852 and when a second Boer republic – the Orange Free State – emerged in 1854 British authorities recognized that too. Reflecting the importance of racial hierarchy to the voortrekkers, the constitution of the South African Republic stated that "The people desire to permit no equality between coloured people and the white inhabitants either in church or state."[14] It seemed as though the relationship between Boer and Briton had reached an agreed-upon impasse that suited both sides.

Because the impact of the trans-Atlantic slave trade on Africa varied by region, time period, class, gender, and society, trying to correlate it to subsequent economic developments proves almost impossible. But perhaps considering the slave trade from a demographic perspective provides some clarity. Scholars estimate that the population of sub-Saharan Africa stood at 50 million in 1700 CE. Roughly half this number fell into the orbit of the trans-Atlantic slave trade and still more in the trans-Saharan and East African systems. When potential birth rates are considered next to the export of persons from the continent, our best estimates are that the number of births *just* outstripped the number of slave exports; extreme estimates postulate that the latter outnumbered the former, resulting in an actual decline in the population of West Africa between 1700 and 1850.

The horrors of the human experience of the slave trade should never be forgotten, certainly, but there are also concrete material reasons why this loss of population proved so destructive. As we noted in the Introduction, the hostile environment of sub-Saharan Africa made "wealth in people" a core organizing principle; people were vital to do the hard and heavy labor that the environment forced upon the land's inhabitants. The majority of people taken in the slave trades were young men and women, the most *productive* and *reproductive* members of society. Without their contributions many communities collapsed or disappeared and untold damage was wreaked upon systems of social and political ordering.

The British abolition of the slave trade in 1807 – and slavery in the colonies in 1834 – did not, however, represent a disengagement with the continent. Missionaries, explorers, and "legitimate" traders poured into Africa, seeking to take up the "White Man's Burden" or simply earn money or fame. The British presence – first informally and then under colonialism – provided African peoples with extraordinary opportunities. They sought to negotiate the best possible circumstances with the pale-skinned foreigners in a wonderfully complex and diverse set of interactions that constantly shifted along fault lines of gender, race, geography, religion, culture, and more.

Notes

1 We have avoided the loaded term "human sacrifice" here. In many parts of West Africa, it is difficult to separate whether killings were for "customary" purposes and involved people already convicted of capital crimes, served to bolster state control, were "judicial executions," or some combination of the above. Ivor Wilks, "Asante: Human Sacrifice or Capital Punishment? A Rejoinder," *International Journal of African Historical Studies* 21 (1988): 443–52; Clifford Williams, "Asante: Human Sacrifice or Capital Punishment? An Assessment of the Period 1807–1874," *International Journal of African Historical Studies* 21 (1988): 433–41.

2 Quoted in PBS, *Wonders of the African World*, Episode 2: *The Swahili Coast*, DVD with Henry Louis Gates, Jr. (1999).

3 The database of slave voyages compiled by Stephen Behrendt, David Eltis, Manolo Florentino, and David Richardson catalogues the journeys of more than 35,000 slave ships. It is available online at www.slavevoyages.org.

4 See P.J. Cain and Anthony G. Hopkins, *British Imperialism, 1688–2000* (London: Longman, 2002).

5 Robin Law, *The Slave Coast of West Africa, 1550–1750: The Impact of the Atlantic Slave Trade on an African Society* (Oxford: Clarendon Press, 1991), 346.

6 Basil Davidson, *The African Slave Trade* (Boston, MA: Back Bay Books, 1980), 217.

7 Paul Edwards, ed., *Equiano's Travels: The Interesting Narrative of the Life of Olaudah Equiano or Gustavus Vassa the African* (Long Grove, IL: Waveland Press, 1996 [1789]), 22.

8 Ralph Austen, *Trans-Saharan Africa in World History* (London: Oxford University Press, 2010), 31.

9 Hannah More, *Slavery, A Poem* (London: T. Cadell, 1788), 8.

10 Quoted in Howard Temperley, *White Dreams, Black Africa: The Antislavery Expedition to the Niger, 1841–1842* (New Haven, CT: Yale University Press, 1991), 15.

11 Quoted in Temperley, *White Dreams, Black Africa*, 157, 162.

12 Quoted in Patrick Brantlinger, *Rule of Darkness: British Literature and Imperialism, 1830–1914* (Ithaca, NY: Cornell University Press, 1988), 178.

13 Quoted in Leonard Thompson, *A History of South Africa*, 4th edn. (New Haven, CT: Yale University Press, 2014), 55.
14 William Worger, Nancy Clark, and Edward Alpers, *Africa and the West*, Vol. I: *From Slave Trade to Conquest, 1441–1905*, 2nd edn. (New York: Oxford University Press, 2010), 190.

Bibliography

Austen, Ralph. *Trans-Saharan Africa in World History*. London: Oxford University Press, 2010.

Behrendt, Stephen, ed. *The Diary of Antera Duke, an Eighteenth-Century African Slave Trader*. New York: Oxford University Press, 2010.

Brantlinger, Patrick. *Rule of Darkness: British Literature and Imperialism, 1830–1914*. Ithaca, NY: Cornell University Press, 1988.

Cain, P. J., and A. G. Hopkins. *British Imperialism, 1688–2000*. Harlow, UK: Longman, 2002.

Davidson, Basil. *The African Slave Trade*. Boston, MA: Back Bay Books, 1980.

Diouf, Sylviane, ed. *Fighting the Slave Trade: West African Strategies*. Athens: Ohio University Press, 2003.

Edwards, Paul, ed. *Equiano's Travels: The Interesting Narrative of the Life of Olaudah Equiano or Gustavus Vassa the African*. Long Grove, IL: Waveland Press, 1996 [1789].

Elphick, Richard, and Hermann Giliomee, eds. *The Shaping of South African Society, 1652–1840*, 2nd edn. Middletown, CT: Wesleyan University Press, 1989.

Eltis, David, and David Richardson, eds. *Extending the Frontiers: Essays on the New Transatlantic Slave Trade Database*. New Haven, CT: Yale University Press, 2008.

Hall, Catherine. "'From Greenland's Icy Mountains . . . to Afric's Golden Sand': Ethnicity, Race and Nation in Mid-Nineteenth-Century England." *Gender and History* 5 (1993): 212–30.

Hempelmann, Ernst, and Kristine Krafts. "Bad Air, Amulets and Mosquitoes: 2000 Years of Changing Perspectives on Malaria." *Malaria Journal* 12 (2013), DOI: 10.1186/1475-2875-12-232.

Klein, Herbert. *The Atlantic Slave Trade*, 2nd edn. New York: Cambridge University Press, 2010.

Law, Robin. "Between the Sea and the Lagoons: The Interaction of Maritime and Inland Navigation on the Precolonial Slave Coast." *Cahiers d'Études Africaines* 29 (1989): 209–37.

Law, Robin. *The Slave Coast of West Africa, 1550–1750: The Impact of the Atlantic Slave Trade on an African Society*. Oxford: Clarendon Press, 1991.

Law, Robin, and Paul Lovejoy, eds. *The Biography of Mahommah Gardo Baquaqua: His Passage from Slavery to Freedom in Africa and America*. Princeton, NJ: Markus Wiener Publishers, 2001.

Manning, Patrick. *Slavery and African Life: Occidental, Oriental, and African Slave Trades*. Cambridge: Cambridge University Press, 1990.

Northrup, David. *Africa's Discovery of Europe, 1450–1850*, 2nd edn. New York: Oxford University Press, 2009.

PBS. *Wonders of the African World*, Episode 2: *The Swahili Coast*, DVD with Henry Louis Gates, Jr., 1999.

Peires, J.B. "The Late Great Plot: The Official Delusion Concerning the Xhosa Cattle-Killing, 1856–1857." *History in Africa* 12 (1985): 253–79.

Rodney, Walter. *How Europe Underdeveloped Africa*. London: Bogle L'Ouverture Publications, 1972.

Shell, Robert C-H. *Children of Bondage: A Social History of the Slave Society at the Cape of Good Hope, 1652–1838*. Hanover, NH: Wesleyan University Press, 1994.

Temperley, Howard. *White Dreams, Black Africa: The Antislavery Expedition to the Niger, 1841–1842*. New Haven, CT: Yale University Press, 1991.

Thompson, Leonard. *A History of South Africa*, 4th edn. New Haven, CT: Yale University Press, 2014.

Thornton, John. *Africa and Africans in the Making of the Atlantic World, 1400–1800*, 2nd edn. Cambridge: Cambridge University Press, 1998.

Wilks, Ivor. "Asante: Human Sacrifice or Capital Punishment? A Rejoinder." *International Journal of African Historical Studies* 21 (1988): 443–52.

Williams, Clifford. "Asante: Human Sacrifice or Capital Punishment? An Assessment of the Period 1807–1874." *International Journal of African Historical Studies* 21 (1988): 433–41.

Wright, Donald R. *The World and a Very Small Place in Africa: A History of Globalization in Niumi, The Gambia*. Armonk, NY: M.E. Sharpe, 2004.

2 Missionaries, merchants, and explorers, 1840s–1880s

In 1874, Samuel Crowther journeyed up the Niger river to meet the emir of Bida, ruler of a territory situated in the west-central portion of what would soon become the colony of Nigeria. On his trip, he wore three hats. The first, a bishop's miter, signaled his position as an Anglican bishop and head of the Church Missionary Society in West Africa, in which capacity he sought to extend Christianity to the largely Islamic northern parts of the region. The second, a Victorian top hat, marked him as a representative of Her Majesty's government, charged with strengthening diplomatic ties with the emir by presenting him with gifts and entreaties to end slave trading. A broad-brimmed straw hat designated Crowther as an agent assisting a contingent of European traders, translating for them as they sought to gain the emir's permission to expand commerce inland from the coast.

The Very Reverend Crowther had a long talk with the emir, King Omoru. He explained how British efforts to bring railroads to such places as Persia (contemporary Iran) had opened up commerce and communication and "improved" the area immeasurably. Certainly so astute a ruler as the emir could appreciate what advantages he stood to gain from similar initiatives in his domain, suggested Crowther. "I then showed him a lump of coal," Crowther noted, ever alert for commercial opportunities, "as the fuel with which steam work is done in England, and [proposed] that he should show it to his subjects; perhaps they might come across such a thing as that in the country one day, [and if they did] to report it to him." In a letter to the official consul in Lagos requesting a yearly stipend for the emir, the bishop put on all of his hats at once. "If Her Majesty's Government would continue to show their recognition of his [the emir's] earnest wishes to promote the interest of trade and more extensive cultivation of produce suitable for European markets by a moderate annual remuneration," he allowed, "I believe good benefits will accrue from it both to commerce and Christian civilization of this extensive portion of interior Africa."[1]

A man of numerous talents, Crowther in many ways embodied the relations between Africans and Britons in the years prior to the scramble for Africa, when missionaries, explorers, and traders constituted the primary British presence there but the British government itself showed little interest

Figure 2.1 Samuel Crowther, c. 1880

in the affairs of the continent. In one respect, however, he belied all expectations: for Crowther was African, a Yoruba man who as a 15-year-old boy was captured by Portuguese slavers and placed on a ship bound for Brazil. Rescued by a captain of the West African Squadron, Ajayi, as he was known, landed in the colony of Sierra Leone, where he found himself one of the "liberated Africans." A missionary family by the name of Davey took him into their school and trained him in English and the Anglican religion. At the end of 1825, at the age of 19, Ajayi received baptism and his new English name.

Crowther's story epitomizes the state of African-British relations in the middle decades of the nineteenth century. They were characterized by possibilities, contradictions, tensions, opportunities, and misunderstandings. Within these sometimes uncertain conditions Africans negotiated their circumstances ably. Some men took on Christianity as a way to procure religious succor and financial benefits, using their education to press for rights from their colonial masters. Some women won success in "legitimate" trade, exchanging palm oil with European traders. And in southern Africa, African peoples formed modern states out of the ravages of the *mfecane*, a period of warfare and upheaval in areas barely penetrated by Europeans.

Krios and Christianity

Before 1800, slavers and traders comprised the largest number of Britons arriving on Africa's shores. But after 1800, Protestant Christian missionaries began appearing in ever-increasing numbers. Their arrival was spurred by an evangelical revival in Britain that had gained a tremendous following from its central role in the abolitionist movement. The revival was focused around the teachings of John Wesley, the founder of Methodism, but it also galvanized other Protestant sects to mobilize missionaries to spread the word of Christ. The Anglicans dispatched members of their Church Missionary Society (CMS) and Congregationalists sent out their own adherents of the London Missionary Society (LMS). Baptists and Presbyterians quickly followed suit. At the core of evangelical fervor was a requirement to proselytize the faith and to baptize heathens in the teachings of Christ. British missionaries, by and large, believed that Africa's "heathens" were stuck in ways of "superstition" and viewed Africa as a fertile ground for conversion.

Africans received Christianity in a variety of ways. Certainly some were genuinely attracted to its message. For many others Christianity provided an opportunity to gain logistical security or an advantageous position in difficult times. By and large, Africans little converted wholesale to the new religion; most maintained long-held cultural practices (relating to the veneration of ancestors, for instance) and layered Christian practices over these existing belief systems. For many peoples living in West Africa's interior or at the Swahili coast of East Africa, Christianity's monotheistic message was nothing new. Islam was widespread in both areas from the fourteenth century onward and for far longer among elite clerics, traders, and court officials.

West Africa was one of the earliest regions for missionizing owing to its closer proximity to Britain and to the high numbers of freed slaves residing there. Initially known as the "Province of Freedom," Sierra Leone became a crown colony under a British governor in 1808 following the abolition of the slave trade the previous year. Ships from the Royal Navy attempted to prevent slave traders operating from West African ports in defiance of abolition and though they met with limited success, their efforts still landed 84,000 freed slaves at the new port of Freetown over the following half-century. These "liberated Africans" were an extraordinarily diverse mixture of peoples from across West Africa, ranging from Igbo and Yoruba to Hausa and Bambara. They joined with a variety of free blacks from the United States, the Caribbean, and Britain (see Chapter 1) to form a new society.

Right from the beginning British influence prevailed in the creation of this new society. The freed slaves settled in parishes named Leicester, Wilberforce, Hastings, and Waterloo, and they received advice and pastoral care from the CMS of London. Early governors in Sierra Leone strongly supported CMS efforts, believing that they would assist in smoothing potential divisions among Africans and creating a successful (preferably Christian) society. Under these governors the British brought western education to Africa for the first time. Fourah Bay College opened in 1827 (though its previous manifestation opened as early as 1816) and became the continent's earliest university modeled on the western tradition. Other schools and colleges followed as Sierra Leone became a magnet for West Africans desiring a British education.

By the second half of the nineteenth century the liberated Africans and earlier settlers had come to constitute a distinct "creole" population called "Krio." By and large, these Krio were educated; most were wealthy from business, which was often trade in palm products or timber; they attended church avidly; and many took English names like Wright, Williams, and Johnson. Above all else they respected education. As Akintola Wyse, one of Fourah Bay's most highly respected alumni and foremost authority on the Krio, put it, "every Krio child . . . grew up to hear and tremble at the words *Bɔbɔ [titi] lan buk* (pay attention in school to reap the benefits of education)."[2] By mid-century some children of Krio elites had traveled to Britain to study medicine and law. Nathaniel King, for instance, attended King's College, London and then moved on to Aberdeen, where he completed his medical degree in 1876. Sylvester Cole also earned his medical degree from Aberdeen in 1883.

The Krio were staunch advocates of British notions of "civilization" and many were grateful for the benefits of British overrule. As S.J.S. Barlatt put it, British civilization "had lifted him to a 'higher plane than that occupied by my fathers.'"[3] But even among the Krio, one of the most seemingly "westernized" peoples following their initial contacts with British governance, the tenets of British culture, religion, morality, and thought rarely supplanted existing practices or beliefs; rather, they were added to them, as was the case among many African peoples in the nineteenth century. Some families, for instance, did not convert to Christianity but preferred to remain Muslim, something that apparently caused little friction. Similarly, when people took English names or those of classical origin, they often maintained their use of local names in conjunction with the new ones (like Aaron Belisarius Cosimo Sibthorpe). Hybridity in terms of dress, religious practices, and funeral rites was also evident, as well as membership in voluntary associations: men would commonly belong to the Freemasons while also receiving initiation into the *Gunungu* or *Ojeh* secret societies. Marriage practices, of course, reflected this mixture of customary and new:

> The bride groom sends his relatives with a calabash covered with white cloth, containing needle and thread, kola nuts and a few domestic items to confirm his intent towards the girl. . . . A Bible, a ring, and "trousseau money" [bedclothes and items of linen] are sent with these items; and after an elaborate exchange of traditional courtesies and speeches by articulate and humorous speakers on both sides, the bride's people signal their approval. Before the wedding-day an *awujoh*, a big feast [to honor dead ancestors], is celebrated.[4]

The Krio certainly viewed themselves as superior to those living in the interior who had had no exposure to Christianity or western education, but they were far from the "black Englishmen" that British officials derogatorily labeled them.

The Krio impact on West African history is significant for two more reasons. First, their convictions about the merits of British practices and notions of "civilization" inspired them to help disseminate these notions. Krio willingly assisted in the spread of British influence during the nineteenth century (for example, participating in the Niger expedition of 1841), leading some African historians later to label them "collaborators." Many became assistants and junior officials in the colonial administration of Sierra Leone and the colony of Lagos from 1861. (In 1851, the British had landed troops in and occupied Lagos, one of the principal centers of the slave trade that persisted after abolition; ten years later, Britain made it an official colony.) Second, the Krio diaspora that began in 1839 had tremendous political and economic repercussions for other parts of the African continent. Many Krio wanted to return to areas from which their fathers and mothers had departed as slaves, and many journeyed between Freetown and Badagry in the Bight of Benin, where they established themselves and traded. This occurred, it is important to note, entirely outside the influence or say of British officials. In Lagos and other parts of Nigeria they were known as the "Saro" and came to control significant portions of commerce in the region. Others saw it as their role to spread the word of God to their new communities or to set up schools. Krio traveled throughout West Africa and some went even further afield.

Krios were also among a handful of West Africans who traveled to and sometimes made their homes in Britain. Records, though scant and unrepresentative, show that Africans lived and worked in places like London in the first half of the nineteenth century. Most men served as seamen in the employ of firms trading out of Liverpool or as domestic servants but a few held skilled artisanal and even professional positions. Many were literate. African women tended to occupy lower-status occupations than African men and their poverty seems to have been greater. By comparison to Irish immigrants in London or Liverpool, Africans fared far better, though their numbers were considerably smaller. They found avenues for self-improvement, which may suggest that in the first half of the nineteenth century, at least, Britain offered a more welcoming environment to Africans than we have previously thought.

Missionaries

The story of Samuel Ajayi Crowther provides an apt illustration of the dynamics described above. In 1826 he accompanied the missionary family that had befriended him to London and spent some eight months at school there. He returned to Freetown in 1827 to attend Fourah Bay College as its very first student and ultimately became a tutor there. Called to the life of a missionary, Crowther joined the Niger expedition in 1841, impressing his CMS employers with his careful and detailed reports of the events we saw unfold in the previous chapter. The CMS then called him back to London for more formal training. Ordained first as a deacon and then a priest in 1843, Crowther returned to West Africa, where he established the Niger mission for the CMS in 1857. In 1864 he was appointed bishop of West Africa, a sprawling territory encompassing lands from the equator to the Senegal river.

The unsuccessful Niger expedition had convinced Crowther that if missionary work among Africans was to succeed Africans themselves would have to undertake it. Certainly Europeans' difficulty in handling the climate of the region informed his thinking but he also recognized the cultural, social, and political obstacles that would stand in the way of European efforts to Christianize Africans. He differed from most of his European counterparts in stressing the role that education should play in the process: where they emphasized preaching the word of God, Crowther underscored the importance of teaching, out of which ultimately the word of God would come. He understood that the first difficulty to overcome would be attracting people to the mission. Once there, he confidently believed, they would gradually – but eventually – come to accept the doctrinal instructions of the Anglican Church.

Crowther thus put his energies into persuading local rulers and elders to allow the CMS to build schools in their territories. He counseled his missionaries to focus their attention on developing these schools, an instruction that provoked a great deal of criticism from his European colleagues. One white missionary protested that the black bishop rarely spoke of God when talking with local rulers, instead presenting the benefits of a mission "as an inexpensive way to enable their children to get good pay as clerks or engineers with the traders." But Crowther knew his audience. He knew that these material advantages would appeal to chiefs and elders where liturgy would not. And, he trusted, the curriculum would work in the missionaries' favor, for "all the elementary school books are extracts from the Holy Scripture inculcating all virtues and condemning all vices, and vividly pointing out the folly and superstition of idolatrous worship."[5] Whether or not his confidence in this was well placed, his strategy worked. In the years following the establishment of the Niger mission in Onitsha in 1857, Crowther expanded CMS activity across southern Nigeria, finding particular success in establishing missions throughout the Niger Delta region.

The British public, however, heard little about Samuel Crowther, the Krio/Saro, or any other African personages when it came to the spread of Christianity. That was the remit of heroic white missionaries, displaying British vigor and grit for all to see. In southern Africa, these qualities were encapsulated in a Scottish doctor (who never actually completed medical school) named David Livingstone. But despite what contemporary recollections suggest, Livingstone was not the originator of all missionary works in southern Africa; in fact he was following in a long tradition of LMS work in the region, the tone of which was set by Dr. John Philip.

Philip was another Scotsman whose activities – like those of Livingstone later – will be forever associated with pressing for the rights of Africans. He took charge of the LMS in South Africa in 1822 and immediately set to work trying to convince the government of the Cape Colony to offer better protections for its non-white population. The British had taken steps to protect African workers in 1809 with the passage of the Caledon Code, but Philip and his compatriots viewed it as insufficient as it also required workers to carry passes that restricted their movement (a later staple of apartheid). In 1828 Philip secured the passage of Ordinance 50, a tremendous achievement for African rights. The ordinance, passed into law on July 17, proclaimed that "Hottentots [Khoikhoi] and other free Persons of colour" could own land and did not have to carry passes. Moreover, it improved the colony's labor contract laws (although it stopped short of being genuinely "colorblind"). Philip was no fool when it came to protesting slavery. He took a leaf from the abolitionists' playbook and spent much of his time arguing that systems of slavery or servitude were in fact highly uneconomic.

But it was Livingstone whose face became attached to the missionary enterprise in Africa. Sporting a thick, walrus mustache set below a permanently furrowed brow, Livingstone was notoriously publicity-shy despite the fame that seemed to follow him around. He ultimately spent the better part of three decades living throughout southern Africa before his death in

Zambia in 1873. His greatest achievements came as an explorer rather than as a missionary; he believed that Africans should convert other Africans, and it is possible that he converted only one person during his career. Livingstone was the first European to set eyes on Victoria Falls (known to the locals as *Mosi-oa-Tunya* – the "water that thunders"), opened the Kololo kingdom of southern-central Africa, traveled west as far as Luanda, and explored many of the continent's central and eastern lakes in a search for the source of the Nile.

Livingstone expressed his views on the British presence in Africa in three words, inspired by evangelicals like Thomas Fowell Buxton, the abolitionist and promoter of the 1841 Niger expedition: "Christianity, Commerce, and Civilization." He and many other missionaries such as Samuel Crowther believed fervently in the doctrine of free trade espoused by Adam Smith. Based on the classical liberal principle of the right of individuals to possess things, free trade held an almost holy status among evangelicals. They believed that the unrestricted amassing of capital, the rational utilization of labor and resources, the pursuit of self-improvement through education and training, and the cultivation of personal responsibility, morality, and self-restraint were the hallmarks of enlightened, godly people, and their inculcation in Africans would bring civilization to the peoples of the dark continent. Most importantly, the benefits of free trade would rapidly end the trade in human beings. Livingstone was deeply troubled by the slave trade that still marred parts of West Africa and much of East Africa, where it had shifted after 1850 or so. He believed that creating viable systems of "legitimate commerce" (probably in ivory) across sub-Saharan Africa would ensure that better options than slave trading prevailed, though he accepted that slavery *within* Africa might exist as a necessary evil for truly ending the export of people from the continent.

Livingstone garnered extraordinary fame during his career. His book *Missionary Travels and Researches in South Africa* (1857) – which sold an extraordinary 70,000 copies – played an important role in catapulting him to prominence. The British public lauded his efforts in Africa, which contemporaries held up in contrast to the journeys of more violent explorers. Livingstone represented the highest degree of selflessness: in 1854, after traversing the continent to Luanda, he refused free passage back to Britain from a vessel in port because he had to guide his African porters home. He routinely refused to accept that expeditions were "his," instead regarding them as the expeditions of the African chiefs or leaders who provided supplies for them. According to some sources he never lost an African porter during a journey. The tragedy of Livingstone's legacy was that after his death in 1873, recognized by a state funeral at Westminster Abbey, his name was used to justify some of the worst abuses of colonization, undertaken to fulfil his purported desire to bring the "Three C's" to Africa.

Livingstone was not just highly respected in Britain but also in Africa. One need only take a tour of the Livingstone Museum (in the town of

Livingstone, on the Zambian side of Victoria Falls) to appreciate the admiration many still have for the man. His name is spoken in hushed, almost reverent tones. The respect is due in large part to Livingstone's views and actions during his lifetime. Unlike the majority of Britons who arrived on the continent during the century, Livingstone tried to master several African languages, becoming fluent in Tswana; he studied local customs and practices in great depth; and he learned about African religious beliefs, an almost unheard-of notion for a Christian missionary. His abilities and approach differed strikingly from those expressed by the majority of explorers who arrived on the continent, as we will see below.

The arrival of Christianity in southern Africa proved particularly attractive to those segments of society that could most directly benefit from the advantages it offered, particularly security. In the early nineteenth century this category of converts was greatly enlarged as a result of the *mfecane*. The term refers to a period of difficulties centered on Nguni-speaking peoples in the southeastern part of the continent during the 1810s and 1820s (modern-day Kwazulu-Natal), when warfare created extraordinary chaos and disruption. During and after the *mfecane* thousands of people scattered north into the heart of Africa in a process that continued for several decades. They fled the violence and formed states to defend themselves.

Shaka was the central figure associated with the *mfecane*. Though relatively little is known about Shaka the man, his image has been used more than perhaps any other figure from nineteenth-century Africa. Apartheid-era historians called upon him to demonstrate the apparent bloodthirstiness of Africans; Zulu nationalists have evoked him in support of Chief Buthelezi's political ambitions in South Africa over the past two decades; and more recently Durban named its newest transport facility the King Shaka International Airport. Older generations of historians laid the *mfecane* directly at Shaka's feet, claiming that new military tactics he used – including the raising of state regiments (*amabutho*) – provided the impetus for violence carried out by his Zulu armies. While this was certainly a part of the intellectual puzzle that is the *mfecane*, there was more to it than one man's ambitions.

A variety of other factors contributed to the creation of new African states during the period. The expanding trade out of the Portuguese port of Delagoa Bay (now Maputo) – especially in ivory but also in a variety of other items – gave the leaders of proto-states incentives to militarize, build regiments of young men, and try to dominate the new business. They had begun this process in the late eighteenth century and the arrival of new trading opportunities galvanized it. Slave trading may have also played a role, and periods of drought in 1800–1807 and 1820–1823 certainly raised the stakes. Armed bands competed for the remaining cattle, fighting one another to control larger sections of the ivory trade.

The *mfecane* inspired the appearance of a variety of "new" African states. The Zulu – a small sub-section of the Mthethwa – under Shaka and his

Figure 2.2 Cover page from *The Life and Explorations of Dr. Livingstone* (1874). A staunch opponent of the slave trade and advocate for African rights, Livingstone is still revered in parts of southern and central Africa today.

successor Dingane (the assassin of Piet Retief) were the most prominent. Following their defeat by Shaka's forces, the Ndwandwe fled north where the main group, led by Soshangane, established itself in southern Mozambique as the Gaza empire. The Ngwane, led by Sobhuza, found refuge in modern-day Swaziland, becoming the "Swazi" later in the century. The former Zulu general Mzilikazi led his people north to Zimbabwe where they became the Ndebele; and Moshoeshoe, utilizing a combination of diplomacy and the purchase of guns and horses, protected the Sotho on a mountaintop called Thaba Bosiu. Four decades later, in 1868, Moshoeshoe – by then an old man – invited the British to declare his kingdom the formal colony of Basutoland, replacing its protectorate status, believing it the best option to secure his people from the depredations of Boers and other African peoples of the interior. Though the boundaries of the new colony excluded much of the land the Sotho had long enjoyed, the decision was the foundation for the modern country of Lesotho, the tiny nation entirely land-locked within South Africa.

Throughout the region refugees fled to whomever could offer them protection. Demonstrating the flexibility of "tribe" in nineteenth-century Africa, many refugees easily "became" Sotho, Zulu, or Swazi as they found new homes. Others such as the Mfengu and Xhosa fled into the Cape Colony seeking protection from the British and established themselves as workers there. And more arrived on the doorsteps of mission stations, looking for a place to find food and security. Mission stations had first appeared in southern Africa during the early nineteenth century, most started by British and American missionaries and a few by French Protestants. The number of early African converts to Christianity was tiny but within several decades they would carry inordinate amounts of power and wealth.

Communities developed in and around the mission stations, with some stations boasting populations as large as 1000 by the end of the century. A typical station included a home for the foreign missionaries, a small school, and perhaps a few basic outbuildings, one of which would house a clinic. For the majority of the nineteenth century, a husband and wife team usually staffed the stations but in its last quarter, single American and British women missionaries became especially active. (Consider, for example, the female American Congregationalists who founded Inanda Seminary outside Durban in mid-century, or those working further afield in places like Uganda and Madagascar.) African chiefs were often happy to grant land to the missionaries for their presence brought advantages. Clinics helped care for the sick and missionaries proved particularly helpful as delegates who could present a case to a British magistrate in the event of a dispute. Moshoeshoe, for example, had invited French and Swiss missionaries of the Paris Evangelical Mission Society to establish themselves at Morjia in 1833. Reverend Eugene Casalis represented the chief's desires to foreigners for the next two decades. Moreover, the missionaries provided a measure of security, as any invaders who caused the injury or death of a missionary might invite British reprisals.

Those who arrived at the stations were almost never the children of chiefs or other prominent persons; they were usually poor and destitute. In some cases they had lost their families in the upheavals of the *mfecane*; others were ostracized by accusations of witchcraft. Some parents dropped their children at the mission stations because they could no longer afford to feed them; others because a woman had borne twins, an occurrence regarded by many peoples in southern Africa as unlucky. Leaving one child for the missionaries to raise could erase the misfortune. These outcasts and rejects received religious and material succor from their new protectors.

In Xhosa areas in South Africa's eastern Cape the arrival of missionaries caused tensions, largely owing to misunderstandings that arose between missionary and Xhosa. Initial interactions between the two sides involved a gift-exchange. The LMS representative, for instance – Dr. Johannes van der Kemp, the eastern Cape's first missionary – gave the Xhosa chief Ngqika some tobacco in 1799, receiving cattle in return following their initial negotiations. Van der Kemp failed to realize that the exchange cemented his place as a political subordinate to the Xhosa chief, a situation that proved awkward in subsequent dealings. Poor relations persisted into the first decades of the nineteenth century as disgruntled Xhosa fled to the stations to evade punishment or regulations imposed by their people. Some women arrived in order to avoid having to marry older men they did not desire. In the minds of many Xhosa chiefs and parents, the mission came to represent a place of rejection of customary authority.

In Xhosaland, as elsewhere across the continent, forms of religious syncretism developed. Missionaries viewed Xhosa country as an "extensive moral Wilderness," devoid of any "knowledge of the *true God*, but [also] without the knowledge of *any* God true or false."[6] But their binary view of belief ("Christian" versus "pagan") left them blind to the realities of the new religious mixings. As among the Krio, Christianity provided Xhosa peoples with new options to add to their pantheon of belief. We see such syncretism in the beliefs of the prophet Nxele, who became a close associate of Chief Ndlambe. Nxele inspired the joint attack of the Ndlambe and Gcaleka against Grahamstown in 1819 (see Chapter 1). His preaching involved railing against "witchcraft, polygamy, adultery, incest, warfare and the racing of oxen." He strongly promoted the biblical creation narrative as well as the story of the resurrection, but his "God" was not that of the Christians but Mdalidiphu, the "creator of the deep."[7]

In mission stations converts learned to read and write in English under missionary supervision, quickly becoming fluent as they listened to sermons from the pulpit and read passages from the Bible. Their lives were ordered by the ringing of church bells. They awoke to the first peals of the morning and organized their daily duties around the sounds that reflected a European sense of time and discipline. And they dressed like Europeans, the men sporting long trousers, waistcoats, and even top hats while the women draped themselves in the long gowns worn by Victorian women across the western world (much to the amusement of those who continued to wear skins). In Zululand converts were laughingly called *amarespektabili* – the "respectable ones" – and their trappings and their lifestyles appeared to pose little threat to the established order.

The term *respectable* was a significant one. Converts consciously viewed themselves as "respectable," "civilized," "black Englishmen." They reflected this status in part by building European-style cottages (though this was difficult and expensive in many areas), wearing tailored and well-maintained clothes (especially at Sunday services), serving tea from china cups in their homes, and avoiding drunkenness. They typified what one historian describes as "creole elites" that appeared across Africa during the nineteenth century: "Westernized black elites" who had taken on the trappings of British society. They shared much in common with the Krios of West Africa, the Cape Coloured in South Africa, and the suited lawyers in Gold Coast. As they became educated and grew wealthy over time they believed themselves deserving of the same legal rights colonial settlers possessed.

As the century progressed the originally precarious livelihoods of the "outcasts" faded into dim memory as first under missionary supervision and then, not long afterwards, outside it these Christians became economically prosperous. Many turned to farming. Whereas the majority of Xhosa or Zulu concentrated their energies on cattle, some converts took inspiration from missionaries' neat, well-tended gardens to establish themselves as successful agriculturalists. Others built trading companies or established sugar mills. Some learned bookkeeping and clerking skills or became lawyers. Some sent their children to colleges in the United States and Britain to do their undergraduate studies.

A significant proportion of the early converts in South Africa were girls and women. Mission stations were certainly attractive to them (for reasons noted above) but their majority at the stations also derived from the fact that boys were expected to look after the herds and undertake migrant labor, both activities that precluded them from attending school. There was a clear distinction in the experience of boys and girls in mission schools in the later nineteenth century. Boys were given minimal education, designed only to enable them to function as migrant workers. Girls on the other hand received more advanced curricula, especially training in domestic skills. Officials believed that learning to cook, clean, and look after their families would encourage a transition to monogamy and prepare women to provide comfortable, stable homes, minimizing potential discord caused by male, educated elites. (Girls trained in professions like nursing and teaching would later use their positions to challenge segregation and apartheid in South Africa by means of various women's groups – especially prayer unions – ultimately leading to the "feminisation of schooling" in the late twentieth century.)[8]

But it is too neat a distinction to separate people into different worlds of "Christian" and "non-Christian"; the two overlapped and lines between them blurred. In Zulu areas, for instance, converts rejected such cultural practices as polygyny, the taking of multiple wives. But other practices persisted, despite missionaries' disapproval. *Lobola*, in particular, was a deeply embedded institution involving the payment of bridewealth in cattle by a man's family to that of his prospective wife. It proved highly resistant to change and remains in many communities today. Similarly, while missionaries preached against the brewing and consumption of beer, its role as an important cultural symbol meant that its production and use continued.

This cultural mixture was perhaps best represented in the figure of Reverend John Dube. Described by one scholar as the "leading spokesman of his day of Natal's African Christian elite," Dube was from a family with the closest possible ties to Inanda Seminary and became the first president of the African National Congress (ANC), then called the South African Native National Congress, in 1912.[9] Like many of these Christian Zulu elites – soon known as *amakholwa* – he was highly educated and attended Oberlin College in Ohio in the 1890s. But the authority he commanded and position of power he was able to maintain were due to more than just his status as a Christian leader. Dube was also tightly linked with the elites of the Zulu-speaking Qadi chiefdom, whose authority assisted him in his rise to power during the late nineteenth and early twentieth centuries. Dube was thus "doubly elite," a man who bridged two ostensibly different worlds in a somewhat ambiguous manner; from this position he won tremendous success.

While the converts played a vital role in rapidly changing social ordering in Xhosa and Zulu areas, further to the west they could play a political role as well. The system known as Cape liberalism – established when the Cape government issued a new constitution in 1853 that included a nonracial franchise for its residents – made it possible for Africans with property worth more than £25 to vote. The Cape Colony enjoyed one of the most liberal constitutions in the world at the time, though voters only ever elected two men of color to parliament. The relatively low bar for property ownership created controversy among many landowners; one, in fact, had joined the colony's legislative council two years before the new law to try to prevent this "torrent of democracy with which we have been threatened."[10] The new constitution gave Christian elites, who often owned businesses, the opportunity to participate in the politics of the Cape, along with those former slaves, Khoisan (a term used to describe Khoikhoi and the few San people, known as "Coloureds"), and other non-white peoples who met the standard.

Christian elites, most of whom were Mfengu and Xhosa, seized the chance to become active citizens in the colony's political and intellectual life. For all intents and purposes election to the Cape parliament was impossible, but they worked to gather votes for white politicians whom they believed would best represent their interests. These politicians, indeed, provided the monies for the publication of *Imvo Zabantsundu* ("Native Opinion," the first African newspaper independent of the missions, edited by John Tengu Jabavu) and *Izwi Labantu* ("The Voice of the People," edited by A.K. Soga), newspapers in which African intellectuals aired their grievances and put forward their political arguments. Their views were conservative. They fought for rights within the constraints of the political system, believing that British liberalism provided the best way forward for Africa. The poet I.W.W. Citashe, writing as Isaac Wauchope, articulated the position of most Christian Africans in a famous poem, published in *Isigidimi samaXhosa* ("The Xhosa Messenger") in 1882. He challenged his fellow men to become educated, express their views in writing, and behave respectably. Conflict was no way to bring political change, he argued vociferously:

> Your cattle are plundered, compatriot!
> After them, after them!
> Lay down the musket,
> Take up the pen,
> Seize paper and ink:
> That's your shield.
>
> Your rights are plundered!
> Grab a pen,
> Load it, load it with ink;
> Sit in your chair;
> Don't head for Hoho [a forest in Xhosaland]:
> Fire with your pen.
>
> Put pressure,
> Engage your mind;
> Focus on facts,
> And speak loud and clear;
> Don't rush into battle:
> Anger stutters.[11]

Men like Jabavu, Sol Plaatje, and Dube – the latter two both founding members of the ANC – were all prolific authors, exemplifying the explosion of African intellectual production that took place among Christian Africans in the late nineteenth century.

Explorers

David Livingstone considered that his explorations of southern and central Africa ran a poor second to his missionary activities, especially his efforts to help end the slave trade. Average Britons on the other hand found tales of "discoveries" by intrepid explorers – of Mount Kilimanjaro, Lake Victoria, or the source of the Nile – far more to their taste, however much they applauded the humanitarian efforts of men like the good doctor. Stories about the exploits of African explorers riveted the readers of newspapers and broadsheets, who endowed their new heroes with the qualities that they prided themselves in possessing – manliness, individualism, courage, morality, patriotism, and a penchant for scientific inquiry. Explorers were the rock stars of their time and their tales of solitary derring-do against man-eating wild animals, raging rivers, blazing hot deserts, and bloodthirsty and cannibalistic savages thrilled readers at home. British schoolboys knew every detail of Richard Burton and John Speke's hunt for the source of the White Nile in the late 1850s, and they could recount the details of Henry Morton Stanley's 999-day journey from Zanzibar across the continent to the mouth of the Congo river (1874–1877) by heart.

The exploits of these intrepid explorers had an academic aspect to them, for the Geographical Society of London (GSL) commissioned and subsidized many of their expeditions. Formed in 1830 for the "advancement of geographical science," the GSL later changed its name to the Royal Geographical Society; it is still active today. The inaugural issue of the society's journal claimed that "interest excited by this department of science is universally felt . . . [and] its advantages are of the first importance to mankind." The society's first two aims were to spread geographical information to the public, who had hitherto experienced difficulty accessing it, and to collect charts and maps of little-known parts of the world.

The foundation of the GSL represented a moment of extraordinary fascination with Africa's geography. Its members funded a variety of explorers' expeditions to the continent – including at least two to try to find Livingstone – and provided a forum for the dissemination of information they gathered. Letters and bulletins dispatched from afar were published in the pages of the GSL's journal long before the explorers themselves returned. While the explorers were still absent in Africa, often for several years at a time, "armchair" geographers fiercely debated one another about the source of the Nile or the location of the Mountains of the Moon. When the explorers finally returned they delivered lectures to sold-out audiences, the members of which hung on their every word.

The "scientific" findings and testimonies of these explorers provided the body of knowledge – the imperial archive – on the basis of which imperialists would later found their enterprises. Their descriptions of their travels and their accounts of the means by which they obtained information about the continent's flora, fauna, geography, topography, environment, peoples, cultures, societies, and raw materials turned out to be highly problematic, as we now know. For one thing, explorers were not the self-reliant individuals courageously cutting through unknown territory that they made themselves out to be. Rather, they traveled in commercially-run and -organized caravans along well-trodden paths, that – in many cases – Arab and Swahili traders had used for centuries. Many explorers did not know how to use their scientific instruments; even when those instruments functioned properly (and they often did not), in the hands of inexperienced practitioners they produced inaccurate measurements and findings. Maps were often

Figure 2.3 A typical expedition caravan in central Africa during the nineteenth century. This image shows one of Britain's most famous explorers, Henry Morton Stanley.

wildly inexact, but once drawn they tended to be used over and over again. Perhaps most strikingly, we cannot regard the state of explorers' minds as they mapped, measured, observed, collected, recorded, named, and classified the peoples and things they came across as rational in any conventional sense, let alone objective or scientific.

Much of the time explorers suffered from dysentery, which produced terrible bloody diarrhea. To treat it they took copious doses of laudanum, otherwise known as tincture of opium. They contracted severe fevers that produced hallucinations and took quinine to prevent or treat deadly fevers such as malaria, which created its own mind-altering effects including ringing in the ears, blurred vision, impaired hearing, and confusion, and even occasionally temporary blindness. Explorers drank heavily and regularly amongst themselves and as part of the social niceties preceding negotiations with African rulers. And they took drugs, often partaking in the hemp-smoking or chewing of the stimulant *khat* in which many Africans engaged. In other words they were literally "out of their minds," as one anthropologist has noted, for a good portion of their travels.[12] Yet it was their "science" that informed subsequent imperialist ventures.

Explorers were especially important in spreading beliefs about race that circulated throughout Europe and the United States in the nineteenth century, on the basis of which British imperialists would soon justify their actions. One of the major contributors to what we now call "scientific racism" was a British officer with the East India Company who became an explorer, ethnographer, and diplomatic consul over the course of his colorful career. Richard Burton's accounts of his many adventures in Africa – fighting off attackers in Somalia, seeking out the source of the Nile in East Africa, and serving as consul in West Africa in the early 1860s – contain detailed descriptions of the "barbaric" peoples he moved among. His writings clearly demonstrate that he was, very often, out of his mind with delirium or drunkenness, but that did not prevent Britons accepting his statements as true and reliable observations of Africa and Africans. Burton portrayed himself as a practiced and professional ethnographer whose findings on race should be given the highest scholarly consideration. They often received it, even if some thinkers took issue with his findings.

Few figures presented a more striking contrast to the saintly David Livingstone than Burton. The two men might have shared in the public acclaim heaped upon them by the Victorian populace but there any similarity ended. Where Livingstone regarded Africans as intrinsically valuable and deserving of his respect, Burton scorned them, viewing them as poor specimens of beings hardly rising to the level of humans. And where Livingstone saw in Christianity, commerce, and civilization sources for the improvement of Africans, Burton saw only wasted efforts at best and a positively harmful set of practices at worst. He felt only contempt for Christianity and missionaries, the former for its subversion of the "authentic" character of African societies and the latter for creating a class of westernized Africans who sought to behave like Europeans, crossing racial boundaries that should have been held inviolable. He saw these "black Englishmen" as ridiculous, hybrid creatures that could only vitiate further the inferior stock of African people. As he put it, "there is nothing to cheer us in the conversion of the negro, because when converted he becomes worse than before." Livingstone grew tired of Burton's persistent slandering of missionaries, calling them "monstrous and false," and Burton himself "an awful ruffian."[13]

Though he himself did not subscribe to it and in fact advocated to the contrary, Burton's writings embellished a theory of race developed during the eighteenth century, when scientific principles and practices of taxonomic classification were applied to human beings. This theory sought to explain racial and sexual difference and different stages of societal and political development on the basis of habitation in one of three climatic zones: torrid, temperate, or frigid.[14] In the writings of a number of prominent Enlightenment figures, including those of Adam Smith, David Hume, and Edward Gibbon, hot climates – those found in the torrid zones immediately adjacent to the equator – stimulated inordinate sexual desire and behavior; the populations residing there displayed few inhibitions and in fact regularly indulged in riotous sexual activity. The further one moved away from the equator, toward Europe say, in the temperate zone, the degree of sexual passion exhibited by populations diminished or at least was much more readily controlled. Further north, in the frigid zone, men and women were so indifferent to passion as to practically ignore each other. These various regimes of sexual desire and activity correlated with the extent to which the societies participating in them had developed their social, economic, and political systems. As Adam Ferguson claimed in 1767,

> The burning ardours, and the torturing jealousies, of the seraglio and the haram, which have reigned so long in Asia and Africa, and which, in the Southern parts of Europe, have scarcely given way to the difference of religion and civil establishments, are found, however, with an abatement of heat in the climate, to be more easily changed, in one latitude, into a temporary passion which ingrosses the mind, without enfeebling it, and which excites to romantic achievements: by a farther progress to the North, it is changed into a spirit of gallantry, which employs the wit and the fancy more than the heart; which prefers intrigue to enjoyment; and substitutes affectation and vanity, where sentiment and desire have failed. As it departs from the sun, the same passion is further composed into a habit of domestic connection or frozen into a state of insensibility, under which the sexes at freedom scarcely chuse to unite their society.[15]

Civilization and political liberty scarcely existed, according to these thinkers, in the hot climates of the torrid zone, where heat and uninhibited sexual activity sapped the energies of individuals and rendered them lethargic and compliant. In the more temperate regions of Europe, climate and sexual restraint enabled the development of societies that enjoyed the energy, productivity, and discipline necessary to produce political liberty and civic virtue. The commercial society of Britain, noted these philosophers, characterized by wealth, industry, political freedom, polite social relations, and the benefits of domesticity and separate spheres for men and women – and the "backward" societies of Africa, populated by indolent, slavish, lascivious men and women – provided a vivid contrast of the differential effects of climate and geography on progress and civilization.

Eighteenth- and nineteenth-century writers also sought to categorize human beings on an evolutionary scale that placed Europeans at the pinnacle and Africans at the bottom. In this representation of humankind, Africans served to delineate the place where humans and animals merged, establishing the African as the "very embodiment of savagery," as Jean and John Comaroff put it.[16] In the minds of the British, Africa came to signify unalterable, fundamental difference from European social and gender roles, morals, mores, customs, values, and traditions. This difference was usually explained by the disordered gender system and promiscuous sexuality attributed to Africans, and especially to African women, by writers and explorers. One English observer writing in *The Universal History* (1760) embedded his description of African sexual practices within a long list of qualities believed to be the antithesis of those characterizing the manly English gentleman and the proper English lady: the African was "proud, lazy, treacherous, thievish, hot and addicted to all kinds of lusts, and most ready to promote them in others, as pimps, panders, incestuous, brutish, and savage, cruel and revengeful, devourers of human flesh, and quaffers of human blood, inconstant, base, treacherous, and cowardly." One could no more "be an *African* and not lascivious" than "be born in *Africa* and not be an African."[17] So overwhelming was the sexuality of African women in the minds of British men that it exceeded all bounds. "If they meet with a [white] Man," William Smith averred in a 1745 account of his experiences in Guinea, "they immediately strip his lower Parts and throw themselves upon him."[18]

The conflation of primitive savagery and sexuality appeared early on in the stories about "Amazons" who inhabited West Africa and would ultimately be called upon to justify violence against those who resisted British efforts to expand their control of the area. Adventurers and government officials brought home to Britain tales of "scantily attired," tattooed, female soldiers in Dahomey, which excited the colonial imagination about Africa and African women. Since the late seventeenth century armed, uniformed, disciplined women had served as palace guards to the king of Dahomey. By the time Europeans arrived in the eighteenth century they had taken on the functions of warriors. Their size, strength, and demeanor led Europeans to dub them "Amazons," after the ancient Greek stories of savage women warriors. The gender and sexual disorder exemplified by Amazon women could be readily adduced by their "masculine physiques" and "unwomanly" traits. "Such . . . was the size of the female skeleton, and the muscular development of the frame," observed Richard Burton in 1863, "that in many cases femineity [*sic*] could be detected only by the bosom."[19] Europeans regarded Amazons as superior to male soldiers in discipline, skill, loyalty, effectiveness, and ruthlessness. By the late nineteenth century stories circulated widely in Britain of Amazons who engaged in horrific hand-to-hand combat using sharpened fingernails and razors to kill, mutilate, and then eat their foes and brought back the scalps, genitals, and internal organs of their fallen enemies to display as trophies. As Burton's widow claimed, Amazons were "crueler and fiercer than men," creatures who tortured their prisoners and cut open the bellies of pregnant women.[20]

These descriptions reduced Africans and African societies to the level of primitive savagery, a state of being that had excused British involvement in the slave trade on the grounds that Africans could hardly be counted as human. The same reasoning was soon used to justify nineteenth-century efforts to subdue and control the peoples of Africa through a system of imperial rule that promised to raise Africans up to "civilized" status. By mid-century, as we saw in Chapter 1, the conviction that Africans could be tutored in British norms and standards was being challenged. Burton played a crucial role in the transition to a way of thinking that precluded such a possibility. He fervently and loudly trumpeted the claim that black Africans did not share human origins with whites and that they in fact emerged from a completely separate and decidedly inferior species of humankind. As one of the founders and then vice president of the Anthropological Society in London, his views enjoyed a wide audience and he convinced a significant portion of British society of their validity.

Commerce

Though they often despised one another, or at least despised the values and concerns each represented, missionaries and explorers shared a common interest – commerce. Men like Richard Burton, John Speke, and Henry Morton Stanley were certainly inspired to undertake their journeys by dreams of adventure and glory but the material support underwriting their efforts derived from entities seeking to enlarge their profits by expanding trade to the interior of Africa. Missionaries like Samuel Crowther, John Philip, and David Livingstone might decry the greed disguised as profit apparent in the activities of merchants plying their trade but they fully embraced the conviction that commerce in "legitimate" commodities was the only way that the trade in human beings could be stopped. For their part merchants and traders might express contempt for do-gooders devoted to converting heathens but they, too, recognized that missionaries played a crucial role in opening up the continent to trade. Missionaries and traders depended on each other for support in their respective enterprises, no matter how much they protested to the contrary (such as when Crowther lamented that some of the

British merchants were "members of the Anthropological Society and disciples of [Richard] Burton," who felt only contempt for missionary work.)[21]

Crowther in fact proved a key actor in opening the Niger interior to European commerce. In 1851 he and the CMS leadership endorsed and lobbied on behalf of Scottish merchant MacGregor Laird's bid to secure a contract from the British government for his African Steamship Company. Laird won a five-year contract to send monthly steamers up the Niger during and after the rainy season when navigation was possible and in 1854 dispatched the first of them, the *Pleiad*. Crowther was aboard along with a good number of Europeans (who did *not* succumb to disease, owing to Laird's practice of dosing them with quinine). Over the next seven years Laird's steamers voyaged up and down the riverway, carrying mail, cargo, Europeans, emigrants from Sierra Leone (who sought new trading opportunities inland), and African missionaries under Crowther's supervision who established and ran new missions.

Laird died in 1861. When no European merchant stepped in to replace his transport business, Crowther proposed that the CMS purchase its own vessel and, under the auspices of the Native Agency committee, take over the ferrying of people and products up and down the river. In 1863, with funding from humanitarians in Britain, the West African Company began operation, setting up depots at the main mission stations that dotted the Niger and carrying goods and people to and fro. It succeeded in large part because of its connection with Crowther's Niger mission. While the management of the West African Company fell to people independent of the mission some of them enjoyed close personal relations with the bishop. His sons, Josiah and Samuel Jr., served as agents for the company at Lokoja, while his son-in-law, James Thompson, ran the depot at Onitsha. Crowther placed the resources of his mission at the disposal of the company, helping to ensure that it survived because he realized how much his mission depended upon it. When, later, French and German trading interests sought to establish their own presence on the Niger in the run-up to what would become the scramble for Africa, they found that the success of the West African Company had precluded them from being able to do so.

But by that time the mutually beneficial commercial relationships between Africans and Britons in West Africa had changed. After 1875 competition from local and emigrant African traders had reduced British merchants' profits. West African Company officials resented the space taken up by missionaries on their steamers, space that could better accommodate clients who would pay full price for it. And they bristled at missionary insistence that they not work on Sundays or require their employees to do so. Over the next decade Europeans displayed increasing hostility toward Crowther's missionaries. The head of the company, George Goldie, sought to establish a new system of rule that would brook no disloyalty, a view that led him to regard the Niger missionaries as suspect owing to their often intimate connections with certain African traders he thought they favored. Goldie fired Crowther's sons and other Africans who held similar posts from the company's ranks. In 1886 Goldie went further still, categorizing Africans from the Niger Delta or emigrants from Sierra Leone as "foreigners" who had to purchase a license if they wanted to engage in the river trade. The new licensing system, he insisted, would work

> to exclude from the Territories . . . a class of men . . . who were formerly the worst enemies of civilization in Central Africa. These were disreputable coloured men (in the past they were generally inferior clerks dismissed for peculation) who . . . lived, by surreptitious dealing in slaves . . . stirring up the natives to discontent and bloodshed . . . under a mask of ardent piety.[22]

This slandering of the very people who had opened up the Niger to British commerce – and the inflammatory language Goldie used to explain his decision – reflected a real shift in the way Britons had come to regard their relationship with African peoples. A virulent racism accompanied this transition, as Goldie's words bear out.

CMS officials, despite their earlier enthusiasm for facilitating "African advancement" through precisely the kind of local trading Goldie now sought to eliminate, tended to support European traders who came into conflict with their own African missionaries. This new attitude within the CMS mirrored that of the general British public, for whom Africans had come to signify savagery and barbarism. Even long-standing CMS authorities harbored suspicions that African missionaries were "not yet proven," and when European traders and newly appointed European missionaries began to level charges of drunkenness and private trading against Crowther's subordinates CMS officials listened. Ultimately they appointed a lay secretary for the Niger mission who was responsible for all of the secular work Crowther had undertaken in the past. Undercut by his superiors and under fire from new European missionaries who attacked him for defending African pastors who were removed from their posts, the bishop of West Africa felt compelled to resign his position. He did so in 1890, his ouster from the church reflecting the broader imperial impulse that emerged with the scramble for Africa. As was the case in commerce and administration, Africans lost ground in church and missionary work, the highest offices going almost exclusively to Europeans. Not until 1953 would Africans celebrate the appointment of another black bishop.

With industrialization well underway in Britain, commerce with Africa thrived. The suppression of the West African slave trade had the effect of increasing the demand for waged and indigenous slave labor in Africa itself as trade in palm oil and then palm kernels came to replace that in human beings. The insatiable call for palm oil to lubricate the machines of industrialization in Europe and the subsequent use of palm kernels to make margarine, a new commodity that found an avid consumer base, stimulated the creation of sizable plantations that required a large workforce. Thousands of European ships from Liverpool or Southampton, bankrolled by financial firms in the City of London, arrived in West Africa to trade. Over the course of the nineteenth century these interactions brought Africa further and further into the world economy. In these interactions "legitimate" trade gradually replaced slave trading, though the two systems coexisted in areas like the Upper Guinea Coast and Dahomey far into the century. Europeans were certainly attracted to the Niger Delta's palm oil but also to products like peanuts from the Gambia and groundnuts and rubber from the Upper Guinea Coast.

The trans-Saharan trade – though it was still important and continues to operate today – gradually became less significant than the trans-oceanic trade during the nineteenth century. European ships docked in towns like Porto Novo and Lagos in ever-increasing numbers and these cities developed into centers of power and wealth. British firms built trading houses and warehouses for the storage of their goods and crown agents made treaties with local leaders that sometimes included financial payments for not trading in slaves. The entire coastal region of West Africa, indeed, saw the migration of large numbers of people from the interior as a result of conflict there and the better economic conditions at the coast. It became far wealthier than the interior, something that is still characteristic of West Africa today.

The European desire for products like palm oil and groundnuts had a significant impact on the organization of societies in West Africa, which varied by region and decade. In Old Calabar, as well as in towns further west in the Niger Delta like Bonny, slave trading elites simply "switched over" from slaves to palm oil, thereby maintaining their positions of high status. In some cases ex-slaves themselves became wealthy trading elites but usually only when their masters supported their rise. Large-scale, wealthy producers acted to cement their positions in towns like Old Calabar, where they forced through a law requiring that every trader pay £1000 for a permit to trade in palm oil. This, clearly, aimed to exclude small-scale producers and increase the profits of the bigger operations.

One of the main differences between slave and palm oil trading was that if the playing field was level (unlike in Old Calabar) large-scale operations offered few advantages over small-scale setups. Palm oil production did not require hundreds of slaves; families could undertake it with their relatives at the household level. In many areas this provided a tremendous economic opportunity for the poor to seize their chance to become better off. Throughout the century Europeans traders paid high prices for palm oil from traders in West Africa, and at the same time the cost of manufactured goods from Europe dropped, giving Africans more buying power. Many became "middle class" through this trade, buying European fabrics, brandy, or iron products as suited their interests.

Legitimate trade also had an important impact on the status and roles of women in many West African societies. The growth and production of palm oil often fell into women's remit because agricultural work was widely considered the preserve of women. In some areas, like Igboland, men prevented women from controlling the products of their labor in palm oil production and it is likely that their exploitation in such circumstances was widespread. But in other places women were more successful in winning economic success. On the border areas between Dahomey and Yorubaland women comprised the majority of small-scale traders. From the capital of Dahomey (Abomey) to the port of Ouidah, European observers in the nineteenth century noted how women dominated "petty trading" and men were barely present in that occupation. Women manufactured the oil and transported it to trading centers or the coast. When a Yoruba chief called Shodeke was told by a British representative that he should sell palm oil instead of slaves he asked, "Is not a woman to sell palm oil, how can a man sell oil like a woman?"[23] This economic system enabled women to maintain a degree of autonomy from their husbands and male relatives, with free women keeping control over their earnings. Some female slaves were even able to earn enough money to purchase their freedom. Though the evidence is scant, one historian suggests that men may have created or raised the importance of "masquerade societies" at the time to try to restrict female movement and trading, which they felt were increasing dangerously. As the American missionary William Clarke noted, "by this means the female population is kept in subjugation. . . . If she dares resist, Egungun [one such society] gives her a drubbing not to be forgotten."[24]

But while "legitimate trade" gradually supplanted slave trading in most areas during the course of the nineteenth century, in some – like Dahomey – slave trading declined hardly at all. Elites continued to export slaves despite abolition, often commanding prices as high as during the peak of the slave trade, given slaves' increased rarity and the dangers of "illegitimate" trading. Dahomey had close connections with Brazilian slavers, most prominently the viceroy Felix de Souza, who ensured that the majority of slaves for export went to Brazil. But Dahomey's elites also reoriented much of their trading internally. The number of domestic slaves skyrocketed, as did the activities of slavers who looked to profit from the business of providing them. Slaves worked on plantations, such as those owned by the king of Dahomey, established on the West African coast to grow palm products. In fact the number of slaves laboring on plantations in West Africa increased during the nineteenth century (with more working there than in the Americas). Livingstone and other missionaries and humanitarians found no shortage of objects for their attention.

One British officer serving on a Royal Navy anti-slavery patrol off the coast of Sierra Leone in the 1860s recorded how slaves fetched higher prices within Africa than from European buyers. "The reason," he observed,

> is the great increase of trade, and all labour being required for the cultivation principally of ground nuts, palm nuts, and palm oil . . . the legal trade and the increasing communication has made the slaves

> much more valuable, so many being required for home slavery that the increased price would not pay any one exporting slaves from this part of the coast.[25]

One chief living in the region explained that he made an annual profit of £7 10s per slave from the sale of the rice they grew on his land. The going rate for the sale of a slave was only marginally more at £10, so it made better economic sense for him to keep his slaves than export them.

This increase in domestic slavery was especially clear in the interior. Many peoples there struggled to turn from slave trading to legitimate trade; their connections to potential European traders were too distant and agricultural products – of high weight and relatively low value – did not bear the costs of transport from the interior to the coast. Moreover, the lower demand for slaves at the coast meant that much of the slave trade turned toward the Sahara, and the prices for slaves in the interior may well have increased during the nineteenth century. But at the same time the Saharan littoral saw an increase in legitimate trading, especially in gum products that traveled east to west into the Senegal valley. This provided enough revenue to increase the supply of guns to the Sahara, the presence and increased use of which caused instability.

The increase in the numbers of firearms was an important factor in creating and maintaining a level of endemic conflict throughout the middle Niger region during the nineteenth century. The economy of the kingdom of Segu (or the "Bambara Empire"), for instance, which arose under the Coulibaly dynasty during the eighteenth century, was based on slave raiding, the sale of captured slaves, and the products of their labor. Similar modes of production and heavy involvement in slaving characterized the economies of the two states that together caused Segu's downfall, Masina and the Tukolor empire. They were two of a number of Islamic theocracies established in West Africa during the eighteenth and nineteenth centuries, their creation based around the ideology of *jihad*. In the Tukolor empire, for instance, the state that sacked Segu in 1861, elites received land and slaves for their services in producing grain for trading. The Tukolor empire offered protection for trade routes to the west into the Senegal valley, where grain was exchanged for guns and other products. Other states, like Samori Toure's Wassoulou empire based in Guinea, for example, followed the same course.

Disease

Perhaps the greatest factor in determining trading relations – and later the imposition of British control in Africa – was not goods or guns but disease. Without European advancements in learning to survive the diseases that afflicted them in Africa, there would have been no British empire in Africa. For traveling in Egypt or on short expeditions up the Niger river was a far cry from the sort of penetration that would be required for colonization.

Before the mid-nineteenth century Africa was aptly known as the "White Man's Grave." About half of all Europeans who ever set foot on the continent died, most of "fever" (usually malaria). Europeans had little immunity to the continent's diseases, unlike Africans.[26] Between 1816 and 1837, for example, Africans serving in the Sierra Leone Command died at a rate of 26.5 per 1000. For Europeans the incidence of death stood at 478 per 1000. There could be no "scramble for Africa" until Europeans learned how to control the disease environment that seemed almost purpose-built to thwart them.

The chief slayer of Europeans was malaria though yellow fever was an ever-present danger too. Malaria is transmitted to humans from the bite of several types of the female Anopheles mosquito. *Plasmodium falciparum*, the most common form of the malarial parasite across sub-Saharan Africa, is more virulent and deadly than the malarial parasite in Europe, *Plasmodium vivax* (although *P. vivax* and another parasite called *P. malariae* also exist in parts of the African continent). But Europeans in the mid-nineteenth century understood neither malaria's vector nor the kind of parasite whose predations inspired Burton to describe the consulate at Lagos as a "corrugated iron coffin or plank-lined morgue, containing a dead consul once a year."[27]

Although missionaries, explorers, and merchants little comprehended malaria's transmission they did learn to treat it. Europeans had experimented with quinine – derived from the ground-up bark of the cinchona tree – since the seventeenth century when Jesuit missionaries in South America had drawn attention to it. True breakthroughs came in the early nineteenth century when quinine entered commercial production in Britain after 1827. Quinine still had its detractors until the middle of the century but its efficacy was finally proven on two expeditions up the Niger river. In 1841, 82 percent of the crew of the three ships that comprised the expedition fell ill with malaria. One traveler, Dr. T.R.H. Thomson, had taken quinine throughout the voyage and avoided the illness (until he returned home and stopped taking the drug!). When MacGregor Laird headed back to the Niger again in 1854, he required everyone to take quinine as a *preventative* measure before exposure to the disease. No Europeans died.

Malaria was not the only problem, though it was responsible for the vast majority of European deaths in Africa in the nineteenth century. Waterborne diseases such as typhoid, cholera, hepatitis A, diarrhea, and dysentery proved just as debilitating and were often fatal. In these cases as well the nineteenth century saw a revolution in treatment, as experts in Britain experimented with ways to treat water to ensure its safety and the improvements were carried to Africa from mid-century onward. A number of scientific breakthroughs inspired the dramatic changes in preventing water-related illness. In the late eighteenth century Antonie Lavoisier discovered that all manner of substances could be dissolved in water. Then John Snow demonstrated that cholera was transported in impure water by means of an analysis of its spread in London during an 1854 outbreak. The development of germ theory soon after, associated with such luminaries as Robert Koch and Louis Pasteur, explained precisely how microorganisms caused disease. As Britons began to take more precautions against waterborne diseases at home, establishing clean sources of water, piping it untainted to homes, and implementing sewer systems, they also transported the improvements to Africa.

This revolution in the treatment of disease advanced significantly after the Asante invaded territory in the southern region of modern-day Ghana in 1873, which the British had purchased from the Dutch just two years earlier (and named "Gold Coast" in 1874). The invasion demanded a response from the British force stationed there under General Garnet Wolseley, an experienced soldier with a reputation for efficiency (and the model for Gilbert and Sullivan's "Modern Major General" in the *Pirates of Penzance*). The "Ashanti Campaign" – the third conflict between the British and Asante – came at the perfect time to test whether improvements in the control of disease were truly effective in Africa. The Asante capital of Kumasi on the northern edge of West Africa's forest region constituted one of the most hostile places for British redcoats to serve. During the first Asante conflict in the 1820s British troops had died at a rate of 638 per 1000. Yet Wolseley insisted on sending British regulars against the Asante because "every native of Africa [has] a superstitious dread of the white man."[28] His troops would have to travel north through humid, moist, and dank forest to reach Kumasi. A number of journalists including Henry Morton Stanley accompanied them in order to observe and report home. The pressure was on: could British troops fight in Africa without the devastating loss of life to disease?

Wolseley took never-before-seen precautions for the march to Kumasi in January 1874. Plans called for the campaign to take place during the dry season to reduce exposure to mosquitos. Seventy-three of the 270 British officers served in a medical capacity, charged with looking out for the health of their men. Several hospital ships stood at anchor off the coast and a series of camps stationed ten miles apart dotted the territory between the coast and Kumasi so that sick men could be hand-carried out rapidly. A medical officer ensured that each man received quinine every day while on land. Extensive precautions related to ensuring the cleanliness of water were implemented. Some men carried special equipment to test water quality; others were issued long tubes through which to procure water from a depth of four to six feet below the soil; and the quartermaster built a distilled water system at the coast. The careful planning and precautions paid off handsomely. Only 27 of every 1000 British troops died over the two-month campaign, *including* those killed in engagements with the enemy.

Wolseley's men had shown that Africa could be penetrated safely. This development had profound consequences for future African-British relationships. The British no longer had to rely so heavily on African agents for a vast proportion of their activities. Increased British intervention in

Africa – in terms both of commerce and actual penetration of the land – gave rise to increased European competition and tension, resulting ultimately in the scramble for Africa, a development that received greater impetus when Britain purchased shares in the Suez canal in 1875.

The Suez canal

Access to the Suez canal would give British military and commercial vessels the ability to move goods and people between India and Europe and Africa speedily and safely. The Suez canal was built in 1869 by a French company, but it appears at first to have made little impression on British strategists, who believed that a railroad across the isthmus linking the Mediterranean to the Red Sea – and thence on to the Indian Ocean – offered the best shortcut to the subcontinent. The completion of the canal, however, and its success in attracting a large amount of British maritime traffic, altered the situation completely. Egypt became the crucial link to India; whoever controlled Egypt controlled the fate of the subcontinent. The Egyptian ruler served, at least theoretically, as a viceroy to the Ottoman sultan, a ruler constantly threatened by Russian efforts to dominate the Dardanelles. Russia, moreover, posed a threat to the British in India. The prospect of this alien power potentially blocking access to the Suez canal caused great anxiety.

The decision to buy in to the Suez canal would prove pivotal in the years to follow. It happened as a consequence of the rise of Conservative leader Benjamin Disraeli to the prime ministership, an office from which he courted Queen Victoria assiduously and positioned her at the center of an imperial policy designed to increase Britain's empire and thereby enhance its status vis-à-vis the other European great powers. His rival for power, the Liberal William Gladstone, often tried to resist the growing demands of both politicians and the people for more and greater imperial adventuring and sometimes succeeded in hewing to a "Little England" line. At other times he could not, and against his own better judgment committed his nation to enterprises that had far-reaching consequences. Together, the two prime ministers engaged their country in a program of "new imperialism" that monopolized British foreign affairs for the remainder of Victoria's life. New imperialism signaled the culmination of a dramatic shift in Britons' understanding of empire. Where it had once connoted a relationship of white colonies of settlement – a union between Britons and their free and loyal kin overseas, best exemplified by the colonies of Canada, South Africa, Australia, and New Zealand – empire now signified possession of and rule over peoples of color.

Gladstone became prime minister in 1868 (the first of his four terms), when a coalition of Liberals and working men newly enfranchised by the Reform Act of 1867 voted the Conservatives out of power. Disraeli nevertheless remained active, embarking upon a series of ventures to further his imperial ambitions for Britain. In 1872 he delivered a speech at the

Crystal Palace in which he asked Britons to decide whether they wanted to live in a "comfortable England" – by which he meant Gladstone's "Little England" – or in "a great country – an Imperial country," from which they would "command the respect of the world."[29] As he had suspected, the public wished for the latter, embracing the idea of empire and expressing enthusiasm for enterprises that would provide a glorious future for the nation. One of Disraeli's first actions when he came to power again in 1874 was to purchase shares in the Suez canal, which became available the following year.

Having spent massive sums – much of it borrowed from British banks – on modernizing their country, the *khedives* of Egypt had built up a mountain of debt. The ruler in 1875 found himself facing bankruptcy. His only assets, his shares in the Suez Canal Company, came on the market and Disraeli jumped at the chance to purchase them. He told only the queen and a few of his ministers of his intentions. Victoria encouraged him to act, applauding his "*very large ideas*, and *very lofty views* of the position this country should hold."[30] Disraeli had to move quickly before any other company or government could upstage him. Parliament was in recess so Disraeli turned to the Rothschild family for the funds, secretly borrowing from the banker the £4 million necessary to purchase the shares. Upon learning that the *khedive* had accepted his offer the prime minister told Victoria, "It is settled. You have it, Madam." The queen was thrilled at the news that Disraeli had won the day but he still had to explain his unorthodox measures to parliament in purchasing the shares, essentially, behind its back. He had done so, he informed members of parliament, because controlling the canal was "necessary to maintain the empire."[31] Some months later, parliament agreed to pay the Rothschilds back. It is hard to imagine that Disraeli's nemesis, the cautious Gladstone, would have ever involved himself in such a reckless venture.

Though Britain had purchased only a minority interest in the company that owned the Suez canal the British public somehow became convinced that it owned the canal itself. Before too many years passed this impression became more and more a reality, as we shall see below, until finally the French company that owned and managed the canal was doing so under the protection of British authorities and the British military.

The middle decades of the nineteenth century saw an increased British presence on the African continent. Missionaries, explorers, and traders – first slavers and then "legitimate" businessmen – all descended upon its shores and began to take the first tentative steps into the interior. Fascinated Britons in the public houses and teahouses of Victorian London followed their progress avidly. Initially, Britons regarded Africans as humans on a lower scale than Europeans; backward but capable under British tutelage of rising to full and complete humanity. But by mid-century, the sympathetic, benevolent (if patronizing) intellectual notions of the abolitionist period had hardened. Britons came to view Africans as degraded and backward, people who would ultimately require "civilizing" at the hands of virtuous Britons.

The greater level of British influence brought new opportunities for different cadres of Africans. In some parts of West Africa women won economic autonomy trading in palm oil, and in others elites built slave plantations to develop crops for sale on the European markets. Across the continent men and women took on Christianity as a way to negotiate famine conditions or simply to win better jobs and livelihoods, adding it to a broad spectrum of beliefs they already held. Many of them were convinced of the merits of "respectability" and strove to become "black Englishmen," though by the later part of the century it was clear that this vision was no more than a mirage. By the 1870s European improvements in disease control – as well as in military, transport, and communication technologies, as we'll see in the next chapter – heralded an entirely new phase in British relations with Africans.

Notes

1 Quoted in Jesse Page, *The Black Bishop: Samuel Adjai Crowther* (Westport, CT: Greenwood Press, 1979 [1908]), 256, 258.
2 Akintola Wyse, *The Krio of Sierra Leone: An Interpretive History* (London: Hurst, 1989), 33.
3 Quoted in Wyse, *Krio of Sierra Leone*, 7.
4 Wyse, *Krio of Sierra Leone*, 11.
5 Quoted in J. F. Ade Ajayi, *Christian Missions in Nigeria, 1841–1891: The Making of a New Elite* (Evanston, IL: Northwestern University Press, 1965), 218–19.
6 Clifton Crais, *White Supremacy and Black Resistance in Pre-Industrial South Africa: The Making of the Colonial Order in the Eastern Cape, 1770–1865* (Cambridge: Cambridge University Press, 1992), 101.
7 Crais, *White Supremacy*, 104–105.
8 Meghan Healy, "'To Control Their Destiny': The Politics of Home and the Feminisation of Schooling in Colonial Natal, 1885–1910," *Journal of Southern African Studies* 37 (2011): 247–64.
9 Heather Hughes, "Doubly Elite: Exploring the Life of John Langalibalele Dube," *Journal of Southern African Studies* 27 (2001), 445.
10 Quoted in Robert Ross, *Status and Respectability in the Cape Colony, 1750–1870: A Tragedy of Manners* (New York: Cambridge University Press, 1999), 169.
11 Jennifer Wenzel, *Bulletproof: Afterlives of Anticolonial Prophecy in South Africa and Beyond* (Chicago, IL: University of Chicago Press, 2009), 77–78.
12 See Johannes Fabian, *Out of Our Minds: Reason and Madness in the Exploration of Central Africa* (Berkeley: University of California Press, 2000).
13 Quoted in James L. Newman, *Paths Without Glory: Richard Francis Burton in Africa* (Washington, DC: Potomac Books, 2010), 219.
14 See Felicity A. Nussbaum, *Torrid Zones: Maternity, Sexuality, and Empire in Eighteenth-Century English Narratives* (Baltimore, MD: Johns Hopkins University Press, 1995).
15 Quoted in Susan Kingsley Kent, *Gender and Power in Britain, 1640–1990* (London: Routledge, 1999), 88–89.
16 Jean Comaroff and John Comaroff, *Of Revelation and Revolution*, Vol. I: *Christianity, Colonialism, and Consciousness in South Africa* (Chicago, IL: University of Chicago Press, 1991), 99.

17 Quoted in Anne McClintock, *Imperial Leather: Race, Gender, and Sexuality in the Colonial Conquest* (New York: Routledge, 1995), 22.
18 Quoted in Kim F. Hall, *Things of Darkness: Economies of Race and Gender in Early Modern England* (Ithaca, NY: Cornell University Press, 1995), 34.
19 Richard F. Burton, *A Mission to Gelele, King of Dahome*, (London: Tylston and Edwards, 1893), Vol. I, 112; Vol. II, 42.
20 Quoted in Burton, *Mission to Gelele*, Vol. II, xi.
21 Quoted in Ajayi, *Christian Missions*, 211.
22 Quoted in Ajayi, *Christian Missions*, 242.
23 Quoted in Robin Law, "'Legitimate' Trade and Gender Relations in Yorubaland and Dahomey," in Robin Law, ed., *From Slave Trade to "Legitimate" Commerce: The Commercial Transition in Nineteenth-Century West Africa* (Cambridge: Cambridge University Press, 1995), 205.
24 Quoted in Law, "'Legitimate' Trade and Gender," 209.
25 Quoted in Law, "Introduction," in *From Slave Trade*, 9.
26 Africans in certain regions that had had long-standing interactions with Europeans were able to resist illnesses of European origin like smallpox, whereas Native Americans, lacking such contact and therefore the build-up of immunity, died from them in huge numbers.
27 Quoted in Robert Smith, *The Lagos Consulate, 1851–1861* (London: Macmillan, 1978), 67.
28 Quoted in Philip D. Curtin, *Disease and Empire: The Health of European Troops in the Conquest of Africa* (Cambridge: Cambridge University Press, 1998), 57.
29 Quoted in Jan Morris, *Heaven's Command: An Imperial Progress* (London: Faber and Faber, 1973), 382.
30 Quoted in Walter Arnstein, *Queen Victoria* (Basingstoke, UK: Palgrave Macmillan, 2003), 140.
31 Quoted in Morris, *Heaven's Command*, 420.

Bibliography

Ajayi, J.F. Ade. *Christian Missions in Nigeria, 1841–1891: The Making of a New Elite*. Evanston, IL: Northwestern University Press, 1965.

Ajayi, J.F. Ade, ed. *UNESCO General History of Africa*, Vol. VI: *Africa in the Nineteenth Century until the 1880s*. Berkeley: University of California Press, 1998.

Arnstein, Walter. *Queen Victoria*. Basingstoke, UK: Palgrave Macmillan, 2003.

Bickford-Smith, Vivian. "The Betrayal of Creole Elites, 1880–1920." In *Black Experience and the Empire*, edited by Philip D. Morgan and Sean Hawkins, 194–227. Oxford: Oxford University Press, 2004.

Burton, Richard F. *A Mission to Gelele, King of Dahome*, 2 vols. London: Tylston and Edwards, 1893.

Comaroff, Jean, and John Comaroff. *Of Revelation and Revolution*, 2 vols. Chicago, IL: University of Chicago Press, 1991–97.

Crais, Clifton. *White Supremacy and Black Resistance in Pre-Industrial South Africa: The Making of the Colonial Order in the Eastern Cape, 1770–1865*. Cambridge: Cambridge University Press, 1992.

Curtin, Philip D. *Disease and Empire: The Health of European Troops in the Conquest of Africa*. Cambridge: Cambridge University Press, 1998.

Dixon-Fyle, Mac, and Gibril Cole, eds. *New Perspectives on the Sierra Leone Krio*. New York: Peter Lang, 2006.

Duffield, Ian. "Skilled Workers or Marginalized Poor? The African Population of the United Kingdom, 1812–52." In *Africans in Britain*, edited by David Killingray, 49–87. Ilford, UK: F. Cass, 1994.

Fabian, Johannes. *Out of Our Minds: Reason and Madness in the Exploration of Central Africa*. Berkeley: University of California Press, 2000.

Hall, Kim F. *Things of Darkness: Economies of Race and Gender in Early Modern England*. Ithaca, NY: Cornell University Press, 1995.

Hamilton, Carolyn. *Terrific Majesty: The Power of Shaka Zulu and the Limits of Historical Invention*. Cambridge, MA: Harvard University Press, 1998.

Hamilton, Carolyn, ed. *The Mfecane Aftermath: Reconstructive Debates in Southern African History*. Johannesburg: Witwatersrand University Press, 1995.

Healy-Clancy, Meghan. *A World of Their Own: A History of South African Women's Education*. Charlottesville: University of Virginia Press, 2014.

Hughes, Heather. "Doubly Elite: Exploring the Life of John Langalibalele Dube." *Journal of Southern African Studies* 27 (2001): 445–58.

Kent, Susan Kingsley. *Gender and Power in Britain, 1640–1990*. London: Routledge, 1999.

Law, Robin, ed. *From Slave Trade to "Legitimate" Commerce: The Commercial Transition in Nineteenth-Century West Africa*. Cambridge: Cambridge University Press, 1995.

McClintock, Anne. *Imperial Leather: Race, Gender, and Sexuality in the Colonial Conquest*. New York: Routledge, 1995.

Morris, Jan. *Heaven's Command: An Imperial Progress*. London: Faber and Faber, 1973.

Newman, James L. *Paths Without Glory: Richard Francis Burton in Africa*. Washington, DC: Potomac Books, 2010.

Nussbaum, Felicity A. *Torrid Zones: Maternity, Sexuality, and Empire in Eighteenth-Century English Narratives*. Baltimore, MD: Johns Hopkins University Press, 1995.

Page, Jesse. *The Black Bishop: Samuel Adjai Crowther*. Westport, CT: Greenwood Press, 1979 [1908].

Prevost, Elizabeth. *The Communion of Women: Missions and Gender in Colonial Africa and the British Metropole*. Oxford: Oxford University Press, 2010.

Ross, Robert. *A Concise History of South Africa*, 2nd edn. Cambridge: Cambridge University Press, 2008.

Ross, Robert. *Status and Respectability in the Cape Colony, 1750–1870: A Tragedy of Manners*. Cambridge: Cambridge University Press, 1999.

Smith, Robert. *The Lagos Consulate, 1851–1861*. London: Macmillan, 1978.

Switzer, Les, ed. *South Africa's Alternative Press: Voices of Protest and Resistance, 1880s–1960s*. Cambridge: Cambridge University Press, 1997.

Thompson, Leonard. *A History of South Africa*, 4th edn. New Haven, CT: Yale University Press, 2014.

Wenzel, Jennifer. *Bulletproof: Afterlives of Anticolonial Prophecy in South Africa and Beyond*. Chicago, IL: University of Chicago Press, 2009.

Wyse, Akintola. *The Krio of Sierra Leone: An Interpretive History*. London: Hurst, 1989.

3 The scramble for Africa, 1870s–1890s

Early in 1867, a South African teenager name Erasmus Jacobs sat down beneath a tree to rest after fixing a water pipe on the "de Kalk" family farm. A *mooi klip* – "beautiful stone" – caught his eye; he gathered it up, took it home, and gave it to his siblings to play with. After some weeks passed Erasmus and his sisters and brother brought out the stone to use in a game they were playing. A neighbor – the former owner of "de Kalk," Schalk van Niekerk – arrived and noticed the stone. He took it to the window of the home and scraped the glass with it to see whether it would cut or mark its surface. It cut. Van Niekerk left with the stone and eventually brought it to Dr. William Atherstone, a mineralogist, for examination.

On April 2, 1867, Atherstone wrote to Richard Southey, the chief secretary of the Cape Colony, reporting that he had received a "fine Diamond" from Hope Town, a settlement on the banks of the Orange river to the northeast of Cape Town. "It *cuts* (not scratches) glass easily," he stated. The following week, the *Colesberg Advertiser* heard the news and published a hastily produced article in time for its weekly print run. "There is a story this morning afoot," began the piece, about a "stone" apparently valued at £800.[1] The *mooi klip* proved to be a 21-and-a-quarter carat brownish-yellow diamond. Later that year it was exhibited at the World's Fair in Paris under the soon-to-be world-famous moniker, "the Eureka Diamond." It set off a diamond rush in South Africa, the impact of which is felt to this very day.

The discovery of diamonds and then gold in South Africa reinforced the centuries-old European belief that Africa was a land of practically limitless wealth that would reward any enterprising European nation that established its presence there. In the late 1870s and early 1880s the various European powers carved out large sections of the African continent that they deemed were their "spheres of influence." Faced with international competition they had not seen since the end of the eighteenth century, British statesmen and politicians responded in kind, formally annexing vast territories across Africa and placing them under administrative control in order to protect British "interests" from encroachment on the part of other European countries. At an international conference held in Berlin in 1884 and

1885 to try to settle conflicts over West Africa, Europeans began the process of recognizing each other's claims to a continent not their own, drawing up maps delineating which power would hold sway where, and establishing the rules to determine how the scramble would take place. This carving up of the "magnificent African cake" continued in a number of later agreements over the next six years, though much of it remained largely confined to paper before World War I, as Africans put up strong resistance against the European presence and the latter did not possess the resources to make good their claims when it came to translating them into actual governance on the ground.

The scramble for Africa took place in a remarkably short period of time. In 1876, Europeans controlled perhaps one-tenth of the African landmass. During the 1880s they claimed five million square miles containing 60 million Africans; by 1900, nine-tenths of Africa had been colonized. On the ground much of the scramble was undertaken by chartered and even private companies, which were granted permission to act as the representatives of European governments, thereby saving taxpayers the costs of empire. This was merely one aspect of a larger imperial impulse – known as "new imperialism" – on the part of the industrialized powers, which by 1900 could boast that fully one-fifth of the land on the globe and one-tenth of the world's population were under their authority. New imperialism had its origins in a number of developments that took place after 1870: widespread industrialization, the unification of Germany and the rise of extra-European nations to great power status, an economic downturn, and the popularization of ideas about race and war that we associate with Charles Darwin's theory of evolution.

Erasmus Jacobs' discovery of the Eureka diamond had monumental repercussions for the lives of Africans in southern Africa. By the 1890s a migrant labor system existed that drew men and women from all over the region to the diamond mines of Kimberley and the gold mines of the Witwatersrand ("The Rand" after 1886). The system caused social pressures and reordering in rural communities as well as in the urban sprawls of Kimberley and Johannesburg, and spurred the formation of a modern sense of "tribe" that we still recognize today. Perhaps most importantly the racialized legislation passed to control black migrant laborers formed the basis for twentieth-century "segregation" and then apartheid in South Africa. Despite these pressures African peoples negotiated the system skillfully. Whether as washermen, prostitutes, beer-brewers, or participants in mine life, workers learned to utilize and shape their situations to create meaningful lives in the midst of a system that was designed to deprive them of this ability.

Britain's second industrial revolution, 1870–1914

The first industrial revolution that began in Britain in the 1760s and ran until the 1860s cannot really be considered "revolutionary." It involved

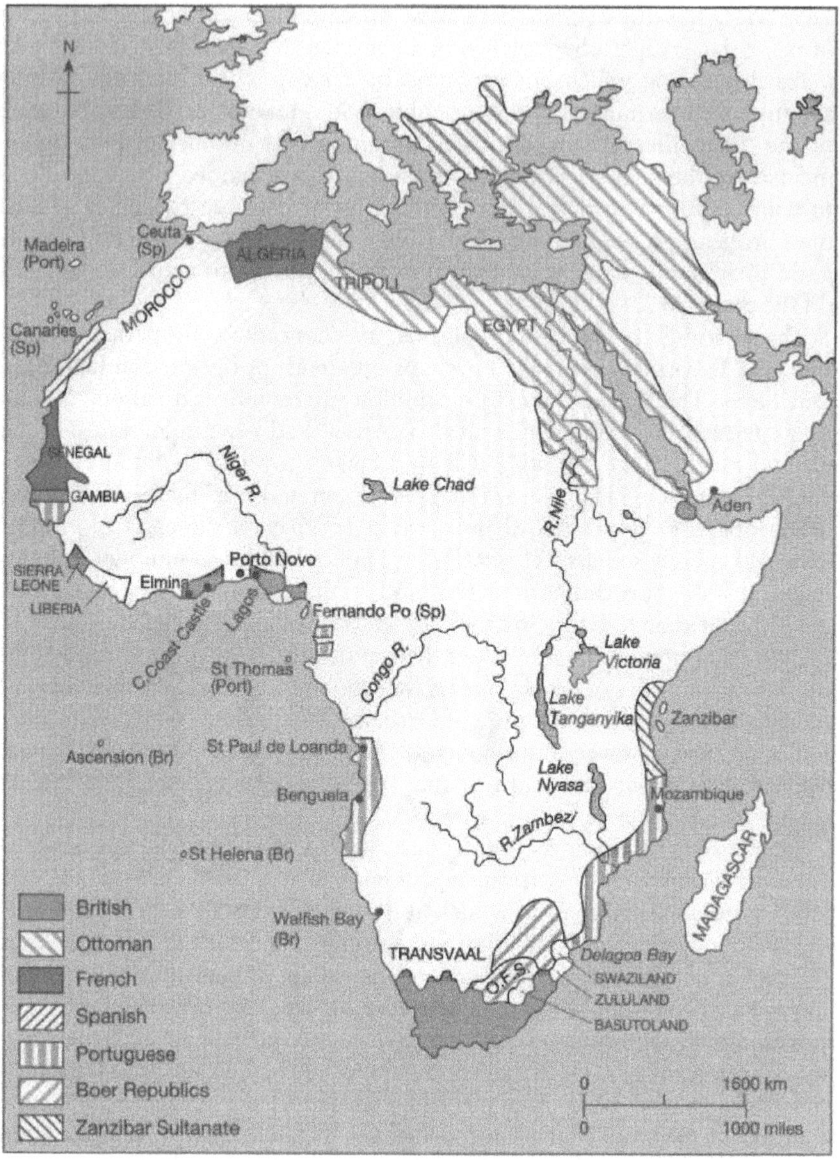

Map 3.1 The European presence in Africa, c. 1870
© *The Scramble for Africa* by M. E. Chamberlain, p. xxxix (Pearson, 2010).

the application of steam power to manufacturing processes, raising output and productivity astronomically in *already existing* industries such as textile production and mining, and it occurred over such a long period that people had time to become accustomed to the changes it wrought. The second industrial revolution in Britain on the other hand was scientific in

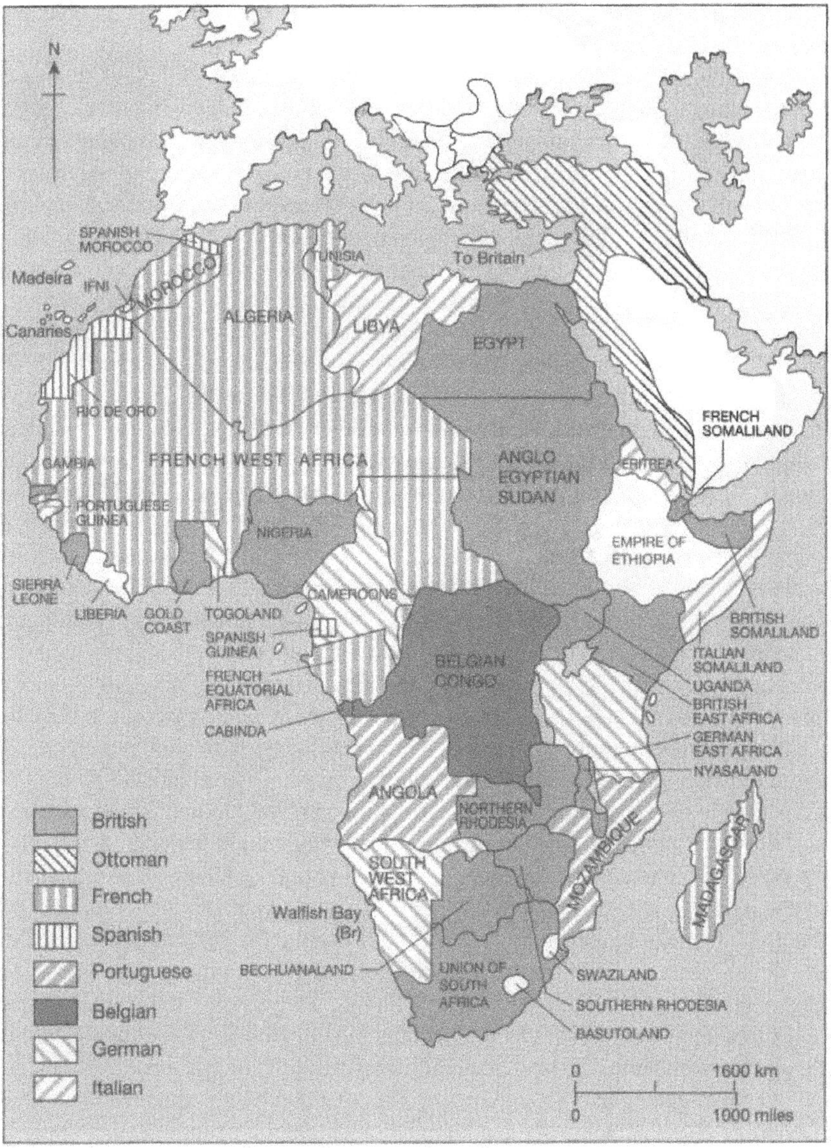

Map 3.2 European colonies in Africa, c. 1914
© *The Scramble for Africa* by M. E. Chamberlain, p. xl (Pearson, 2010).

nature. It entailed the creation of entirely *new* products, transforming the way individuals lived their lives in the space of a single generation. Rubber for tires, minerals that made possible the cost-effective development of strong and lightweight metals like steel and aluminum, petroleum products to fuel automobiles – these and countless other discoveries and innovations introduced westerners to consumer goods that we now take for granted and created an insatiable demand for raw materials.

New technologies appeared in almost every aspect of life. New modes of transportation and conveyancing – bicycles, trams, trolleys, buses, refrigerator ships, automobiles, airplanes, the Panama and Suez canals, and tunnels through the Alps – enabled people and goods to move and be moved quickly from formerly distant parts of the world. New forms of communication – the telephone and telegraph, typewriters, mass newsprint – brought individuals, groups, and nations into almost instant contact with one another, exposing formerly isolated peoples to one another and making the long-distance governance of vast non-European populations by small numbers of Europeans possible in ways it had never been before. New medicines, food stuffs, preservatives, and purification practices improved the health and longevity of the European population, vastly increasing its size despite a falling birth rate among middle- and upper-class families and a tremendous outflow of migration to North America and white colonies of settlement such as Australia, New Zealand, and Canada. Factories and firms became massive in scale and scope, employing thousands of workers who were situated together in huge agglomerations, where they were distant from management but proximate to one another. Cities grew rapidly in terms of numbers and of space, producing vast urban corridors where farm and pasturelands and forests once existed. Electricity provided lighting for homes and streets and brought recorded music into private homes by means of the gramophone, paving the way for the later twentieth-century development of consumer items like radios, washing machines, vacuum cleaners, and other household appliances.

Dramatic developments in chemistry transformed medicine, hygiene, and nutrition, all of which had a marked impact on the longevity and the quality of people's lives. Joseph Lister – after whom Listerine was branded – advocated the use of antiseptics in 1865. New dyes made it possible for scientists to stain bacteria and differentiate them from one another, enabling the development of the fields of microbiology, biochemistry, and bacteriology. Scientists developed antibacterial drugs: Salversan, used to treat venereal disease, appeared in 1909. Vitamins and hormones were discovered in the early twentieth century, and the identification of the mosquito as the carrier of malaria in 1897. Aspirin, the wonder drug, appeared on store shelves in 1899. Anesthesia and the use of antiseptic practices turned medical practice from an iffy proposition at best to a profession that could actually improve peoples' lives. Hospitals were once places where people went to die, largely owing to the rampant infections coursing through them; aseptic and antiseptic methods reduced the dangers considerably.

The new fields of microbiology, biochemistry, and bacteriology provided the knowledge that enabled significant improvements in food production and preservation. Sterilization and pasteurization made preserved foods safer and tastier; they could be produced in bulk now and supplied in large volume to large numbers of people at a reasonable price. Transportation innovations

Figure 3.1 Stringing telegraph wire, c. 1874. British imperialism in Africa was built upon the foundation of technological innovation.

improved food supplies as well. Steamships could carry thousands of tons of goods and when refrigerated they could bring fresh beef to Europe from Argentina and Kansas City or fresh mutton from New Zealand. Tunnels bored through the Alps brought fresh fruits and vegetables from the Mediterranean in record time and the cutting of the Suez canal in 1869 markedly reduced the time it took to move goods from Europe to the east and back again. All of these inventions and innovations revolutionized the feeding of industrialized, urbanized populations throughout Europe and the United States, contributing to a vast increase in population growth there and in other parts of the world.

The second industrial revolution dramatically increased the integration of the world. The new industrialism created enormous demand for raw materials that could not be found at home or in other parts of Europe. No part of the world remained unscathed as European, American, and Japanese industrialists sought to supply their factories. The acquisition of nickel from Canada; nitrates from Chile; copper and gold from South Africa and Australia; zinc, tin, and rubber from Malaya and Africa; wheat and other foodstuffs from a variety of areas – all these and much more brought far-flung territories into the world economy, creating a single economy on a global scale and a world market driven by world prices. Tied to one another by economies and finances the countries of the world became interlocked in the space of a single generation.

Economics played an important role in the "new imperialism." Beginning in 1873 what Europeans perceived to be a depression took hold of the world's capitalist economies for over two decades. Shrinking markets and falling profits led business leaders to seek new opportunities abroad where they hoped to find new outlets for their goods. European nations and the United States and Japan had become increasingly reliant upon foodstuffs and raw materials obtained from overseas. Fearful that these supplies might be cut off by other powers they determined to obtain colonies whose trade they could control. The depression compelled – and the developments in technology permitted – many European powers and the United States and Japan to embark upon the path of "new imperialism."

Britain faced competition from Europe and the United States in the geostrategic as well as economic realms. In 1871 the German states had unified under the leadership of the kingdom of Prussia. Now a large and mighty German empire occupied what had formerly been a vacuum of power in central Europe. International rivalries generated by the recent appearance of a powerful Germany on the continent – and a dynamic America across the Atlantic – reinforced European impulses to expand in Asia and Africa and helped to instill a sharp sense of competition and conflict among the western powers. In cultural and intellectual life the promulgation of Darwinist and Social Darwinist theories of evolution and "racial" deterioration accompanied these developments, legitimizing some initiatives already under way and spurring others into action.

New imperialism prompted a new, more self-consciously imperialist phase of colonial acquisition that Disraeli had suggested was Britain's destiny if it was to retain its status as a preeminent world power. Placed on the defensive by the rise of the new industrial powers Britons responded with an aggressive display of imperial might designed to counter any notion of economic or military weakness. Poets and writers told of indescribable wealth and unparalleled adventures to be had in the frontier areas of Asia and Africa, and celebrations like that of Queen Victoria's Diamond Jubilee in 1897 made manifest the power and glory of empire. Politicians, military men, and commercial adventurers extolled the virtues of imperial power for national health, seeing in empire and imperial rule the means by which Britain was to preserve its international standing. Men like Joseph Chamberlain, Lord Rosebery, Cecil Rhodes, and Lords Curzon and Milner regarded the empire as central to Britain's very survival, and the training ground that would prepare it, Rosebery insisted, "for the keen race of nations."[2]

Although Britain's population had grown dramatically in the late nineteenth century it was dwarfed by those of the United States and the continental powers, and its birth rate had slowed considerably. Fears of population decline joined concerns about the quality of the British population, especially in light of a growing awareness of the degree and depth of poverty in cities where sanitation was poor and life spans short. For despite the improvement in real wages enjoyed by those who had regular work, poverty levels increased during the 1880s and 1890s and urbanization made this poverty far more visible than it had been when most people lived on the land. Twenty-eight percent of York's population earned incomes insufficient to maintain a household; London's percentage was even higher. Perhaps one-third of all Britons lived below the poverty line. Moreover, infant mortality rates were on the rise. In England and Wales in the 1880s, 142 of every 1000 infants born died within the first year of life; that figure increased to 154 during the 1890s until by 1899 it had reached 163.

The existence of so much poverty, disease, and death in the midst of such plenty demanded explanation. Physicians, scientists, politicians, churchmen, authors, and moralists believed that cities depleted the health and vigor of populations, regarding them as "the graves . . . of our race," as the dean of Canterbury put it in 1887. The *Fortnightly Review* warned its readers of the effects of urban life in its description of the "town type." "The child of the townsman is bred too fine, it is too great an exaggeration of himself, excitable and painfully precocious in its childhood, neurotic, dyspeptic, pale and undersized in its adult state, if it ever reaches it." The conditions of city life, many believed, enervated formerly healthy specimens, demoralizing them and causing physical deterioration. The solution lay in gathering up the remaining "unoccupied" territories of the world and peopling them with Britons. It was through acquisition, possession, and the rule of colonies overseas that Britain's health was to be maintained. "New imperialism" gained momentum from the Social Darwinist theories that saw in competition with the other European powers, the United States, and Japan the means by which to create a robust society of virile men and proper, moral women. As Lord Rosebery, former Liberal prime minister, put it in a letter to *The Times* in 1900, "an empire such as ours requires as its first condition an Imperial Race – a race vigorous and industrious and intrepid. Health of mind and body exalt a nation in the competition of the universe. The survival of the fittest is an absolute truth in the conditions of the modern world."[3]

For others conflict offered the most effective means of strengthening the citizens of a nation. In the eyes of many who embraced Darwin's notions of the survival of the fittest – and applied them to the species of human beings – war constituted a positive good, an arena in which men could be hardened and those who were unfit selected out and prevented from procreating, and thus from passing on inferior or degenerate traits to a subsequent generation. Through war the "effeminate" could be weeded out, the manly preserved. "The stimulus of a great patriotic excitement," wrote one apologist for war and empire,

> the determination to endure burdens and make sacrifices, the self-abnegation which will face loss, and suffering, and even death, for the commonweal[th], are bracing tonics to national health, and they counteract the enervating effects of "too much love of living," too much ease, and luxury, and material prosperity. . . . Strength is not maintained without exercise.[4]

With new imperialism came a new model of masculinity, one characterized by racial superiority over "blacks," action, and physical force, and one which recognized working men as manly as much by virtue of their "sinew and muscle" as by their temperance, self-reliance, and possession of women in the home. The liberal gentleman of the 1830s and 1840s – morally and spiritually earnest, rational, and convinced of the inherent equality of all men – would not disappear entirely but he was increasingly overshadowed by the new man of body, a figure who would most vividly appear in the guise of the imperial pioneer and hunter. Drawn from the stereotypical images that populated the adventure stories of writers like H. Rider Haggard and G.A. Henty, the quintessential hero countered the image of the narrow-chested, puny, flat-footed tubercular urban male that so haunted the imaginations of politicians, statesmen, military officials, scientists, and physicians. He acted in a natural world free of the contaminations of urban industrial society according to strict rules about class and gender that seemed to be under assault from so many avenues in Britain. Like the white characters in Haggard's *King Solomon's Mines* and *Allan Quatermain*, he was honest, independent, self-reliant, and among "the most generous and chivalrous of [his] race." A gentleman, he demonstrated the qualities of honor, decency, courage, physical strength, and endurance that had enabled Britain to obtain its empire in the first place. Now, if the nation was to hold on to it in the face of international rivalries and urban deterioration, it would have to build up a race of men from all classes schooled in the lessons of the frontier.

The imperial frontier and one of its most cherished activities, hunting, provided the best means short of actual war itself for developing an imperial race. In hunting the frontier man learned how to train for war. He tracked, stalked, and observed the habits of his quarry and he possessed skill in marksmanship. A man of action rather than reflection, he relied on his senses and his wits, lived off the land, endured nature's dangers, and ultimately triumphed. Free of women and of the society they inhabited he displayed a virility that "town types" could not possibly possess, a manliness upon which the survival of Britain and the empire depended.

The ability of Europeans to seize control of and rule over the lands of Asia, Africa, South America, and Oceania stemmed in large part from the new technologies in transportation, communications, medicine, and armaments thrown up by mature industrialization. For the first time Europeans had the means of administering millions of people with a relatively small number of officials and soldiers. Railroads and steamships enabled explorers, entrepreneurs, and settlers to open up country that had barred their passage in earlier years. The telegraph kept colonial officials in contact with their subordinates in the "bush" and outlying regions and with their superiors in the metropolitan capitals. New medicines like quinine enabled Europeans to cope with diseases like malaria that had so mightily thinned their ranks. But above all the invention of new modes of firepower made it possible for small numbers of Europeans to impose their will over indigenous peoples armed mostly with ancient muskets, spears, and bows and arrows. The breech-loading rifle, the "repeating" machine gun, the gunboat – these weapons gave Europeans the power to destroy those who resisted their onslaught. As one African put it, "The whites did not seize their enemy as we do by the body, but thundered from afar. Death raged everywhere – like the death vomited forth from the tempest."[5] At the battle of Omdurman in 1898, for example, when 40,000 Sudanese soldiers bearing muskets and spears attacked a small force of British troops traveling up the Nile, more than 11,000 Sudanese lost their lives at the hands of machine gunners and artillery officers. Only 48 British and Egyptian soldiers, by contrast, lay dead.

The tools of empire enabled the industrial nations to colonize much of the rest of the world but they were aided in their conquests by a series of weather-related famines that swept across much of what came to be called the "third world" in 1876–1879, 1889–1891, and 1896–1902. Afflicting the entire tropical monsoon belt and northern China and North Africa, these famines were produced by El Niño events – the rapid warming of the eastern tropical Pacific Ocean that reduced the strength of the monsoon rains, bringing drought to broad swathes of the globe. In 1876–1879 drought and famine devastated the populations of Egypt, India, China, Java, the Philippines, New Caledonia, Korea, Brazil, southern Africa, and the Maghreb, killing off perhaps ten million people. The 1889–1891 drought hit India, Korea, Brazil, Russia, Ethiopia, and Sudan; its counterpart in 1896–1902 ravaged virtually all the tropical lands and northern China, bringing epidemics of dysentery, smallpox, malaria, cholera, and bubonic plague in its wake.

Somewhere between 30 and 50 million people died in these crises of mass starvation, which, though they appeared to be "natural," were in fact tragedies that could have been avoided had state power and world commodity markets not operated to prevent intervention. Certainly the droughts and crop failures were massive in their destruction; some of them, in fact, were the worst seen in centuries. But in only one instance – Ethiopia in 1889 – was total lack of food the issue. In virtually every other case, grain surpluses existed elsewhere that could have alleviated the famines. The existence of a world market in commodities that encouraged price speculation – and the failure of state governments to intervene to block these deleterious effects – made the difference between who ate and who didn't. For at precisely the time when nations of the west had eliminated famine, the world market wreaked havoc on the colonial world. Where once, under a system of subsistence farming, villages responded to local crises by providing relief to the poor from their extra food stores, now, under commodity agriculture, markets and price speculation governed the movement of food elsewhere, and there was little extra to spare for those in need. The existence of the world market system meant that food ended up circumventing the local populations that actually produced the crops. In a tragic irony, the railroads that were touted as a modern improvement were actually used to take food *out* of the afflicted areas so that it could be sold on the global market.

These deadly famines coincided with some of the most ambitious expansions undertaken by Europeans as they embarked upon their policies of new imperialism. It is difficult to argue with one historian who sees in "each global drought . . . the green light for an imperialist landrush." The incursions of the British in southern Africa in the 1870s provide one of the most telling examples of this kind of exploitation of distressed peoples. The drought of 1876–1879 dramatically weakened African and Boer peoples, rendering them far more susceptible to British incursions than they might otherwise have been. Moving speedily, the British took the Transvaal from the Boers in 1877; suppressed a rebellion by the Griqua acting in part from drought-related grievances; and turned on the Zulu kingdom, Britain's erstwhile ally against the Boers. Hit hard by drought and famine, Zululand could not hold out for long against the British, who burned their villages, captured their cattle, and destroyed their economic system. Overwhelmed "as much by famine as by firepower," as this historian puts it, the Zulu surrendered to the British in July 1879.[6]

The scramble for Africa

The scramble for Africa is the subject of countless studies, and historians do not agree on what exactly caused it. No single event, certainly, set off the scramble, which is fitting given the size of the continent and the number of players – African and European – involved. But we can identify four sites involving British interests that contributed to the furious stampede toward colonization: southern Africa, West Africa, Egypt, and East Africa.

By the early 1870s, South Africa consisted of two British colonies, the Cape Colony and Natal; two republics independent of Britain and controlled by the Boers, the Orange Free State and the Transvaal (also known as the South African Republic); and a number of African polities, the most prominent of which were the Xhosa, Zulu, Pedi, Tswana, Sotho (most living within the British protectorate of Basutoland), Swazi, and Venda. In 1871 diamonds were discovered in the area that became named Kimberley in Griqualand West, which the generally friendly Orange Free State and the generally antagonistic Transvaal claimed for themselves. Faced with this competition from the independent republics, the British seized the territory and annexed it, engendering the enmity of Boers across the entirety of southern Africa and helping to initiate the stirrings of an Afrikaner nationalism that would have profound consequences. The rivalry between the British and Boers intensified as the Transvaal persisted in its efforts to expand its territory to the east, desirous of securing access to the Indian Ocean through a port at Delagoa Bay, held by the Portuguese.

Imperial officials in London were convinced that preventing an independent, powerful Transvaal was crucial for the security of the rest of the British empire, particularly India. The colonial secretary, Lord Carnarvon, who had recently completed the consolidation of the Canadian colonies into a single confederation, believed that British control of the Cape and, by extension, India required the same kind of consolidation of the territories of southern Africa. Boers in the Transvaal felt no inclination to follow along with such a plan but the ill-advised actions of their government gave Carnarvon an opening to advance his initiative. The Transvaal instigated a war against the Pedi, hoping to grab their land, but under the leadership of their chief, Sekhukhune, the Pedi fought back hard and effectively and routed the Boer fighters. Upon hearing of their retreat the colonial secretary immediately petitioned Disraeli for permission to move into the Transvaal. Once granted, Carnarvon appointed Theophilus Shepstone to serve as special commissioner there and secretly ordered him to annex the republic. Fearful of further Pedi attacks, the Transvaal Boers welcomed the presence of British troops but once it became clear that they were there to annex the republic and not simply to protect it, their mood altered abruptly. Too late to prevent the formal annexation of the Transvaal in 1877, Boers registered forceful protest against the action.

Anger against the annexation ranged well beyond the Transvaal. Boers in the Orange Free State were already resentful of the Cape's grab of the diamond mines. Those in the Cape Colony (for not all Boers had trekked off in the 1830s and 1840s and others had migrated into the Cape from the east in later years) feared that their culture would soon be absorbed into that of the British. In the Cape a Dutch Reformed Church minister named Stephanus du Toit embarked upon a project of vitalizing the culture of the Boers – now becoming known as "Afrikaners" – and turning their language – Afrikaans – into one that could be used by all Afrikaners across southern Africa. Du Toit established a newspaper in order to disseminate the language and authored a history of the Afrikaner people that treated them as members of a single nation. His efforts mark the beginnings of a robust cultural and political Afrikaner movement. We will hear much more about this in Chapter 6.

Emboldened by the strength of public support at home for the annexation of the Transvaal, the governor of the Cape Colony, Sir Bartle Frere, determined to expand British territory even further, this time against the Zulu who lived in the lands north of Natal. Under the leadership of Cetshwayo, who had been recognized as king by the representative of the "Great White Queen" over the seas, the Zulu were a powerful warrior society. Their very presence on the borderland of Natal unsettled many Britons. Frere convinced himself that the Zulu had to be "pacified" if British rule were to prevail; moreover, the defeat of the Zulu would force thousands of young men into the Kimberley mines that they had thus far avoided. Frere therefore cooked up an ultimatum demanding that the Zulu disband their armies, reform their system of justice, and permit the presence of a British resident at their capital, Ulundi. When Cetshwayo failed to reply, Frere, without the approval of his superiors in London, ordered an invasion of Zulu lands. He sent 16,000 troops north to defeat this mighty enemy in January 1879 under the leadership of the commander-in-chief of the South African army, Lord Chelmsford, a distinctly incompetent officer who enjoyed the friendship and support of Queen Victoria.

Chelmsford figured on a quick and decisive victory. Instead, the army of 24,000 Zulu divided its forces and drew out two-thirds of the 5000 British troops that were encamped at Isandhlwana. Some 12,000 Zulu set upon the remaining 1760 British and allied African soldiers on January 22. Some Zulu were armed with smooth-bore rifles – effective at a far shorter range than the British Martini-Henry breech-loaders – but their victory was derived from swamping the defenders with constant waves of *assegai* (spear)-wielding warriors who braved efforts to shoot them down before they could reach the British lines. Thousands of Zulu died by rifle fire but thousands more surrounded the British troops and cut them down. It proved an unmitigated disaster. Of the 1760 who had started out that day, only 400 escaped, and 870 Britons and 490 African auxiliaries died. When news of the terrible defeat reached Disraeli in February 1879 he became so depressed that he was forced to take to his bed.

The public reacted with outrage to the news that "spear-wielding savages" had whipped the well-equipped British army. Sentiment against the hapless Lord Chelmsford grew exponentially. By May the outcry against Chelmsford had reached a fever pitch and Disraeli replaced him with General Wolseley, the hero of the Asante expedition of 1873. The prime minister ordered his general to destroy the Zulu state.

Before Wolseley could even reach southern Africa, Chelmsford determined to redeem himself. Ignoring ever more urgent telegrams from Wolseley, he marched 5000 troops onto the Ulundi plain in July with the intention of taking down his nemeses. This time, facing Gatling guns and soldiers with repeating rifles, the Zulu could not prevail. At the end of the day all of them – some 1500 warriors – were killed. Thirteen British soldiers died in the battle. With a British victory in hand Wolseley imprisoned Cetshwayo, divided up Zululand into 13 powerless chieftaincies, called "kinglets," and

Figure 3.2 The British suffered a humiliating defeat at the hands of the Zulu at Isandhlwana on January 22, 1879

placed them under British suzerainty. He gave much of the Zulus' land to the Transvaal, over which he now presided as "supreme civil and military authority." Wolseley then turned on the Pedi, determined to crush Sekhukhune's state in the northeast of South Africa. In November 1879 he led a powerful force against the Pedi capital of Tsate, which fell to British and African troops in a matter of hours. The chief surrendered and was put in prison in Pretoria; his people's lands were confiscated and they were sent to live in scattered and isolated new settlements – reserves – that had little to recommend them. The confiscation of land had a lasting impact on Pedi autonomy (arguably until the present day), and the imposition of heavy taxes (payable in cash, not in kind) forced Pedi men into the diamond mines as laborers. The Pedi war was followed by a series of rolling campaigns against African peoples that culminated in 1897 with the defeat of the Venda.

Threats from the Pedi and the Zulu now eliminated by British force of arms, the Afrikaners of the Transvaal saw their chance. They revolted against British rule in 1880 and declared an independent republic. With an army of perhaps 7000 mounted civilian soldiers, the Afrikaners prepared to defend their republic in what they called their war for independence. The British army fared badly against them, unable to lift the sieges laid to their garrisons by Afrikaner fighters. A relief force suffered numerous defeats, an especially humiliating one at Majuba Hill in 1881 where just 600 Afrikaners – "dressed in civilian corduroy trousers and floppy-brimmed hats," as one historian described the guerrilla force – surrounded the hill and proceeded to destroy their enemy. Nearly 300 supposedly crack British troops were killed or wounded.[7]

Britons at home could not bear the humiliation suffered by an elite force of Scottish Highlanders at Majuba Hill. The army general staff and Conservative politicians demanded redress for the terrible defeat and the re-establishment of British authority. But Gladstone – who had become prime minister for the second time in 1880 – feared that renewed fighting would only lead Afrikaners in the Orange Free State and the Cape to rise up. He chose instead to settle with the Transvaal rather than continue to try to fight it (in any case, the Pedi defeat had guaranteed the diamond magnates the labor they needed for the immediate future). In 1881 the Transvaal regained its independence as the South African Republic. Convinced that the British would not intervene to stop them, Transvaal settlers called "freebooters" immediately expanded their borders to the east and west, grabbing up the land of various chiefdoms there.

One such seizure took place in the lands just north of the Cape Colony in what would soon become Bechuanaland, today's Botswana. Freebooters set up settlements and named them republics, establishing barriers in the way of what Cape colonists regarded as "the road to the north" into the interior. Missionaries who had established mission stations among and friendly relations with the Tswana people feared that Afrikaners would bring destruction to the area and its inhabitants. More compelling to Cape business interests, trade with the interior amounted to some £250,000 per year, a significant level of income. Even more important to men like diamond magnate Cecil Rhodes and imperialists in Britain, the road to the north constituted the only real possible route from the Cape to the Zambesi region, rumored to possess fabulous riches. Afrikaners standing in the way of northern and northeastern expansion blocked access to the territories that would help form the Cape-to-Cairo swathe of British possessions, at least as Rhodes and others envisaged it (we will treat Rhodes in greater depth below).

Facing what they considered a hostile government in the Transvaal, the British moved to shore up their position, sending some 4000 troops north in 1884 to expel the freebooters and secure Bechuanaland. Reviving its "forward policy" in response to perceived Transvaal encroachment, Britain commandeered other territory until all of the unannexed coastal and inland areas between the Cape of Good Hope and Delagoa Bay was in its hands. This aggression drove other Europeans to follow their course, setting the stage for the scramble to follow.

The second area of conflict contributing to the scramble involved rivalry between the British and the French in West Africa. In 1879 the French embarked on a program of expansion throughout the region, seeking to consolidate and enlarge their various holdings in Senegal, Ivory Coast, Dahomey, and the territory north of the Congo river. Their actions and ambitions raised alarms among British traders in West Africa, who were already feeling the pinch of the depression that had created a crisis in the legitimate commerce that had supplanted the slave trade. Demand for palm oil in Europe fell considerably after the discovery of petroleum made it possible to utilize other forms of oil for lubrication. Palm kernels also lost a good portion of their market to new sources of fats coming from India, Australia, and Russia. Prices that Europeans could command for palm oil and kernels fell dramatically, cutting deeply into traders' profits on the West African coast. British traders took steps to reduce competition among themselves and against Africans by amalgamating the four British commercial companies operating in the Niger region. The merger was effected as the United Africa Company in 1879 by an adventurer and former officer in the Royal Engineers, George Goldie, whom we met in Chapter 2.

At just this time two new French trading companies established themselves on the Niger and one went so far as to make a treaty with chiefs in the Bonny region of the Niger Delta. The prospect of French intrusion into an increasingly difficult market heightened British fears, propelling the United Africa Company to seek out its own treaties with local chiefs. These agreements, produced on printed forms in English, appeared to give the company sovereign rights to the territories presided over by the chiefs, who most likely thought they had put their marks on documents establishing trade agreements and friendship. British officials back in London looked at the treaties askance, reluctant to involve the British government in any expansionist schemes. But in 1882 the French government recognized treaties negotiated by a military officer in their employ, Pierre Savorgnan de Brazza, with Chief Makoko on the northern banks of the Congo river. Makoko's concession of huge tracts of land to the French was followed by the French establishment of a protectorate over Porto Novo, situated just to the west of Lagos, in 1883. The British Foreign Office felt compelled to respond to these moves, agreeing with Goldie's assessment of the situation. "To keep France back is a national necessity," he urged.[8]

In 1884 the British government responded with two initiatives designed to block French expansion. In the first the foreign secretary directed the British consul at Fernando Po to conduct additional negotiations with chiefs in the Niger region. The resulting treaties, which were translated into local languages and accommodated some of the chiefs' major concerns, established a British protectorate over the area in 1885. In the second British officials entered into an agreement with Portugal, recognizing that country's ancient claims to control the mouth of the Congo river and setting up a commission that would keep the river open to navigation by all countries. This Anglo-Portuguese treaty prompted the German chancellor, Otto von Bismarck, to call the European powers and the United States to an international conference at Berlin, where the rivalries over Africa could be addressed before they blew up into out-and-out warfare.

The delegates to the Berlin Conference of 1884–1885 drew up a series of agreements to settle the conflicts over the Congo and Niger river basins. These established freedom of navigation on the two rivers but gave administrative control of the Congo region to King Leopold II of Belgium, who had launched a number of commercial ventures in the area. The treaties that Britain had arranged with Niger chiefs in 1884 gave a reality to its claim to be "*the* Niger power." Delegates accordingly acknowledged British predominance on the lower and middle Niger. Separate agreements between the European countries recognized their various claims to territory in other parts of the continent. One of the most far-reaching consequences of the Berlin Conference concerned how new claims to African lands would be handled: the doctrine of "effective occupation" required countries to establish a genuine presence in territory they wished to annex. In the past it was possible to make ambiguous and imprecise claims on areas that few Europeans ever saw; now, to make good their claims Europeans had to actually put down stakes.

For Britain this condition posed problems. It now had to effect actual rather than theoretical control over the Niger region in the face of the reluctance of the Treasury to provide the money necessary to do so. The costs involved in setting up a government and furnishing a fleet to patrol the Niger river seemed beyond what British taxpayers should be asked to bear, so the government was receptive when Goldie proposed that his company receive a charter to rule the territory. He won the charter in 1886, renamed his firm the Royal Niger Company, and took over the responsibility of ruling what became called the Territories of the Royal Niger Company, lands in the middle portion of what would ultimately become Nigeria.

The third set of incidents that triggered the scramble for Africa took place in Egypt, and in this instance India played a crucial role in Britain's acquisitions of northern African territory. Ever since Britain had obtained shares in the Suez canal, Egypt had taken on increasing significance in official thinking about empire. The country remained a vassal state of the Ottomans, with the Egyptian *khedive* serving as the Ottoman sultan's viceroy. So long as he maintained his hold on power British authorities were content to remain at a distance. But the finances of the Egyptian state proved so parlous (owing to the ruinous interest rates levied on loans to Egypt by British and French bankers) and the government so corrupt that France and Britain felt they had to step in to protect their considerable financial interests. In response to this foreign intervention an Egyptian army officer, Arabi Pasha, staged a revolt in 1882 designed to rid his country of outsiders. Prime Minister Gladstone determined that the time had come, regrettably, for a full-on imperial intervention.

Gladstone sent an army under Wolseley to invade Egypt. Wolseley's forces quickly defeated Arabi at the battle of Tel-el-Kebir, inflicting enormous casualties on the rebel fighters and blowing Egypt's cultural center – Alexandria – to bits. The British then marched on Cairo, took it over, and raised the Union Jack above the city. Gladstone and his ministers insisted that their actions did not constitute annexation of the country, only a temporary occupation that would end once stability and order was imposed. "Undoubtedly of all things in the world," the prime minister tried to reassure those who believed Britain sought to permanently seize Egypt for itself, "that is the thing which we are not going to do."[9] The *khedive* remained in power and the sultan retained the title of head of state; but all power rested with the British army and the actual governing of Egypt rested in the hands of British officials. This anomalous situation produced numerous confusions, not least concerning whether Britain had also taken responsibility for ruling Sudan, the land to the south of Egypt that had been an Egyptian dependency for 60 years. British officials in Cairo and at home cared little about the desert country and would have preferred to remain aloof from it. Imperial expansionists, however, insisted that control of Suez required not simply control of Egypt but of Sudan as well. For this was a territory constantly in revolt against Egyptian authority. Led by a charismatic Muslim holy man called the mahdi ("guided one"), Sudanese rebels meant to end rule by the Egyptians who, they believed, paid only the slightest lip service to the precepts of Islam. Before they knew it the British had an armed insurrection on their hands and they responded by sending an Egyptian force headed by British officers south to defend the rule of the *khedive*.

The adventure ended in disaster. Some 50,000 Sudanese soldiers met the 10,000-strong Egyptian army at El Obeid and destroyed it. All of the British officers fell to the mahdi's forces and only a few hundred Egyptian soldiers survived. The mahdi gained control of virtually all Sudan, leaving only a few Egyptian garrisons scattered across the countryside. In the wake of the catastrophe Gladstone resolved to abandon further efforts to maintain Sudan for Egypt, a position that frustrated even his supporters who thought it unworthy of Britain, and he ordered the evacuation of the remaining

Egyptian garrisons. To oversee the evacuation he appointed in 1884 a popular and flamboyant – and utterly unreliable – soldier-adventurer, General Charles Gordon.

Gladstone was perhaps clear in his own mind about the necessity for the evacuation but other prominent people felt differently, including Queen Victoria. Indeed, there were sufficient countervailing influences about that it was possible for Gordon to interpret his mission in virtually any way he wished. With encouragement from a number of imperial expansionists he disobeyed orders from London and decided that rather than evacuating the fort at Khartoum – where he had arrived in February 1884 – he would stand and fight in order to keep the Nile valley in Egyptian and British hands.

In March the mahdi's forces laid siege to Khartoum, cutting the telegraph line to Cairo and leaving Gordon isolated. Gordon was playing a tricky and potentially deadly game. He would not evacuate the Egyptian forces at Khartoum or even leave the city to save himself. It gradually became apparent to Gladstone's government that the mercurial general was in effect blackmailing the government into retaking Sudan by allowing the mahdi to hold him hostage. The British public, for whom Gordon was a hero, a perfect Christian gentleman who had given so much of himself to the British empire, would not stand to see him abandoned in the desert by a heartless, cowardly government. Newspapers across Britain and the rest of the western world, the clergy, the army, and the queen herself demanded that Gladstone send a British force to save this most selfless of men. The cabinet realized that if the government did not comply it would be toppled from office. Against all of his principles Gladstone knew he must act, and in the fall of 1884 requested that parliament grant him £300,000 "to enable operations to be undertaken for the relief of General Gordon, should they become necessary."[10]

Wolseley assembled troops in Cairo and after months of painstaking preparation ventured up the Nile. But three days before the expedition force arrived in Khartoum, the mahdi's soldiers attacked the city in the middle of the night, killing the inhabitants and then Gordon himself. In the face of heated public opinion, Gladstone's government ordered a retreat from Khartoum, and Wolseley and his troops returned to Egypt, though as we'll see in the next chapter, Gladstone's view of the wisdom of extricating Britain from Sudanese affairs was not sustained by those who followed him in office. In the meantime the British occupation of Egypt to protect the Suez canal and its subsequent incursions into Sudan provoked other European powers, especially France, to take steps to establish their own spheres of influence in other parts of Africa.

The British presence in East Africa came later than in the west. Further removed from Britain and therefore a more expensive proposition for long-distance trading, British visitors before the late nineteenth century were few and far between, usually restricted to the odd zealous missionary, intrepid traveler, or big game hunter. The spice island of Zanzibar, however, proved the exception to this general rule, attracting Britons seeking trade in the 1830s and 1840s.

Zanzibar held center stage on the Swahili coast, a 3000-mile-long strip running from Mogadishu to Mozambique. The Swahili coast seemed to the British to be "Arab": its merchants and rulers wore the long, white robes characteristic of the Arabian peninsula, were devout Muslims, claimed origins in Persia, and built their homes from whitewashed stone in an Islamic style. In actuality "Swahili culture" was a fusion of more than 1000 years of interactions between Indian Ocean traders – many of whom were from Arabia – and black Africans resident at the coast. The coast's wealth derived from its prominent "big men" serving as middlemen in trade between the East African interior and the Indian Ocean world. Caravans carrying ivory, dye, gums, and slaves traveled for months from the interior to the coast, where Swahili merchants bought their goods to sell to arriving ships at a profit.

Under the Omani sultan Seyyid Said, Zanzibar had become a trading center of wealth and prestige, so much so in fact that Said moved his capital from Muscat in Oman to Zanzibar in 1840, where he sustained himself and his position with a vast fleet. He held total control over Zanzibar and the nearby Pemba as well as a variety of fortified cities on the East African coast. Said invited Indian money-lenders and traders to reside in his cities – always guaranteeing the rights of religious expression to all – and by 1860 more than 5000 had taken up residence there. He earned vast profits from trade. In 1859 his kingdom exported £755,666 in goods (including £146,666 in ivory) and imported close to £1 million worth of products, including £185,232 in cloth from the United States, France, and Britain.[11]

The British opened diplomatic relations with Zanzibar in 1822, and the sultan permitted a British consul to reside at his court from 1840 onward. British efforts to influence policy in Zanzibar were largely restricted to trying to persuade the reigning sultan to abandon the slave trade, something that had flourished since abolition in West Africa in the early nineteenth century. They met with little success until 1873 when a combination of insecure rulers and a cyclone that destroyed the reigning sultan's clove plantations forced him to accept a strict British treaty on the control of the slave trade. British officials began training the sultan's troops and, in concert with the Royal Navy, they acted to cut slave trading.

Chastened by what had happened in Egypt, Gladstone's government initially refused to entertain any kind of expansionist programs in East Africa. That changed in 1884, however, when a German explorer, Karl Peters, obtained from a number of local chiefs treaty rights to land in what would become Tanganyika. He returned to Berlin with these agreements in early 1885, and on the day after the Berlin Conference that had adjudicated the Niger and Congo conflicts adjourned, the German government announced that it would place those areas gained by Peters under its protection.

The declaration shocked Britain and prompted another round of boundary-making among the Europeans. In two agreements in 1886 and 1890 Britain and Germany divided East Africa between themselves. Britain took what became Kenya and Uganda and Germany annexed the lands south of them, including Mt. Kilimanjaro. Sultan Barghash's territories – the coastal islands and a strip of land on the mainland – were left temporarily intact until 1890 when the British declared Zanzibar and Pemba a British protectorate, giving a formal stamp to their increasingly influential hold over the sultan and finally ringing the death knell for the institution of slave-trading and slavery in East Africa. Drawn into Britain and Germany's wranglings, the sultan had little chance of maintaining his autonomy. He was, as one historian aptly noted, "but a pawn on this wide chessboard, to be sacrificed if necessary."[12]

In conformity with the doctrine of "effective occupation" set up by the Berlin Conference but confronted by the desiderata of colonialism on the cheap, the British government set up a chartered company to act as its agent. The Imperial British East Africa Company (IBEAC), founded in 1888, took over responsibility for governing a vast tract of land extending westward from the Indian Ocean 600 miles to the lakes region of east-central Africa. We will see its progress in the following chapter.

Cecil Rhodes and the British South Africa Company

Chartered companies established to rule territories claimed by Britain appealed to the government on the grounds of economy. Treasury officials especially worked tirelessly to keep British subjects from having to shell out tax revenues to pay for empire but the Colonial Office also had good reasons for preferring to outsource its administrative and military responsibilities to people already there on the ground. The colonial secretary's obligations to his worldwide empire at the end of the nineteenth century far outran the resources he could mobilize to meet them; chartered companies appeared to be the perfect solution to a variety of problems.

The most ambitious and far-reaching chartered company proved to be the last one set up in Africa, Cecil Rhodes' British South Africa Company, established in 1889. Rhodes had arrived in southern Africa in 1870 at the age of 17. When diamonds were discovered at Kimberley the next year, he and his partner, Charles Rudd, garnered the contract to provide one of the most important processes of any mining operation, that of pumping water out of the mines. With profits generated from this vital service and a multitude of other wheeling-and-dealing transactions, Rhodes was able to ultimately establish the De Beers Company. Ownership of the firm gave him a near-monopoly on diamonds mined in southern Africa and provided him with a vast fortune and the political influence that went with it. Rhodes became the prime minister of the Cape Colony in 1890, and used his power to advance the interests of his company and of his country.

The discovery of gold on the Witswatersrand of the Transvaal in 1886 increased the likelihood in the minds of many Britons and Afrikaners – not least of them Cecil Rhodes and Paul Kruger, president of the Transvaal – that magnificent riches lay to the north in the lands known vaguely as Zambesia. Tales of great treasures in the area had circulated for decades; Haggard's *King Solomon's Mines*, published in 1885 to wildly popular acclaim, was only the most recent account of the fantastic wealth that might be acquired by anyone with the courage and the means to journey north. Rhodes determined to be that man. But he faced a number of obstacles.

First, to the north the Ndebele people held the territory of modern-day western Zimbabwe, which the British called Matabeleland. Their chief, Lobengula, was the son of Mzilikazi, who had migrated out of Zululand in the aftermath of the *mfecane* (see Chapter 2) in the earlier part of the century. Lobengula commanded a powerful army comprised of fierce warriors who had extended the chief's influence north and east into Mashonaland and south into parts of Bechuanaland. Lobengula extorted tribute from the Shona and the Tswana as well as a number of other groups in the Zambesia region. He exercised a careful watchfulness over his lands, building military posts along his borders to control the influx of whites and Africans from other areas. He permitted some missionaries to work within Matabeleland and occasionally allowed white hunters to pursue big game. But for the most part Lobengula only rarely allowed visitors into his jurisdiction, or, as he put it, "gave them the road" to Mashonaland to the east.[13]

In 1887 Transvaal president Paul Kruger dispatched two brothers, Pieter and Frederick Grobler, to Lobengula to make a treaty of friendship with the chief. The Groblers returned to Pretoria with what they claimed was Lobengula's approval, prompting Rhodes and other Cape officials to take action in response. They turned to a missionary named John Moffat who was friendly with Lobengula to conduct their own negotiations, and Moffat's influence with the Ndebele chief paid off. At the end of December Lobengula repudiated the Grobler treaty and, hoping to rid himself of Europeans pestering him for concessions, acknowledged that his chiefdom of Matabeleland – and territory he did not possess, much of Mashonaland – fell within Britain's sphere of influence. The chief miscalculated, as it turned out, but in establishing Britain as the effective European presence in Zambesia, Rhodes had ensured that others would be kept out. He had cleared his first hurdle.

The second obstacle would require Rhodes to pull all the political strings he held in Cape Town and London. The British government had no desire to set up another protectorate that would require a great deal of money to administer but yield little in the way of revenue. Rhodes, having seen how chartered companies in West Africa and East Africa promised to resolve that dilemma, proposed to create his own. He lobbied influential newspapermen and politicians in London and gained their support; Cape officials, too, came on board to endorse his project. But before he could get any further he needed to secure a mining concession from Lobengula that would undergird his proposed charter. Once again Moffat worked his magic with Lobengula, persuading him that granting a single mining concession to Rhodes would eliminate all the other petitioners who sought his permission to set up shop on his lands. Lobengula, in his capacity as "King of Matabeleland, Mashonaland and certain adjoining territories," signed an agreement on October 30, 1888, to give Rhodes "the complete and exclusive charge over all metals and minerals situated and contained in my kingdoms, principalities and dominions together with full power to do all things that they may deem necessary to win and procure the same and to hold, collect and enjoy the profits and revenues . . . from the said metals and minerals."[14] In return the chief was to receive a monthly cash payment and a one-time grant of 1000 Martini-Henry breech-loading rifles, plus 100,000 rounds of ammunition. Moreover, Rhodes' agents promised Lobengula – though the chief failed to get it in writing – that only ten white men would be allowed to dig in Matabeleland and then only under the jurisdiction of Ndebele laws. The chief had been duped and when he realized his mistake he disavowed the agreement that became known as the Rudd Concession.

It was too late. Concession in hand, Rhodes hurried back to London to obtain his company charter. With the support of prominent bankers, businessmen, journalists, and politicians, he succeeded in persuading the colonial secretary, Lord Salisbury, to grant it to him. In October 1889 the queen formally recognized Rhodes' British South Africa Company as the governing entity of the lands of Zambesia, authorizing it to build an infrastructure of roads, railways, telegraph systems, banking services, and police and charging it with the responsibility of establishing laws and awarding land grants to immigrants. Rhodes rounded up some 200 whites – pioneers, he called them – to invade and occupy Mashonaland. Promising them mining claims and 3000 acres of land each, he supplied the pioneers with uniforms and weapons and primed them with tales of the untold wealth that could be found right near the surface. On June 27, 1890, escorted by 500 military police with artillery and machine guns, the pioneers set out to make good their claims on Lobengula's lands. They set up headquarters at Fort Salisbury, a base that would become the capital of what was starting to be called Rhodesia.

Africans and the mines

In the face of European domination, both actual and impending, Africans continued to make wide-ranging, complex, and often ambiguous responses. A wealthy sugar-mill owner in southern Africa, marketwoman in Gold Coast, or military leader like the Zulu king Cetshwayo all responded to the new presence in ways that they believed best suited their circumstances. But in southern and southern-central Africa, African autonomies were restricted to an arguably greater degree than anywhere else as a result of the mining industry. The repercussions of this system are felt in the region even today.

The diamond and gold mining industries drew African workers from as far away as contemporary Tanzania into a migrant labor system. The system has had a tremendous impact on Africa's modern history. It helped create modern notions of ethnic identity among the peoples who experienced it; it caused tremendous social dislocation in many communities; and it laid the foundation for the most rigid systems of racial division on the continent, in twentieth-century South Africa, beginning with "segregation" and transforming into apartheid.

South Africa defies the simple categorization that fits the rest of the scramble for Africa. The diamond mines at Kimberley came under British rule only after 1871 with the annexation of Griqualand West, and the gold mines were never part of the British empire: the Witwatersrand was located well within the Afrikaner-ruled Transvaal, though the British occupied much of this territory during the South African War (1899–1902). The important factor in play in South Africa, then, was British capital and influence; actual territorial acquisition was to some degree irrelevant. British capitalists and Afrikaner politicians often clashed over the administration of the territories in which the mines were located and had different ideas about the oversight of the mining operations. They did find common ground on which they could agree, however – restriction of the rights of African laborers directly benefitted both parties.

There was little hint in 1870 that the diamond fields would produce the monstrous conglomerate of De Beers. Production was small-scale; the earliest prospecting was alluvial and took place along the Vaal river. The maximum size claim a digger could own was only 20 square feet. Even when diggers turned to the mines of Dutoitspan, Bultfontein, De Beers, and Kimberley – the latter where the majority of diamonds were discovered – the claims were only 31 feet in size and diggers were restricted to a maximum of two each. This was a genuine "rush": by late 1871 50,000 people had arrived at the mines, 20,000 of them white fortune-seekers from as far afield as Australia and 30,000 of them black. People made and lost fortunes overnight. One man sold a 28-square-foot claim for £900. Soon the cost of claims began to drive out all but the wealthiest prospectors.

We tend to view the South African mining system as one that crushed Africans beneath its machinery but the reality was more complex. Black laborers found their labor in ever-increasing demand and leveraged their position to claim – and receive – ever higher wages (they doubled in 1872 alone). Blacks commonly switched employers if their requirements were not met, causing a headache for the claim owners. Nor was there any restriction on them owning claims beyond those that applied to whites. Thousands of Africans made money by selling food, wood, clothing, or other supplies to the expanding mine towns. Others established themselves as carpenters, stoneworkers, builders, artisans, and publicans.

Over the following several years, however, the mines underwent a transformation that ushered in the era of De Beers. By the mid-1870s life had become more difficult for the small-scale owners. The price of diamonds dropped, claims increased in price, and the tiny claims often collapsed in on themselves as workers tried to negotiate the system of rickety pulleys and wooden-plank bridges that hung precariously above their claims. Poverty and even starvation increased. In 1876, in an effort to put the system on better footing, the governor of the Cape Colony passed legislation permitting the free trading – and unlimited purchases – of mining claims. Companies trading on the London Stock Exchange took over multiple failed claims and consolidated them, using machines powered by steam to dig deeper and deeper.

As white diggers faced difficulties in the mid-1870s they came to assert that their problems arose from lazy and unreliable black workers, who, in reality, simply refused to work for minimal wages and quickly left poor working situations for other employers. White diggers and company officials pressured the government to restrict the movement of black laborers. Many of their demands became law, although the legislation placed these restrictions on "servants" so as to avoid any suggestion that they might be racially based. Thus a whole system of law effectively based on race came to dominate the running of the mines. "Servants" could be strip searched; they could not own mining claims; they could be whipped up to 50 times if they could not "satisfactorily account" for diamonds found in their possession; they were paid less than white miners or overseers; and they had to carry passes that limited the times and places they could move. These curbs contributed to circumstances in which 8 percent of Africans employed in the mines in the late 1870s died every year.

As large companies came to dominate the landscape they tightened the limitations on Africans. The police began to act at the behest of mine companies. One H. Green at Dutoitspan, for instance, wrote to the governor of Griqualand West asking, "Could not the police put a little gentle pressure on these gentlemen [Africans] to oblige them to enter service?" The governor responded by ordering the police to conduct a series of raids to check employees' passes.[15]

By 1884 racialized legislation reached its peak with the creation of "closed compounds," the most prominent means through which employers controlled black labor in Kimberley. As one of the most renowned historians of the period states, white miners had finally "created a pervasive ideological equation of black workers with criminals."[16] The compounds were attached to the diamond mines and black workers could not leave them for the duration of their contracts, which usually lasted six months. Workers went from the mine into the barracks where they lived without ever leaving the company's control. At home wives and grandparents bore the burden of raising and supporting the children while their menfolk toiled in the mines, enabling the mining companies to skimp on costs by providing only for their male workers. Diseases like smallpox and pneumonia were a constant presence. The white overseers of African workers suffered none of these depredations. Because of the color of their skin they enjoyed a relaxed style of living in the leafy suburbs.

When gold was discovered on the Rand in 1886 established capitalists like Rhodes – who became known as the "Randlords" – transferred their Kimberley operations some 300 miles to the northeast, turning the small town of Johannesburg into a bustling city. By 1899 mining companies employed 100,000 Africans and produced close to one-third of the world's gold. Mechanisms for controlling African labor in Kimberley came to the gold mines and a formal color bar was introduced. Black workers could not hope to hold either the same jobs – or receive the same pay – as their white counterparts, who earned eight times more than they did and received subsidized housing.

The type of ore on the Rand in part determined the experience of the workers there. The ore was highly consistent and plentiful and would reward the patient (and wealthy) mining company. But it was extremely low grade: in order to produce an ounce of gold one had to mine three tons of rock at a depth of two miles beneath the surface. Enormous quantities of labor and vast stores of capital were required to mine the precious metal. Moreover, because gold was practically the only commodity on the world market for which there was a fixed price (the "gold standard"), mine owners could not hope for an increase in the price their product could command. Instead they had to do everything they could to lower costs. First and foremost this entailed cutting the price of African labor.

Figure 3.3 African and European miners outside a South African gold mine, 1888
© Bettmann/Corbis

The mines on the Rand voraciously and unceasingly consumed African labor. Nothing could satisfy their demand, it seemed, especially once the requirements of Kimberley were added in. Mine owners recruited African men from throughout southern and even central Africa. Hugh Masekela, one of Africa's most famous jazz musicians, put it best in his 1990s hit *Stimela*, which bears quoting at length here, though the black-and-white of this page are a poor substitute for Masekela's passionate vocals.

> There is a train that comes from Namibia and Malawi,
> There is a train that comes from Zambia and Zimbabwe,
> There is a train that comes from Angola and Mozambique,
> From Lesotho, from Botswana, from Swaziland,
> From all the hinterlands of southern and central Africa.
> This train carries young and old, African men,
> Who are conscripted to come and work on contract,
> In the golden mineral mines of Johannesburg,
> And its surrounding metropoli, sixteen hours or more a day,
> For almost no pay.

Africans came to work on the mines for a variety of reasons, and two classes of Europeans played important roles in encouraging their employment. First, labor recruiters traveled far and wide across southern Africa, promising good wages and living conditions in exchange for their labor. The realities of mine life – the venereal disease, starvation wages, and 50-person dorms with stacked concrete bunks – did not enter the conversation. For many chiefs and "big men" across southern Africa, sending "their" young men to the mines brought significant rewards. The recruiters offered generous incentives to chiefs, many of whom implemented an informal "tax" on the meager wages of returning workers.

Missionaries, too, encouraged their charges to undertake mine labor. They viewed wage labor as the sort of activity that "civilized" men did. Wages enabled converts to buy the trappings of respectability: "whiteman's trousers," neckerchiefs, hats, and ties, and stoves, chairs, tables, and paraffin lamps for their homes. Protestant missionaries saw nothing wrong with the accumulation of capital from hard work. Indeed, they viewed the devotion to work and the discipline it required as qualities that brought people closer to God. Thus missionaries ended up indirectly supporting the colonial system by influencing their followers to go to work for the mines.

But perhaps the most powerful impetus driving Africans into the mines was related to cattle. An extraordinary outbreak of cattle diseases – redwater fever, lungsickness, and rinderpest – assaulted southern Africa during the second half of the nineteenth century. Rinderpest, a viral disease that kills practically every beast it contacts, obliterated more than 90 percent of the cattle in southern Africa during the 1890s. The loss of cattle undermined the basis of political and social organization across the region. For many communities the status of senior men derived from their ownership of cattle and as the animals died social ordering came under great stress. Cattle permitted the accumulation of "wealth in people"; because cattle were necessary for the payment of bridewealth, their possession enabled older men (and sometimes women) to control younger people and their labor.

Migrant labor and the decrease in the numbers of cattle spurred generational squabbles between young and old. Elders became unwilling to spare the few cattle they had remaining, meaning that young men could not get married, that all-important step into adulthood. In many communities, marriage rates decreased significantly, and many young men came to feel that their passage to adulthood was blocked. Many viewed the mines as a potentially winning lottery ticket: if a man could make his fortune there he could return home and purchase the cattle necessary to become a "big man," freeing himself from dependence on his male elders. Such a prospect attracted many youth who gawked open-mouthed at men in their twenties who returned from the mines with names like Jack, Tom, Sixpence, or Shilling – names connoting that they had become "men of experience."[17] But even here the returning migrants' options were restricted. In chiefdoms surrounding the port of Delagoa Bay – modern day Maputo – older men resisted the pressure to replace brideprice in cattle with brideprice in cash, which would have suited the young men. Where the change *did* occur elders often increased the cash rates beyond the reach of returning migrants.

The experience of migration and mining played an important part in the shaping of ethnic identity across southern Africa. British mine owners and colonial officials assumed that Africans lived in neat, distinct "tribes" and ordered them as such. In the diamond mines in Kimberley, the gold mines of the Rand, and later the copper mines of Zambia, officials housed African peoples based on their perceived "tribe": Zulu here, Xhosa there, Venda here, Pedi there. Migrants came to learn this new identity as they struggled to survive in the mines. Young men came to consciously view themselves as members of a "tribe" as opposed to an extended family, village, or clan, a situation that provided solace, a way to sustain one's social life amidst the chaos of the drilling and blasting. The flexibility that characterized "tribe" – where it existed – in precolonial Africa fell by the wayside; it became more difficult for a "Zulu" family to move from Natal to the Highveld and become "Sotho," discarding one "tribe" for another. Soon, though, African peoples would utilize the power conveyed by the notion of tribe to press against colonial governments across the continent for more political and economic benefits.

Despite the challenges of the all-encompassing mining world African peoples often created vibrant, economically successful lives for themselves. Some survived by simple good business sense: one Zulu guild called the *amaWasha* came to realize that there was money to be made in laundry. Because Johannesburg had no decent water source, municipal ordinances stipulated that washing had to take place on the outskirts of the city so as to avoid contamination and dirty water build-up. In 1890, the *amaWasha* – laundrymen – took advantage of the difficulties created by the ordinance to establish a monopoly on washing clothes for the gold miners. Middle-aged men from a select number of clans in Zululand traveled together on foot to Johannesburg and set up shop, often with their sons. By 1896 some 1200 *amaWasha* plied their trade in Johannesburg, often enriching property-owning Europeans who leased parcels of land they held along rivers in the area to the laundrymen. Concordia Mining Company, for instance, earned £350 per year from *amaWasha* rents. During the 1890s the *amaWasha* enjoyed extraordinary privileges. They could carry weapons, brew their own beer, and even enjoyed exemption from the pass laws. Ultimately, however, they found themselves squeezed out by French and American steam-powered laundries backed with significant capital and favored by municipal authorities as more "hygienic." By 1906 the *amaWasha* could no longer compete in the laundry business.

Other Africans turned to occupations in the towns that grew up around the mines. Mining compounds on the Rand could not be "closed" as they were at Kimberley – the sheer logistical challenge would have been mind-boggling. Each weekend the miners emptied out of their underground tunnels and headed for the towns. One observer described the scene as one in which "ancient Nineveh and Babylon have been revived. Johannesburg is their twentieth century prototype. It is a city of unbridled squander and unfathomable squalor."[18] As in any prospecting rush, boozing and sex occupied the minds and emptied the wallets of men of all colors. Despite the entreaties and lamentations of the missionaries, many African women traveled to the mines to brew beer or work as prostitutes, sometimes earning enough money to buy entire buildings. Close to 1000 European women also traveled to South Africa to take advantage of the various entertainment industries that sprouted in the mining centers.

Sometimes Africans' abilities to shape social life were more subtle, as one historian has shown with his research on same-sex relationships between men on the Rand's gold mines. In the absence of women many men took "wives of the mine," younger men who did chores for them (like cleaning clothes or cooking food) and who acted as sexual partners as well. The rules that governed these relationships were strict and known to all: the relationships were discreet, took place in certain designated areas, and were limited to the mines themselves. This was – as one man recalled – "only friendship on the mines."[19] Some began their relationships out of boredom, others out of a fear that women in the towns and away from the compounds might rob them, trick them, or give them venereal diseases.

These relationships served to give men control over a variety of aspects of their lives. They precisely mirrored the relationships that men and women had in the rural areas: each partner was meant to act in precisely the same way, conforming to customary ways of interaction. Even the kind of sex they had – the Xhosa called it *hlobongo*, the Zulu *metsha* – was non-penetrative intercourse, common among young, unmarried couples throughout southern Africa. Men, young and old, thus ordered their unstable lives in ways that replicated their experiences at home. And the marriages served to enable them to become full adults: the money they earned from their "boyfriends" allowed them to go home and marry women. From the perspective of mine owners these relationships posed no problem. On the mines and in the compounds workers could be controlled; away in the towns, at the mercy of prostitutes and other dodgy people, they might drink excessively, spend all their money, and not come back to work.

In 1898 the president of France made a rather extraordinary statement as he reflected on his country's recent involvement in Africa. "We have behaved like madmen," he declared.[20] For while the scramble for Africa took place for a variety of economic, political, strategic, and social reasons, it also seemed to resemble a bizarre game of one-up-manship as European powers fell over one another to claim chunks of a continent about which they knew very little. Their conquests were made possible by advances in medical, military, transportation, and communication technologies. As we have seen in this chapter, and will see to a greater extent in what follows, Africans responded to European incursions sometimes by force of arms and at other times in more subtle ways as they sought to maintain social and economic order in their communities in the face of drastic changes.

From the perspective of the European powers, their tasks now gained a new level of complexity. They now had to occupy – and "pacify," in the parlance of the times – huge blank areas on maps of dubious accuracy, all the while spending as little cash as possible.

Notes

1 Quoted in Marian Robertson, *Diamond Fever: South African Diamond History 1866–9 from Primary Sources* (New York: Oxford University Press, 1974), 38–40.
2 Quoted in *The Liberal Magazine* 10 (1903), 141.
3 Quoted in Richard A. Soloway, *Demography and Degeneration: Eugenics and the Declining Birthrate in Twentieth-Century Britain* (Chapel Hill: University of North Carolina Press, 1990), 39 and Bernard Porter, *The Lion's Share: A Short History of British Imperialism, 1850–1983*, 2nd edn. (London: Longman, 1984), 130.
4 Quoted in Porter, *Lion's Share*, 129.
5 Quoted in Lynn Hunt, Thomas R. Martin, Barbara H. Rosenwein, and Bonnie G. Smith, *The Making of the West: Peoples and Cultures*, 4th edn. (Boston, MA: Bedford St. Martin's, 2012), 770.
6 Mike Davis, *Late Victorian Holocausts: El Niño Famines and the Making of the Third World* (London: Verso, 2001), 103.
7 Martin Meredith, *Diamonds, Gold, and War: The British, the Boers, and the Making of South Africa* (New York: Public Affairs, 2007), 104.
8 Quoted in M.E. Chamberlain, *The Scramble for Africa* (London: Longman, 1999), 55.

9 Quoted in David Levering Lewis, *The Race to Fashoda: European Colonialism and African Resistance in the Scramble for Africa* (New York: Weidenfeld and Nicolson, 1987), 7.
10 Quoted in Jan Morris, *Heaven's Command: An Imperial Progress* (London: Faber and Faber, 1973), 510.
11 Marie de Kiewiet Hemphill, "The British Sphere, 1884–94," in *History of East Africa*, Vol. I, eds. Roland Oliver and Gervase Mathew (Oxford: Oxford University Press, 1963), 219.
12 Quoted in John Flint, "The Wider Background to Partition and Colonial Occupation," in *History of East Africa*, Vol. I, 370.
13 Quoted in Meredith, *Diamonds, Gold, and War*, 208.
14 Quoted in Meredith, *Diamonds, Gold, and War*, 219.
15 Quoted in William Worger, *South Africa's City of Diamonds: Mine Workers and Monopoly Capitalism in Kimberley, 1867–1895* (New Haven, CT: Yale University Press), 122.
16 Worger, *City of Diamonds*, 110.
17 Patrick Harries, *Work, Culture, and Identity: Migrant Laborers in Mozambique and South Africa, c. 1860–1910* (Portsmouth, NH: Heinemann, 1994), 157.
18 Quoted in Charles Van Onselen, *Studies in the Social and Economic History of the Witwatersrand 1886–1914*, Vol. II: *New Nineveh* (Harlow, UK: Longman, 1982), vi.
19 Quoted in T. Dunbar Moodie, "Migrancy and Male Sexuality on the South African Gold Mines," *Journal of Southern African Studies* 14 (1988), 232.
20 Quoted in Douglas Porch, *Counterinsurgency: Exposing the Myths of the New Way of War* (New York: Cambridge University Press, 2013), 45.

Bibliography

Barraclough, Geoffrey. *An Introduction to Contemporary History*. New York: Basic Books, 1965.

Chamberlain, M.E. *The Scramble for Africa*. London: Longman, 1999.

Comaroff, Jean, and John Comaroff. *Of Revelation and Revolution*, 2 vols. Chicago, IL: University of Chicago Press, 1991–97.

Curtin, Philip, et al. *African History: From Earliest Times to Independence*, 2nd edn. New York: Longman, 1995.

Davis, Mike. *Late Victorian Holocausts: El Niño Famines and the Making of the Third World*. London: Verso, 2001.

Flint, John. "The Wider Background to Partition and Colonial Occupation." In *History of East Africa*, Vol. I, edited by Roland Oliver and Gervase Mathew, 352–90. Oxford: Oxford University Press, 1963.

Forman, Ross. "Randy on the Rand: Portuguese African Labor and the Discourse on 'Unnatural Vice' in the Transvaal in the Early Twentieth Century." *Journal of the History of Sexuality* 11 (2002): 570–609.

Harries, Patrick. *Work, Culture, and Identity: Migrant Laborers in Mozambique and South Africa, c. 1860–1910*. Portsmouth, NH: Heinemann, 1994.

Hemphill, Marie de Kiewiet. "The British Sphere, 1884–94." In *History of East Africa*, Vol. I, edited by Roland Oliver and Gervase Mathew, 391–432. Oxford: Oxford University Press, 1963.

Hernon, Ian. *Britain's Forgotten Wars: Colonial Campaigns of the 19th Century*. Stroud, UK: Sutton, 2003.

Hunt, Lynn, Thomas R. Martin, Barbara H. Rosenwein, and Bonnie G. Smith. *The Making of the West: Peoples and Cultures*, 4th edn. Boston, MA: Bedford St. Martin's, 2012.
Kent, Susan Kingsley. *Gender and Power in Britain, 1640–1990*. London: Routledge, 1999.
Lewis, David Levering. *The Race to Fashoda: European Colonialism and African Resistance in the Scramble for Africa*. New York: Weidenfeld and Nicolson, 1987.
Meredith, Martin. *Diamonds, Gold, and War: The British, the Boers, and the Making of South Africa*. New York: Public Affairs, 2007.
Moodie, T. Dunbar. "Migrancy and Male Sexuality on the South African Gold Mines." *Journal of Southern African Studies* 14 (1988): 228–56.
Morris, Jan. *Heaven's Command: An Imperial Progress*. London: Faber and Faber, 1973.
Porch, Douglas. *Counterinsurgency: Exposing the Myths of the New Way of War*. New York: Cambridge University Press, 2013.
Porter, Bernard. *The Lion's Share: A Short History of British Imperialism, 1850–1983*, 2nd edn. London: Longman, 1984.
Robertson, Marian. *Diamond Fever: South African Diamond History 1866–9 from Primary Sources*. New York: Oxford University Press, 1974.
Rotberg, Robert. *The Founder: Cecil Rhodes and the Pursuit of Power*. New York: Oxford University Press, 1988.
Soloway, Richard A. *Demography and Degeneration: Eugenics and the Declining Birthrate in Twentieth-Century Britain*. Chapel Hill: University of North Carolina Press, 1990.
Thompson, Leonard. *A History of South Africa*, 4th edn. New Haven, CT: Yale University Press, 2014.
Vail, Leroy, ed. *The Creation of Tribalism in Southern Africa*. Berkeley: University of California Press, 1988.
Van Onselen, Charles. *Studies in the Social and Economic History of the Witwatersrand 1886–1914*, 2 vols. Harlow, UK: Longman, 1982.
Worger, William. *South Africa's City of Diamonds: Mine Workers and Monopoly Capitalism in Kimberley, 1867–1895*. New Haven, CT: Yale University Press, 1987.

4 Violence, negotiation, and consolidating British rule, 1890s–1914

In August 1895 three Tswana paramount chiefs – Khama, Sebele, and Bathoen – left their homes in the protectorate of Bechuanaland and journeyed to London to meet with the new Conservative secretary of state for the colonies, Joseph Chamberlain. The chiefs had heard rumors that either the Cape Colony – under the prime ministership of Cecil Rhodes – or Rhodes' British South Africa Company planned to absorb the protectorate and they determined to do all they could to prevent this taking place. In June they had signed a petition addressed to Chamberlain objecting to any kind of annexation and then they had resolved to make their case in person, hoping to raise support for their cause across Britain and put pressure on the government to uphold its promises to protect them; to let them, as the petition read, "remain under the Government of the Great Queen" and not be annexed to the Cape Colony or taken over by Rhodes' company.[1]

Chamberlain greeted his visitors on September 11, 1895, spending two hours with them as he heard their grievances. He then departed for a two-month vacation in Europe, during which time Khama, Bathoen, and Sebele toured the British countryside, meeting with and speaking to local clergy and their congregations, missionary societies, and prominent figures in the humanitarian and progressive worlds concerned about the administration of British colonies in Africa. In their top hats and their bespoke suits these educated, Christian chiefs made a deep impression upon everyone they encountered. In the last days of their visit they breakfasted with guests hosted by the duke of Westminster, among them the future archbishop of Canterbury, the bishop of London, Canon Wilberforce of Westminster Abbey, the marchioness of Ormonde, and two Ladies Cavendish from the prominent family of the duke of Devonshire. A more distinguished and high-born gathering would have been difficult to assemble. Moreover, the interests these breakfasters represented were precisely those Chamberlain looked to for electoral support. Khama, Sebele, and Bathoen had gathered to their side the very people the colonial secretary could not ignore, however much he might have liked to in this particular instance.

For Chamberlain was up to his eyeballs in a conspiracy with Cecil Rhodes and Dr. Leander Starr Jameson to foment revolution in the Transvaal, and the plans called for an invasion from Khama's lands in the Bechuanaland Protectorate. Rhodes and Jameson required these lands as the staging ground for what would be called the Jameson Raid into Afrikaner territory, and Rhodes expected to be able to annex the entirety of the protectorate to his company or to the Cape Colony. But when the chiefs finally sat down with Chamberlain in November 1895 they were able to negotiate terms that at least partially recognized their concerns. Their successful delegation to Chamberlain also held up the planning for the Jameson Raid long enough to help bring about its ultimate failure.

These sorts of negotiations between Africans and Britons characterized the 1890s and 1900s. They shaped the final moves in the scramble for Africa and the way that colonial administration could be imposed upon the continent. For Britain might have asserted its claims to spheres of influence over a number of African territories in the 1880s but it could not make good those claims for many years, often not before 1914. The chiefs' response to British rule was carried out in the realm of high politics; in other places, however – Benin City or the Transvaal, for example – those who had little interest in becoming British subjects took up arms against their purported overlords. In these instances success in establishing effective British control required the use of violence.

Chiefs seeking diplomatic relief, kings leading their people into battle, Afrikaner commandoes fighting British domination, and young men and women in the villages negotiating new threats and opportunities all sought to respond to the British presence in ways that best suited their specific circumstances. As the red ink dried on the map of empire in Africa the situation on the ground reflected these efforts. At times the presence of other European nations determined British actions, but more often than not African peoples did.

Avenging Gordon

The failure of British-led troops to rescue General Charles Gordon in Khartoum from the mahdi's forces in 1884 left a bad taste in the mouths of many Britons who hankered after revenge. This kind of sentiment was not enough to move a succession of Liberal prime ministers to action, however, and for ten years the humiliation of the affair was allowed to stand. In 1895 the Unionist-Conservative government of the marquess of Salisbury came to power and the post of colonial secretary went to the committed and vocal imperialist, Joseph Chamberlain. Dubbed "Josephus Africanus" for his forward program of expansion on that continent – what one Liberal politician described as "killing people because it is good for trade" – Chamberlain frequently set the agenda for his sometimes reluctant prime minister. Salisbury complained that his colonial secretary "wants to go to war with every Power in the World, and has no thought but Imperialism."[2]

French actions in central Africa gave Salisbury's government all the justification it needed to pursue Chamberlain's expansionist goals. Ever since Britain's 1882 occupation of Egypt, France had nursed fantasies of challenging its erstwhile enemy there. One plan had even involved damming the Nile river at Fashoda in Sudan (near the modern-day border between Sudan and South Sudan) so as to destroy the lands through which it coursed to the north, thereby threatening the British position in Egypt. Such an eventuality was not technologically feasible at the time but Britons worried nonetheless, ever wary of anything that might compromise their control of the Suez canal, the lifeline to India. British fears intensified when the Italians invaded Ethiopia and were defeated at Adowa in 1896 at the hands of the Abyssinians, who seemed willing to support French expansion in Equatoria, which lay just to the west of Sudan. British officials determined to seize the moment and at one blow avenge Gordon's death, establish control over Sudan, and render Egypt safe from any further onslaughts. In doing so they also took dramatic steps toward realizing Cecil Rhodes' dream of building a railway that would run from the Cape to Cairo.

In 1896 the commander – or sirdar – of Egypt's forces, General Horatio Herbert Kitchener, ordered his army to advance toward Omdurman, the capital of mahdist Sudan some 1000 miles south of Cairo. In the course of 1896 Kitchener had captured a major northern Sudanese stronghold at Dongola but had had to halt in Wadi Halfa to build the railway that would transport troops across more than 200 miles of punishing desert. Kitchener pushed his workers ruthlessly in the 130 degree heat, driving them to lay as much as a half-mile of track a day. By the end of October 1897, following several successful battles against the armies of the Sudanese *khalifa* (who had succeeded the mahdi following his death in 1885), the railway had reached Abu Hamed, an extraordinary feat of both engineering and effort.

Kitchener's army, comprised of 8200 British and 17,000 Egyptian soldiers, continued south along the Nile, battling for and winning a number of mahdist strongholds. At the beginning of September 1898, encamped just north of Omdurman, the troops came under attack from mahdist forces. They rode into battle on camels wielding swords, spears, and a few antiquated rifles. Armed with Maxim guns and repeating rifles and backed by gunboats equipped with howitzers, Kitchener's army mowed down its attackers, leaving over 11,000 of them dead. Fewer than 50 Britons and Egyptians lost their lives that day in what one war correspondent called "not a battle but an execution."[3] Winston Churchill, who was part of the expeditionary force, decried the "inhuman slaughter" carried out by men Kitchener had trained "to regard their enemy as vermin – unfit to live."[4] For his part, Kitchener ordered the destruction of the mahdi's tomb, looted it of the religious leader's bones, and threw them into the Nile. His well-publicized plans to make a drinking bowl out of the mahdi's skull came to naught when the outcry in Britain caused him to scuttle them, though his

Figure 4.1 The British and their Egyptian allies slaughtered over 11,000 of the mahdi's followers at Omdurman in 1898, losing just 48 men

successor as sirdar, General Reginald Wingate, followed through and crafted for himself a noteworthy trophy from the *khalifa*'s skull.

Kitchener's campaign destroyed the forces that had murdered Gordon, as Britons saw it, cemented British control over Sudan, and secured Egypt. It also marked the effective end of the scramble for Africa, for when the sirdar finished up his work at Omdurman, he journeyed south to Fashoda, where French troops waited. The French hoped that their military presence in lands sought by the British would give them a bargaining chip: recognize our claims in Morocco, the idea went, and we'll retreat from your sphere of influence. A standoff between the European powers ensued, with war a genuine possibility. But before long the French commander, who had marched his little regiment some 2000 miles across Africa from the Congo river, bowed to Britain's superior force and communications and relinquished the ground. Neither country really wanted war; the denouement allowed Britain to proclaim Sudan an Anglo-Egyptian condominium, thus drawing the last of the boundaries that delineated colonial Africa.

Conflict, collaboration, and control

Endemic conflict in Buganda during the late 1880s spurred the Imperial British East Africa Company (IBEAC) to send Frederick Lugard to "pacify the natives." The ancient highlands kingdom of Buganda, a land torn between

Christian and Muslim, was engaged in almost-constant warfare that often involved its neighbor, Bunyoro. (The *mukama* (king) of Bunyoro – Kabarega – reportedly abandoned his capital and shifted its location as many as six times in three years during the fighting.) Lugard arrived in 1890, supported by armed porters from Zanzibar and a handful of Sudanese and Somali soldiers, not to mention a Maxim gun, though it had seen better days. His forces installed a faction of Buganda's Protestant Christians in power and formally established the Uganda Protectorate in 1894. Lugard later rewarded Buganda's assistance in putting down a mutiny of Sudanese in 1897 by setting the kingdom's borders at a far greater geographical extent than they had existed at any point over the previous centuries, incorporating a great deal of Bunyoro territory into the

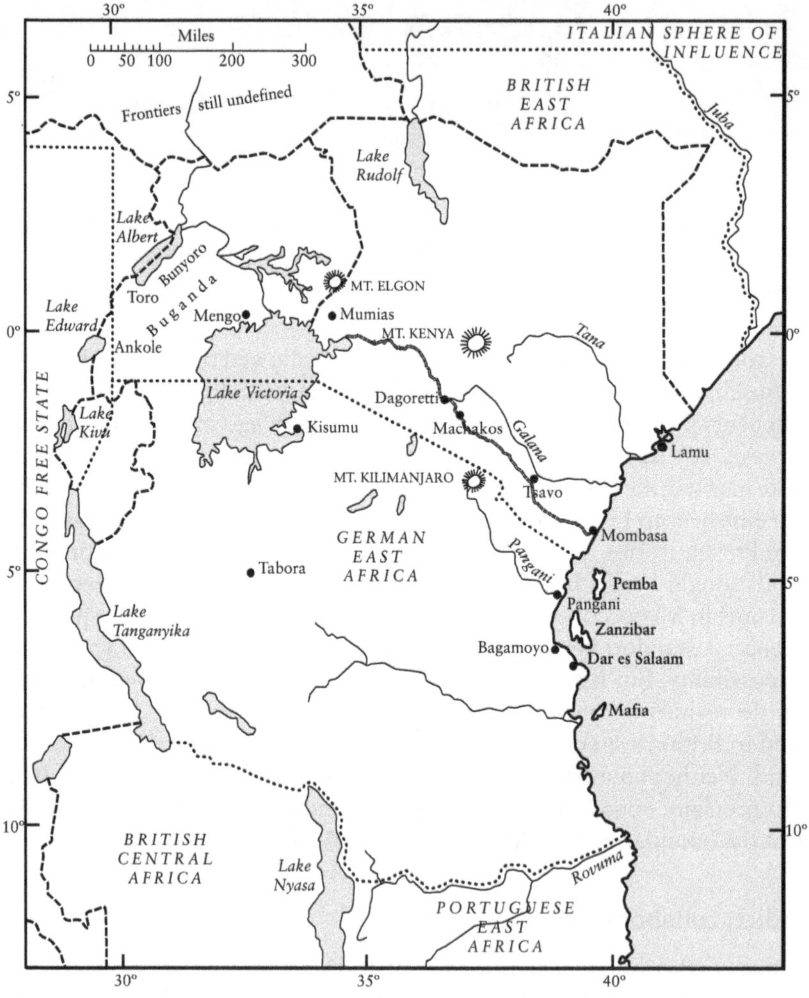

Map 4.1 East Africa, c. 1890

Buganda kingdom. The "special relationship" forged between the British and Buganda, formalized in a treaty in 1900, became a bone of contention later in Uganda's history.

Despite the creation of the new protectorate the elites of the kingdoms of Buganda, Ankole (Nkore), Toro, and Bunyoro were far from helpless. Chiefs seized the opportunity presented by the imposition of British administration to solidify (and in some cases create) political power. Their actions reflected their relationship with the colonial power; they never simplistically "collaborated" with or "resisted" the British but instead negotiated with them in a constantly shifting, fluid process, sometimes accepting parts of western culture, bureaucracy, or regulation and sometimes not. For instance, in Ankole, Enganzi Mbaguta – a "great commoner" – produced a "revolution" in the kingdom's politics between 1899 and 1901.[5] He recognized the prospects that a close association with the British presented and used his connections with colonial officials to drive out the old royal ruling class – the Hinda – setting up his own puppet on the throne. Those who acted most quickly and effectively in the new circumstances prospered.

From the perspective of the IBEAC, the finances of East Africa hinged on Buganda. Officials believed that with its excellent climate, centralized government, and relatively stable political atmosphere the kingdom's peasants could produce goods that would make the entirety of East Africa financially sustainable. The problem was getting those products to the coast so they could be sold on the world market. The company's directors therefore hatched a plan in the mid-1880s to build a railway between Mombasa and Lake Victoria to move peasant produce and people quickly between Buganda and the coast. Quickly dubbed the "Lunatic Express" because of the logistical difficulties in its construction, the Uganda Railway would pass through Kenya on its way to Lake Victoria. At the time the IBEAC still had no blueprint for the white settlement that would soon appear in Kenya (known as the "East Africa Protectorate" until 1920). The initial British administration in the East Africa Protectorate extended little beyond the handful of government stations established near the railway line. Tsavo, west of the Taru desert, was the first major port of call; Machakos (the company's first "capital" from 1889) sat further along in Kamba country; Dagoretti (and later Fort Smith) was established by Lugard in 1890 in southern Kikuyu territory; Fort Hall was situated further to the north; and in the west stood a station at the Wanga *nabongo* (king) Mumia's home close to Lake Victoria on the River Nzoia.

The IBEAC's agents brought with them pre-established views about how African peoples organized themselves politically. Kingdoms like Buganda, Bunyoro, Ankole, and Toro, with their centralized governments, "made sense" to company employees who considered their more "modern" systems of statehood a sign of intelligence and advancement. They felt most comfortable dealing with such kingdoms, seeing in them classic candidates for "indirect rule," which we will discuss below. The disposition and organization of most "tribes" further to the south and east, in contemporary

Kenya, was less clear to Britons. Europeans had certain notions of ordering. They considered Nilotic peoples – often taller, thinner, and possessed of more aquiline features (like "the Maasai") – more "advanced" than the squatter, blacker peoples of central Kenya like the Kikuyu. But these characterizations little aided youthful administrators who arrived on the continent expecting to find discrete, governable "tribes," each with a chief that would facilitate the imposition of British control. They tried to identify tribes as they went and recorded tribal "customs" they assumed had been practiced in precisely the same way since time immemorial.

In actuality few living in the East Africa Protectorate viewed themselves as members of a "tribe," as distinct from a village, extended family, clan, or any other unit of organization. People oriented their lives in a local way and their social circles rarely ranged far from their homes. Given the insecure environment of the region – often beset by drought or famine – people needed to be able to move between different areas (and ostensible "tribes") at a moment's notice. This was usually easier for women than men; their abilities to work *and* reproduce made them especially valuable to other groups. In short, ethnic identity, where it existed, was innately flexible. It was one of a series of potential options a person might use to negotiate his or her circumstances and it could be thrown off when required. The misunderstandings between Africans and Britons over this issue were vast. In 1889, for example, IBEAC expedition leader Frederick Jackson made a treaty with Mboli – a "big man" among the Kamba – near the company's new post at Machakos. Jackson believed he had made an arrangement with "the Kamba," but in fact Mboli's influence probably extended little beyond his own village.

Reflecting the fact that few unified "tribes" existed, different sections of each reacted in different ways to the presence of Britons. In Kamba country "big men" in the vicinity of the station at Machakos (including Mboli) allied themselves with the company administrator, John Ainsworth. Leading warriors and their juniors formed a militia for Ainsworth that assisted him in campaigns against Kikuyu and Maasai peoples to the west. But farther to the east Mwatu wa Ngoma led his forces against Ainsworth, as did leaders to the south toward the railway line. Ainsworth was viewed, most likely, as simply another "big man" jockeying for position in the political systems of the region.

Britons also often failed to notice or understand the internal political and economic divisions that African peoples experienced in this period. We see this clearly in British thinking about "the Maasai." For company employees no African people held a more fearsome reputation than the spear-carrying, red *shuka*-wearing men. The German missionary Johann Krapf had described them as "dreaded as warriors, laying all waste with fire and sword," a common refrain among nineteenth-century European travelers (though somewhat unfair in its judgment).[6] In actuality "the Maasai" constituted no united group and were riven by political conflict during the mid-nineteenth century. During the 1870s, a period sometimes described as the "Iloikop Wars," a civil war pitted Maa-speaking pastoralist and agriculturalist groups against one another for control of water and grazing resources in the Rift valley and further south.

The Maasai and many other peoples in East Africa encountered the forces of British imperialism at a time of environmental catastrophe. Drought, famine, smallpox, locust swarms, and cattle disease, including rinderpest, assaulted the Maasai economy in the 1880s and 1890s, requiring them to retreat back across the Kapiti plains to the southwest. Maasai peoples called the period "The Disaster," and Kikuyu and Kamba peoples raided them at will. But Kamba peoples did not escape their own devastations. In 1898 and 1899 the famine of *Muvunga* (the term means "rice," which people ate to survive) killed a quarter to a half of the population. Because famine periods typically differed in areas occupied by Maasai, Kikuyu, and Kamba peoples, they acted as a tremendous spur to movement, migration, and shifting of "ethnic" identities. They also compelled young men from all parts of Kenya's central region to take jobs working for the colonizers – especially on the railway – in order to procure wages that would aid survival.

As the 1890s progressed the relationship between Africans and the British in the East Africa Protectorate became increasingly characterized by violence, as we saw in the case of Waiyaki and Lugard in the Introduction. This was especially true in the western part of the colony where the Nandi had escaped the worst travails of disease and internal political intrigue. The Nandi possessed no leaders who seemed to represent the "tribe," nor had they come into contact with earlier British caravans through long-distance trade. The Nandi fought with great success against British forces. It took the British more than a decade after 1895 to "pacify" them in the course of five separate campaigns. But perhaps the greatest indignities were heaped upon the Embu in a campaign that made Richard Meinertzhagen's name notorious for the sorts of violence carried out upon Africans by colonialists who were unaccountable for their actions. Later described by Elspeth Huxley as a man who "killed abundantly and killed for pleasure," Meinertzhagen's bloodthirsty career in Africa belied his upbringing in the Hampshire countryside and his pursuit of zoological studies at Cambridge.[7] After an expedition against the Embu, Meinertzhagen confided in his diary, "To my mind the people of Embo [*sic*] have not been sufficiently hammered, and I should like to go back at once and have another go at them. During the first phase [of the campaign] . . . we killed about 796 niggers, and during the second . . . 250."[8] He represented that cohort of British colonial officials who believed that the only way to rule the African was to beat him violently into submission. Behavior such as Meinertzhagen's would come back to haunt Kenya a half-century later.

British beliefs about "tribes" presented a tremendous opportunity for young, upwardly mobile, wannabe chiefs who saw a chance to gain status. They put themselves forward as "tribal leaders" and eager officials gladly appointed them, especially if they proved that they could assist with procuring men to serve as "native auxiliaries" or laborers. These men usually received a small salary and a token of office, typically a badge or cap. Their appointments often proved disastrous. Because they were men of no status they commanded little respect, and few obeyed them. They often resorted to force and corruption to achieve their goals. "We became saddled with a large number of persons of no importance and possessed of no authority," raged one frustrated official stationed in eastern Kenya in 1910.[9]

At the same time these upstart youths faced competition from older men who themselves viewed the imposition of colonial rule as an opportunity to seize greater control over young men and women by manipulating the notion of "custom." They succeeded in their efforts because British administrators assumed that African peoples held a deep, long-standing attachment to clearly defined forms of "tradition" that were, in fact, rarely the hallmark of pre-colonial African societies. Older men stamped their control on the institution of marriage and the possession and distribution of land. In some areas they insisted that only older men could legally own cattle and imposed "punishments" requiring payment in goats or cattle for perceived offences against "custom." British officials tried desperately to record and codify such "customary laws," sometimes bringing a level of rigidity to a previously flexible system. But as we will see in Chapter 5, women proved particularly adept at negotiating these attempts to restrict their liberties.

In the face of overwhelming technological superiority, African peoples continued to resist British efforts to assert their authority. One such incident took place in Benin City to the northwest of the Niger Delta in 1897. The initial flashpoint involved the killing of a party of Britons by Edo men. The British had tried to extend trading rights into the interior of the Niger Delta area, but in the late fall of 1896 the *oba* (king) of Benin had refused to allow outside traders to do business in his kingdom. The British saw this act as violating a treaty enacted in 1892 that had established British sovereignty over the area (and done away with, for all intents and purposes, Benin's independence). An overzealous official by the name of Phillips, serving in place of the absent deputy consul general, opted to prove his worth to his superiors by taking an unarmed group of men to meet with the *oba* in Benin City to resolve the impasse. The *oba*'s emissaries and others sent a number of warnings to the party to stop their advance but Phillips persisted. In response Edo men attacked the group, killing all but two British officers. The British reacted swiftly. Within three weeks a force of 1500 soldiers was amassed and on February 18, 1897, it raided and occupied Benin City and exacted its revenge, looting the city and shooting many of its inhabitants.

Although the incident arose from British attempts to break the *oba* of Benin's trade monopolies, accounts in the British press glossed over this inconvenient fact and presented the actions of the British as heroic efforts to bring civilization to savage barbarians. As the *Illustrated London News* put it, the Edo engaged in "habits of disgusting brutality and scenes of hideous cruelty and bloodshed, ordained by the superstitions of a degraded race of savages."[10] Presumably such characteristics justified the British in taking away their independence and visiting violent punishment upon them when they resisted encroachment.

Another instance of military resistance to British imperial expansion occurred in Gold Coast in the last years of the century. We saw in Chapter 2 how General Wolseley had defeated the Asante in 1873–1874 and briefly occupied Kumasi, forcing the Asante to renounce any claims to southern territory. The resulting peace lasted for some 20 years but in 1895, fearing that Germany and France might encroach on their sphere of influence, the British government asked the Asante King Prempeh I to allow them to establish a garrison in his capital of Kumasi. The king refused. When repeated requests were similarly denied the British sent a column of troops to Kumasi in 1896 and arrested Prempeh without incident. They exiled him to the Seychelles, built a small fort in the city, stationed a few British officers and a sizeable number of Hausa troops, and posted administrative officers and a British resident. Asante territory became part of a British protectorate.

But it wasn't enough, at least as some officials saw it. Authority in the Asante kingdom resided in the Golden Stool, a symbol of the power of the Asante king and of his close union with his people and his ancestors. The British wanted this authority for themselves and made an ill-considered bid for it in March 1900. The governor of the colony, Sir Frederick Hodgson, an arrogant bureaucrat with little knowledge of the people he sought to rule, traveled to Kumasi and upon his arrival commanded that the Asante bring the Golden Stool to him. "Where is the Golden Stool?" he demanded through translators. "I am the representative of the Paramount Power. Why have you relegated me to this ordinary chair? Why did you not take the opportunity of my coming to Kumasi to bring the Golden Stool for me to sit upon?"[11] He ordered his troops to search the area for the stool.

Hodgson's words caused an immediate stir and his ignorance of the spiritual nature of the stool led him to commit an insult of the highest order. The stool was the repository of the spirits of all the kings who had gone before. It was a sacred object, revered for what it represented; out of respect for the ancestors no mortal was ever to sit upon it. No Asante king had ever done so and certainly no foreigner should have expected to. The exiled king's mother, Nana Yaa Asantewa, rallied her people to fight the insolent British, declaring, "Why should they deport the King Prempeh and then come and take the Golden Stool of Asante? We must fight them."[12]

The resulting siege of the British fort in Kumasi by Asante warriors – and closely fought battles in heavily forested bush – lasted for nine months, during which time the British fared badly. The Asante fought hard and effectively. In July 1900 a relief column reached Kumasi and freed the malnourished and sick Britons inside, but another two months passed before the British could take other Asante strongholds and it wasn't until the end of December that they finally brought the Asante to heel. One thousand

British soldiers and an unknown number of Asante warriors died during the conflict, many of the British from disease. Queen Asantewa, like her son, was sent into exile, a number of local chiefs were stripped of their powers, and the Asante kingdom became a crown colony in 1901. Much as they tried the British never found the Golden Stool, which was hidden away in the hollow of a tree and guarded by successive generations of Asante. They finally gave up the hunt in 1920.

Indirect rule and the creation of Nigeria

In Nigeria efforts to establish effective British rule began with the appointment of Frederick Lugard, who came to West Africa in 1894 in the employ of George Goldie, founder and director of the Royal Niger Company. Lugard quickly became known as an intrepid soldier whose courage and resolve had enabled him to "survive in untamed Africa." These characteristics recommended themselves particularly to Goldie, who needed such a man in the Niger territories to protect and further the interests of his company. Lugard spent five years as the representative of the Royal Niger Company, bushwacking his way through "uninhabited" country to extract treaties from local chiefs that barred French commercial activities in return for the "protection" of the British company.

In 1897 Lugard founded and took command of the Royal West African Frontier Force (RWAFF), which played a direct role in the Benin and Asante campaigns discussed above. With a trained military force comprised largely of Hausa soldiers in hand, he turned his attention to the "Muhammadan emirates" of the interior. These were provinces of the larger Sokoto Caliphate, whose *khalifa* had delegated day-to-day governing responsibilities to a variety of emirs. First Ilorin in Yoruba country and then Nupe farther north fell to British arms in 1897. Because the *khalifa*, fearing an incursion by French or German forces if he left his capital undefended, could not spare his own imperial troops to help defend the provinces, each emir had to face the British alone. Lugard's army of fewer than 1000 soldiers marched through northern Nigeria taking one emirate after another. In some instances the emirs surrendered and were allowed to remain in office under British supervision. In others they fought and lost to Lugard's men. In these cases Lugard deposed them and replaced them with men from different branches of the royal families. By 1906 the emirs had – in the imperial phrase – been "pacified" and were settling into the process of colonization. After their defeat the British permitted the emirs to govern their subjects under Lugard's system of "indirect rule."

The doctrine of indirect rule undergirded British colonial government in this era. The system left indigenous ruling structures in place, and the local British resident or district officer asserted British power through them, administering greater amounts of territory than would otherwise have been possible. The doctrine had a long pedigree and provided the basis on which

British imperialists and, increasingly, the British public had developed particular ideas about themselves "as a ruling race."[13] Developed first in the Punjab in India in the 1840s as the British sought to bring that area under control, the ideal promulgated by indirect rule portrayed British imperialists as men of such strength of character, resourcefulness, and moral certainty that tiny numbers of them could rule over millions of alien peoples without resorting to violence to do so. Such a conceit, as we have seen above, was bunk.

In 1900 the British government had replaced the Royal Niger Company as the administrative power in the northern territories, establishing the Northern Nigeria Protectorate with Lugard at its head as high commissioner. The Southern Nigeria Protectorate came into existence in 1906 with the merger of the Niger Coast, Lagos, and Oil Rivers protectorates, three previously distinct territories administered by both the Foreign Office and the Colonial Office. The British had accomplished much of the "pacification" in the south by 1900 through a combination of treaties with various Yoruba states, the forcible conquest of the Benin kingdom, and the domination of the trading federations in the Niger Delta. The eastern hinterland territories in the south proved far more resistant to British control, however. British forces undertook numerous expeditions into Igbo territory – such as that against the Aro in 1901–1902, whom Lugard thought exercised political control over the Igbo people. But the decentralized Igbo across the region did not surrender when the Aro did; they forced the British to battle them village by village. Britons could not exercise governmental authority in southeastern Nigeria until 1909 or so. To do so, they inflicted a degree of violence in the area that probably surpassed that of any other. Armed troops routinely swept through the villages of the southeast looking for subversives and weapons, while taking as their due whatever foodstuffs and other goods that they could "requisition." These same armed colonial forces considered the able-bodied young men of southeastern villages to be a pool for forced labor under the Roads and Rivers Ordinance of 1908, often sweeping up as many of a particular village's youthful male population as they could find for use as bearers, road and rail builders, miners, and any other type of labor that the colonial authorities deemed necessary.

Men and women learned to flee their towns upon learning of the approach of colonial forces because of the brutality that became commonplace. After the implementation of the Collective Punishment Ordinance in February 1912, punishments were regularized and supposedly imposed only after proper judicial hearings in which villagers could state their cases against the punishment. In practice, however, the colonial "man on the spot" often went ahead and meted out rough justice – burning houses and crops, destroying shrines, markets, or other places where people might congregate, and paying little attention to local property rights. When men (especially local elders) were accused of subversion or armed resistance against the emerging colonial regime they could expect lengthy and physically dangerous stays in the new jails being constructed by forced labor; flogging; and even the possibility of death by hanging. The colonial authorities sometimes flogged or otherwise physically punished women during the implementation of collective punishment; most of their pain, however, went unnoticed in the colonial record.

In 1911 the Colonial Office asked Lugard, who was by then serving as governor of Hong Kong, to return to West Africa in order to consolidate the protectorates of Northern Nigeria and Southern Nigeria into a single administrative entity. Upon at least nominal completion of this task in 1914 Lugard was appointed the first governor of the united Colony and Protectorate of Nigeria, an office he occupied until the end of the Great War. As colonial officials saw it the process of pacification of the "Nigerian" peoples was now concluded.

In their efforts to bring vast amounts of territory, people, and resources under their jurisdiction, British imperialists disrupted local economies, polities, societies, land tenure and legal systems, and cultures. In southeastern Nigeria under indirect rule, for example, the understaffed and overwhelmed British sought to govern through local rulers, as they had in the northern emirates. Believing that chiefs ruled southeastern Nigerian communities as emirs did in the north, British officials appointed chiefs to whom they gave warrants, making them the sole executive heads of their local communities

Figure 4.2 British colonizers appointed "warrant chiefs" to assist in the administration of Nigeria

and entitling them to participate in the trials of cases in the "native courts" that were established. In most instances these were men of no special standing who had put themselves forward – or been put forward by their villages – to negotiate with colonial authorities. Lugard gradually transformed certain warrant chiefs into paramount chiefs, with a concomitant addition of power awarded to those fortunate chosen few. The paramount chiefs were thus meant to become "native authorities" much in the style of the northern emirs but their positions did not look anything like the indigenous political systems that had existed and were now subsumed under the new regime. Most indigenous peoples regarded the native courts as instruments of oppression. Warrant chiefs and other men co-opted into the colonial system as court messengers, court clerks, and the like fared well under colonial rule; village denizens knew these personages well and chafed at their elevation, particularly as that elevation was viewed as undeserved.

Beyond the administrative and judicial systems thousands more became "employees" in the colonial system in Nigeria and beyond. Their positions demonstrate the insufficiency of thinking in simplistic categories like "collaboration" and "resistance." The new colonial world required interpreters, clerks, legal assessors, transcribers, and other general employees – most of whom were male – who occupied the middle ground between the ostensibly separate worlds of colonizer and colonized. The requirement for such employees only increased year by year, particularly by the 1920s. These "middlemen" were in difficult positions, expected to move between the two worlds and balance the needs of both sides; some succeeded and many failed. Those who skillfully negotiated the fraught no-man's-land won advantages for themselves and their communities: a clever translator – aware how much an official in a village hundreds of miles from the seat of government depended on his translator to do his job – could shape both policy from above and its implementation on the ground. In many cases jobs in higher civil service roles were given to Indians – deemed more "civilized" than Africans by the British – who had been brought to Africa to serve as laborers.

In many places education was viewed as a guaranteed route to improvement. It improved one's chances of finding work within the colonial administration and some of those who hailed from relatively elite families even chose to pursue education in Britain, in the very heart of the empire itself. There they found the communities, comradeship, and ideologies that would empower them to claim for themselves the rights and dignities denied under colonialism. They had not necessarily set out to follow such a path when they left their towns and villages but their experiences of discrimination and harassment in Britain led them to use the tools of education to try to eliminate the indignities of colonial rule.

African student organizations appeared in Britain as early as 1897 when Caribbean and West African students formed the African Association. Its membership included those from Edinburgh University such as Moses Da Rocha (from Nigeria) and Richard Akiwande Savage (from Gold Coast).

They helped to organize the first Pan-African Conference that was held in London in 1900. Other students at Edinburgh, among them the Nigerians Bandele Omoniyi and Ayodeji Oyejola, worked in the first decade of the twentieth century to improve living conditions for Africans both at home and in Britain. They and students from Liverpool and other colleges helped create the Ethiopian Progressive Association (EPA) in 1904, a broad-based society that joined with African-American and Afro-Caribbean groups to protect the interests of all those of African descent. The EPA protested against the discrimination within the West African Medical Service, the situation of blacks in Natal, and Lugard's "pacification" campaigns in Nigeria. They also joined with white organizations such as the African Society and the Anti-Slavery and Aborigines Rights Protection Society to promote "inter-racial unity" and eliminate the color bar in Britain. The EPA and other African groups did not seek to end colonialism, from which many of them had in fact benefitted. They sought rather to ameliorate the racism they experienced both at home and in Britain. As Omoniyi put it, "The treatment accorded to Africans in the Nativeland and abroad by the ignorant classes of white men and those who ought to know better generally 'make one's blood boil.'"[14]

These efforts yielded little political change in the years before the outbreak of the Great War in 1914. But Africans in Britain had begun to lay the groundwork for more robust efforts designed to lessen the destructive impacts of colonialism that would mature in the interwar period and set the stage for demands for more profound changes in British rule in Africa.

Bechuanaland, Rhodesia, and the Jameson Raid

In southern Africa the consolidation of imperial rule involved the extension of Cecil Rhodes' British South Africa Company (BSAC) into what was usually described as "Rhodesia" and then "Southern Rhodesia" after about 1900. (The British government only took formal control of this territory – contemporary Zimbabwe – after 1923, at which point it enjoyed self-government in any case.) We saw in the last chapter that some 200 white "pioneers" seeking to make their fortunes by digging for gold traveled into Shona country (Mashonaland) in the eastern part of the country, land claimed by the Ndebele chief Lobengula as his and ceded to Rhodes via the Rudd Concession in 1888. But it turned out that gold was nowhere to be found, a calamity compounded by terrible weather that brought heavy flooding and outbreaks of malaria in its wake. The financial health of the BSAC was at risk from the failure to find gold, which compelled it to change course. Between 1891 and 1893 it carved out huge tracts of land to give out to syndicates and private investors with the proviso that they put money into its development. The land was designated for white farms. Few were actually worked at the time but the scramble for them was on. The Shona people knew that this land grab spelled disaster for them.

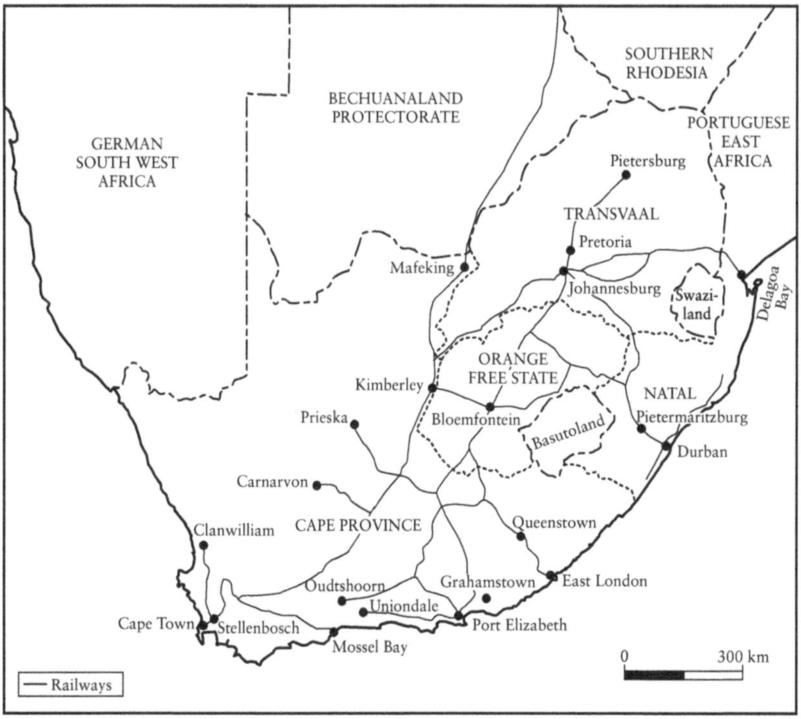

Map 4.2 Provinces and railway lines of South Africa, c. 1908

Stymied in their efforts to get rich quick in Mashonaland white settlers came to believe that Matabeleland to the west presented better chances for finding gold. Under the leadership of Rhodes' friend Jameson they ventured south and west into Lobengula's kingdom. Rhodes had known for some time that war with the Ndebele must come, for not only did they constitute an independent power of not insignificant military might but they also stood in the way of the diamond magnate's ambitions to consolidate British territories in southern Africa: the Cape Colony, Natal, the Bechuanaland Crown Colony, the Bechuanaland Protectorate, Mashonaland, and Matabeleland. Lobengula was under no illusions about the threats he faced from company encroachments on his lands and worked assiduously to keep his proud warriors from engaging in raids that might provoke a military campaign against him. But he also had to protect his authority and when he sent a party to punish a Shona chief for stealing his cattle Rhodes and Jameson used the incident as an excuse to bring war against the Ndebele chief. The fighting did not last long, as Ndebele *impis* – regiments – despite carrying breech-loading rifles received as part of the agreement granting Rhodes his mining concession (see Chapter 3), came up against BSAC forces using machine guns and artillery. They fell to those advanced weapons in the thousands.

Lobengula died shortly after his defeat in 1893. Rhodes and Jameson set up a "Loot Committee" to distribute cattle and land to whites, leaving only two "native reserves" in peripheral areas for the Ndebele. The following year the British government acknowledged the BSAC's authority over Matabeleland, leaving Rhodes to administer the area as he chose.

Rhodes' success emboldened him to pursue the next step in his plan to bring more of southern Africa under the jurisdiction of the British: the incorporation of the Bechuanaland Crown Colony (to the south) into the Cape Colony and the Bechuanaland Protectorate (to the north) into BSAC territory. In September 1894 Rhodes' company began to make claims on lands that Lobengula had contended were his prior to his defeat, including territory held by Chief Khama in the Bechuanaland Protectorate. Khama protested vociferously to the British government against these efforts to steal his land and was backed by the governor of the Cape Colony and high commissioner for the rest of South Africa, Sir Henry Loch, who telegraphed the colonial secretary, Lord Ripon. "Chief Khama has ever been a faithful friend and ally of Her Majesty's Government," Loch noted, "and to hand over that Chief, his people and his territory, to be administered by a commercial company, dependent for their prosperity upon what they may get out of the country, would be a breach of faith such as I am sure the Government would not for a moment entertain."[15]

He was wrong. With the accession of Salisbury as prime minister, the government was fully prepared to entertain the transfer of the protectorate to Rhodes' commercial company. For Salisbury, in addition to holding imperialist sympathies, had married the daughter of one of the Rothchilds, who held a significant stake in the BSAC. Salisbury' government was thus far more inclined to listen to Rhodes' entreaties than earlier governments had been. In 1895 Rhodes leveraged his position as prime minister of the Cape Colony to persuade the legislature to annex the Bechuanaland Crown Colony.

It was no secret that Rhodes intended to do the same with the Bechuanaland Protectorate that he had long coveted, which would allow him to build a railway to Rhodesia. But his motives for taking the protectorate now included a scheme that could not be made public. With Colonial Secretary Joseph Chamberlain's knowledge and support, Rhodes and Jameson were plotting a coup in the Transvaal, desirous of bringing the Afrikaner government under British control. They planned to launch their assault from Pitsane in the Bechuanaland Protectorate.

Here Rhodes' ambitions ran up against the determination of Bechuana chiefs to protect their lands. Khama, Bathoen, and Sebele certainly did not gain everything they asked for when they met Chamberlain in London in November 1895. They had to cede land on which a railroad would be built and those lands would be governed by the BSAC as the representative of Her Majesty's government. But Chamberlain promised that he would take no more land than was needed for the railway and that the government would compensate the chiefs for their losses. Khama maintained control over the lands that Rhodes had tried to claim in 1894 and all the chiefs received assurances that they would be allowed to govern as they always had. "Each of the three chiefs," minuted Chamberlain in his notes on the meeting, "shall have a country within which they shall live as hitherto under the protection of the Queen. The Queen will appoint an officer to reside with them. The chiefs will rule their own people much as at present."[16]

In recognizing the rights of the chiefs to hold on to large portions of their lands – what one historian has described as "Bechuana islands in a Rhodesian sea" – Chamberlain's settlement infuriated Rhodes. "It is humiliating to be utterly beaten by these niggers," he raged.[17] And they had beaten him, for all the other chiefs in the vicinity did indeed lose their lands. Had Khama, Sebele, and Bathoen not been in London at the time it is likely that Rhodesia would have absorbed the entire protectorate.

The Bechuanaland chiefs' deputation to Chamberlain had another important outcome. It held up the preparations for Rhodes' and Jameson's attack on the Transvaal, home to the world's principal supply of gold and an impediment to British imperialists' aim to consolidate all of the territory in southern Africa into a single, British-run confederation. Apologists for empire asserted that the Afrikaners' impertinent independence could not stand, that something had to be done to bring them to heel. But officials worried that however ready the British public was to embrace the bloody conquest of African peoples, blatant aggression against European-descended whites – even if they were Afrikaners – was not something it would countenance. Other methods had to be devised. Rhodes and Jameson, with Chamberlain's unofficial imprimatur, created a plan that would be easier to sell to the British public. They would claim that they were acting to protect the rights of British citizens in the Transvaal who were "discriminated against" because they paid high taxes and possessed secondary status in law. Rhodes and Jameson hoped to spark these people – called *uitlanders* (aliens) by the Afrikaners – into insurrection, at which point Jameson could lead the British South Africa Police into the Transvaal, overthrow Kruger's government, and establish British control. All to defend the "rights" of British citizens.

The Jameson Raid started on December 29, 1895, and it failed spectacularly. The Afrikaners learned of the incursion almost immediately and sent troops to thwart it; British settlers in the republic did not rise up in rebellion. On January 2, 1896, Jameson and his followers surrendered in humiliation and disgrace. Afrikaners in Cape Town, whose political support Rhodes had courted and won through a series of segregationist measures against Africans, turned on their prime minister and ousted him from office. His rivals tried hard to persuade the government to revoke the BSAC's royal charter, but Rhodes had enough dirt on Chamberlain to ensure that didn't happen. The British government condemned the raid; Chamberlain, complicit in the preparations for the raid because he had granted parts of the Bechuanaland Protectorate to Rhodes' company, covered his tracks by extending the terms of his settlement with the Bechuanaland chiefs to cover the entirety of the protectorate. All lands of the protectorate now enjoyed the protection of the British government. The strip of land on which the BSAC had planned to build a railroad reverted to the protectorate, indicating the British government's deep displeasure with Rhodes' actions.

In Rhodesia rounding up a military force for the Jameson raid had left white settlers without protection from the possibility of attack by the Ndebele, whose anger and resentment over the theft of their cattle and land had not diminished. Their losses were compounded by drought, an invasion of locusts, and rinderpest, a disease that killed what few cattle they still owned. When news of the raid's failure reached them in March 1896 the Ndebele rose up, left their native reserves, retrieved the arms they had hidden at the time of Lobengula's surrender in 1893, and attacked whites in outlying farms, mining camps, and trading posts. Within a week they had killed some 200 white settlers, most of whom lived in remote rural areas.

The Ndebele strategy of attacking the outlying areas first allowed whites in the towns to rally and call for help from police and soldiers from the Cape Colony and Natal. Rhodes appeared with a 150-man volunteer force, though Chamberlain – once burned, twice shy – demanded that he place them under the command of imperial officers. The combined forces pushed the Ndebele back from the main settler towns but just when it looked as if the Ndebele could hold out no longer the Shona, who had long lived under the Ndebele yoke, joined the rebellion in June 1896. Their traditional enmity toward the Ndebele overcome by the depredations of white rule, the Shona erupted in violence against white settlers, killing more than 100 men, women, and children. The revolt continued into the fall until Rhodes – whose company was on the hook to pay for the campaign against the Ndebele and Shona – cut a deal with the Ndebele chiefs in October. In return for ending their hostilities the chiefs would go unpunished and those who pledged their loyalty to Rhodes would receive appointments and salaries. The Ndebele would get their land back, Rhodes promised. The scheme worked and Rhodes saved his company, even if he enraged white settler and official imperial opinion with his leniency toward the chiefs. The Ndebele did not get back their land, however; in fact, they lost even more. When they returned to Matabeleland two-thirds of them discovered that they now lived on "white" land. The Shona, less well armed and organized, received no clemency at all. Company and imperial troops hunted them down cruelly, extracting cold-blooded vengeance until they had destroyed all resistance.

The South African War, 1899–1902

With hindsight we can see that the South African War began with the Jameson Raid. Jan Smuts, the Afrikaner commander, certainly thought so. Since 1895 Britain had exerted ever-increasing pressure on Kruger's government, finally forcing the president of the Transvaal into an ultimatum that gave Britain the justification for war it so desired. The war pitted the "phantom commandos of bearded Boers," as one South African novelist later put it, mounted on horseback and armed with rifles, against the might of the British empire.[18] It was a war that could produce only one winner, the British believed; it would be over in time for tea, joked the metropolitan press. The British, however, counted neither on the determination of the Afrikaner horsemen nor the skill of their generals.

The appellations given to wars reveal much about the perspective of those doing the naming. For decades the South African War was known as the "Boer War" in Britain, a label that placed the blame for the conflict on the Afrikaners. Many Afrikaners called it the "Second War of Liberation" from the British invaders (the first was in 1877–1881). A little more appropriately, it later became the "Anglo-Boer War," phrasing that at least accepted that both sides bore burdens for its promulgation. But even the latter phraseology obscured the notion that Africans were involved in any way in the conflict; they were, in large numbers. Today, therefore, we use the term "South African War."

Confident of their success and determined to teach the Afrikaners a lesson about the power and glory of the British empire, politicians and the public were stunned when their armies suffered a series of humiliating and embarrassing defeats in the first months of the war. By late 1900 the British had reversed those losses but the defeat of the 45,000 Afrikaner guerrilla soldiers required an additional 18 months and 450,000 British soldiers.

Britons had viewed war with the Afrikaners as inevitable. As Winston Churchill put it, "sooner or later, in a righteous cause or a picked quarrel . . . for the sake of our Empire, for the sake of our honour, for the sake of the race, we must fight the Boers."[19] It was really for the sake of the gold mines in the Transvaal, but no matter. The presence of so many Britons in the Afrikaner republic, where they constituted a majority of the population, paid 80 percent of the taxes, and yet had no rights of citizenship, provided the "righteous cause." The "picked quarrel" came from the Afrikaners, who after the Jameson Raid saw the writing on the wall and felt they had to move quickly if they were to have any chance of preventing a British takeover of their country. On October 11, 1899, they launched what they regarded as a preventive invasion of Natal and the Cape Colony. Before a week had passed, three divisions of British troops had embarked on their voyage to destroy the Afrikaners and gain fame and glory for themselves and for their queen and country.

For all the talk of the need to prepare for the keen race of nations, British planners had done little to modernize their army. In its attitudes and tactics it harkened back to the days of the duke of Wellington. It possessed modern arms – machine guns and repeating rifles – but employed them in decidedly ancient ways. Soldiers went into battle led by pipers and drummers and only recently had they shed their redcoats for a more drab olive uniform.

They formed up in battle squares and advanced in close order. Moreover, they had not fought Europeans since the Crimean War in the 1850s except for meeting the Afrikaners in the debacle at Majuba Hill in 1881, where the Afrikaners had utterly humiliated them.

The Afrikaners in many ways looked precisely like those imperial pioneers and hunters extolled in British adventure stories. They constituted not an army as much as an irregular commando force almost entirely comprised of Afrikaner men on the backs of their own horses in homespun clothing that barely resembled anything like a uniform, who showed up for service when they felt it necessary and departed when they had more pressing issues elsewhere. Their discipline was lax and they elected their own officers. But in addition to the modern weapons they brought to the battlefield they possessed extraordinary skills of horsemanship and knew the terrain like the backs of their hands. Consummate hunters, they responded to the needs of the moment, flexible in their tactics and responsive to whatever the situation they faced might demand. They knew what they were doing was in defense of their land and their way of life.

Despite being heavily outnumbered the Afrikaners inflicted a series of defeats on British forces. The British performance in the first months of the war proved so inept, indeed, that calls for an inquiry soon arose. The terrible failures only started to turn around in February 1900 when relief forces raised Afrikaner sieges on British garrisons at Kimberley and Ladysmith. In the scheme of things these victories should have been accepted as a matter of course but so bad had the situation been just a month earlier that the British public erupted in wild celebration. Queen Victoria traveled by carriage through London cheered on by thousands of her subjects waving Union Jacks and singing "God Save the Queen." "It was like a triumphal progress," she reported of the huge crowds that surpassed even those of her Diamond Jubilee.[20] The disproportionate response to the victory demonstrates just how bad things had gotten.

The war continued on, the fighting bitter and ugly and seemingly endless. Britain carried out a scorched earth policy, firing farmhouses and sowing fields with salt. Both sides executed prisoners in the field, ignoring international rules governing warfare. The British threw women and children into concentration camps, among the first the world had seen, whose terrible conditions left their inmates diseased and malnourished. Twenty-two thousand Britons died, two-thirds of them from disease. Twenty-four thousand Afrikaners died, 20,000 of them women and children who had suffered in the camps. The remaining Afrikaners found themselves destitute and nearly starved when the fighting stopped in May 1902.

The concentration camps brought women into the narrative of the South African War for the first time. General Kitchener, who became commander-in-chief of the British forces in 1900, established the camps as part of his military strategy. Because "every farm is to [the Afrikaners] an intelligence agency and a supply depot . . . it is almost impossible to surround or catch them," he stated. He therefore ordered the inhabitants of the farms – almost exclusively women and children – into camps where he could keep them from spying and otherwise aiding the Afrikaner cause. In other words, he imprisoned women because they were acting as combatants. When the existence of the camps became known in Britain an uproar ensued and War Secretary St. John Broderick faced awkward questions in parliament. "What civilized Government ever deported women?" demanded Irish MP John Dillon, "Had it come to this, that this Empire was afraid of women?" Broderick replied with the explanation Kitchener had provided him, that "women and children who have been deported are those who have either been found giving information to the enemy or are suspected of giving information to the enemy." This had the effect of spurring Dillon onto even greater rhetorical outrage. "I ask the honourable gentlemen," he sneered, "if any civilized nation in Europe ever declared war against women. . . . A pretty pass has the British Empire come to now!"[21] With no good way out of this gender morass government officials and supporters of the war quickly changed their stories to ones that better fit the gender ideology of Victorian Britain. They insisted now that the camps had had to be built in order to protect Afrikaner women from the unmanly behavior of their menfolk, and, more pointedly, from black Africans.

Afrikaner men had deserted their women, this new narrative asserted, leaving them alone in a dangerous land to starve. Had the men upheld their responsibilities "to provide for their women and children, many of those difficulties which are now complained of would never have occurred," declared Broderick in 1901. And to release those women now, *The Times* insisted, would be to "expose them to outrages from the natives which would set all South Africa in flame."[22] The discourse of new imperialism, in which manly Britons had to take control over unmanly and hyper-sexualized indigenous peoples in defense of white women, took hold immediately. In this instance the terms of the discourse had to be altered slightly, as British women were not themselves at risk from sexually savage peoples. By including Afrikaner women among the ranks of white women, however, the ideology of vulnerable womanhood could be sustained. One passage describing the fate of Afrikaner women being rounded up for imprisonment told of the following:

> On this occasion Kaffirs were used. . . . The women knelt before these Kaffirs and begged for mercy, but they were roughly shaken off, and had to endure even more impudent language and rude behavior. . . . When the mothers were driven like cattle through the streets of Potchefstroom by the Kaffirs, the cries and lamentations of the children filled the air. The Kaffirs jeered and cried, "Move on; till now you were our masters, but now we will make your women our wives."[23]

The gender uncertainties of late nineteenth-century Britain produced by concerns about effeminacy in "town types" and exacerbated by feminist women who refused to play their supposedly God-given gender roles emerged in much of the press coverage of the South African War. Where *The Times* tended to keep its representations of Afrikaner women in line with the ideology of domesticity and passivity for women some of the less "establishment" papers did not. War correspondent Edgar Wallace denounced Afrikaner women for their activities and urged that they be treated as enemy combatants. "There have been many occasions since the war started when I have wished most earnestly that the friends of emancipated womanhood had had their way," he declared, co-opting the rhetoric of feminism in his excoriation of Afrikaner women,

> [and] that the exact status of women had been made equal to that of man. I have often wished her all the rights and privileges of her opposite fellow . . . to be honoured for her gallantry – and shot for her treachery. Especially to be shot for her treachery. Women have played a great part in this war, not so much the part of heroine as of spy. . . . We have decided that we do not make war upon women and children, and if through ill-nature women and children make war on us, we loftily refuse to acknowledge they are making war.[24]

Wallace's rant perfectly exposed the contradictions of Victorian gender ideology at precisely the moment when it was coming under attack from so many quarters. In more ways than one the South African War was certainly the "last of the gentlemen's wars."[25] Britain won, but its grubby victory left Britons with a very bad taste in their mouths.

When the war began the British had expected that the conflict would little involve Africans, but they were wrong. Africans were caught up in the war just as they were in later conflicts that were begun by (and focused on the interests of) European powers, as we will see in the next chapter. There was something of a contradiction here. Many British generals considered it "just not cricket" to use black troops to fight a war against other white peoples but the needs of war and the capabilities of African soldiers often rendered that "nicety" moot. British generals recruited some 20,000 blacks to fight on their side in the war. Afrikaner leaders took great offence at the presence of armed blacks. At the siege of Mafeking in late 1899 Afrikaner commander Piet Cronje was infuriated by Colonel Robert Baden-Powell's decision to give guns to Africans to aid the resistance. Describing it as "an enormous act of wickedness," Cronje suggested to Baden-Powell that "even if it cost you the loss of Mafeking . . . [I suggest you] disarm your blacks and thereby act the part of a white man in a white man's war."[26]

Almost all Africans in the Cape Colony and beyond supported the British in the war in large part because of the indignities they had suffered at the hands of Afrikaners over the previous decades. The view of British rule as preferable to that by Afrikaners was quickly reinforced once the conflict began. Afrikaners summarily shot Africans they discovered with weapons and Afrikaner commandos treated Africans in rural areas abominably. In 1900, when British soldiers finally reached the gold mining towns of the Rand, "crowds of black workers jubilantly burned their passes."[27] But their hopes for change were dashed. The British abruptly halted African efforts to snatch back the farms the Afrikaners had taken from them over the past century and chiefs like the Pedi Sekhukhune II, who had assisted the British against their enemies, found themselves quickly forgotten by their erstwhile allies.

The African experience of the war was mixed. Some producers in rural areas profited handsomely. British troops required enormous quantities of foodstuffs and African peoples catered to their needs in return for high pay. Some succeeded in taking advantage of the conflict to steal cattle from Afrikaner farms, righting perceived historic wrongs. Absent Afrikaner landlords could do little as blacks moved onto "their" farms. By and large, however, the war caused tremendous trauma among African peoples. Many were driven from their land during the fighting and the British scorched earth policy left thousands homeless.

Close to 116,000 Africans ended up interned in concentration camps during the war. Some were the servants of Afrikaner women, others were women struggling from the absence of husbands who were serving in the British forces. But the greatest number were refugees who had fled the war, their livelihoods ruined by the clearing of Afrikaner farms on which they resided or their families threatened by Afrikaner commandoes. Black and white were accommodated together in camps until mid-1901, after which point the British set up a separate system based on race. Conditions were poor. In the Heidelberg camp internees lived on the "carcasses of diseased cattle."[28] The British farmed out as much as half the African camp population for labor service in 1901 and 1902, allowing them to

Figure 4.3 Many Africans fought on the British side in the South African War (1899–1902)

return to the camps every three months to visit their families. Death rates skyrocketed, reaching as high as 436 per 1000 in the Orange river sites. Some 14,000 Africans died in the camps. Most were children, but the British press paid little attention to the terrible straits in which Africans found themselves.

As the war effort staggered toward its ignominious end in 1902 the question of the future of South Africa's black population came to the fore. African intellectuals and chiefs hoped that the peace settlement would contain at least some protections for African rights. But on this score Britons and Afrikaners agreed. As Sir Alfred Milner, the British high commissioner at the Cape, put it, "The white man must rule because he is elevated by many, many steps above the black man; steps which it will take the latter centuries to climb . . . [if] at all." Milner's disinterest in African rights determined the status of Africans under the Treaty of Vereeniging, signed in May 1902 to bring the conflict to a conclusion. He and Chamberlain readily threw out any clauses protecting African rights if they stood in the way of bringing the two sides' positions closer. As Milner put it, "sacrifice 'the nigger' absolutely and the game is easy."[29]

The Treaty of Vereeniging offered generous terms, designed as it was to reconcile the Afrikaners to membership in a union of the four colonies of South Africa. The treaty compensated the Transvaal for the devastation it had suffered, guaranteed full equality for Afrikaners within the union, and formally recognized the Afrikaans language. The British hoped that their magnanimity would enable them to establish a secure Union of South Africa dominated by British citizens who could control the gold fields and provide some degree of protection for Africans from the Afrikaners. But they miscalculated voting patterns. In 1907 and 1908 Afrikaner parties won elections in the Orange Free State, Transvaal, and Cape Colony, with only Natal remaining British-dominated. Ultimately the British left the decision of whether to grant Africans political representation and voting rights to the white populations of the Orange Free State and Transvaal, effectively guaranteeing that they would receive neither.

In 1910 the governments of each of the four colonies created a draft constitution for a union modeled on the British political system. It enacted formal color bars that prevented Africans from voting in the Orange Free State and Transvaal, gave negligible voting rights to those in Natal, and maintained the non-racial franchise in the Cape Colony. The British government accepted the changes in the South African Act and on May 31, 1910, the Union of South Africa came into existence under the leadership of two South African War veterans, Prime Minster Louis Botha and his deputy, Jan Smuts. South Africa became a self-governing dominion of the British empire, a status it shared with Canada, Australia, and New Zealand.

The creation of the Union of South Africa paved the way for segregation in the country for virtually the remainder of the twentieth century. In 1913 the South African government passed the Native Lands Act, placing

7 percent of the country's land in reserves for Africans, who in 1910 comprised two-thirds of the country's overall population of nearly six million (four million Africans, 500,000 "coloureds," 150,000 Indians, and 1,275,000 whites). Africans could only buy or rent land in these crowded "reserve" areas, which frequently contained poor-quality plots. The Native Lands Act, the first in a long line of pieces of racialized legislation, set the tone for the segregationist impulses that would define South Africa for much of the twentieth century.

The ignominies suffered by Britain during the South African War changed the national discourse of empire. At both the official and popular levels of discussion and debate the arrogant and aggressive tone of new imperialism gave way to a more sober set of calculations and less bombastic rhetoric. At the end of the war Britain found itself the target of international condemnation and contempt. Its decision to pick on a small group of backward farmers – as it appeared to the rest of the world – generated disdain among the European great powers and the United States. Its failure to effectively prosecute the conflict against them led its rivals to regard the island powerhouse as something of a paper tiger. So friendless was Britain – and so evident its weakness – that the country that had pursued a policy of "splendid isolation" vis-à-vis Europe for the past hundred years turned almost immediately to its longtime enemy, France, to improve relations. By 1904 they had established the *Entente Cordiale*, which called for both parties to settle colonial disputes but made no provisions for assistance in the event of war. Nonetheless it was quite an achievement, for, as we have seen, Britain and France had come perilously close to war at Fashoda in 1898.

In 1905, provoked by the German build-up of its navy and the kaiser's increasingly bellicose posturing on the world stage, the British Admiralty began to plan for a naval war against Germany in the event that it attacked France, and the War Office started to think about playing a role in potential continental conflicts in France and Belgium. Unofficial conversations between French and British military officials took place, establishing stronger ties between the two countries. In 1907 an Anglo-Russian understanding that resembled the *Entente Cordiale* was reached. Over the next seven years European frictions increased and hostilities intensified; alliances grew more rigid until finally, when a Bosnian nationalist assassinated a member of the Austro-Hungarian royal family in Sarajevo, the world erupted into war.

Despite difficulties during the European "pacification" and consolidation of its colonies, Africans demonstrated an ability to succeed in the face of long odds, from the mines of the Rand to the newly imposed chiefly system of administration in the East Africa Protectorate. The disordering of African lives in virtually every arena also provided a spur to protest, which spread in a variety of manifestations in the first decades of the twentieth century. African men and women were quick to use the imports of the colonial system – the law, Christianity, and the classificatory system of tribes – to resist their subjugation and create new alliances and networks among themselves.

Notes

1 Quoted in Neil Parsons, *King Khama, Emperor Joe, and the Great White Queen: Victorian Britain through African Eyes* (Chicago, IL: University of Chicago Press, 1998), 60.
2 Quoted in Piers Brendon, *The Decline and Fall of the British Empire, 1781–1997* (New York: Knopf, 2008), 206–207.
3 Quoted in Byron Farwell, *Queen Victoria's Little Wars* (New York: Harper & Row, 1972), 336.
4 Quoted in Brendon, *Decline and Fall*, 209–10.
5 Edward Steinhart, *Conflict and Collaboration: The Kingdoms of Western Uganda, 1890–1907* (Princeton, NJ: Princeton University Press, 1977), 154.
6 Johann Krapf, *Travels, Researches and Missionary Labours in East Africa* (London: F. Cass, 1968 [1860]), 359.
7 Elspeth Huxley, "Preface," in Richard Meinertzhagen, *Kenya Diary, 1902–1906* (London: Eland Books, 1983 [1957]), v.
8 Meinertzhagen, *Kenya Diary*, 152.
9 Quoted in Myles Osborne, *Ethnicity and Empire in Kenya: Loyalty and Martial Race among the Kamba, c. 1800 to the Present* (New York: Cambridge University Press, 2014), 66.
10 Quoted in Annie E. Coombes, *Reinventing Africa: Museums, Material Culture, and Popular Imagination in Late Victorian and Edwardian England* (New Haven, CT: Yale University Press, 1997), 7.
11 Quoted in Ian Hernon, *Britain's Forgotten Wars: Colonial Campaigns of the 19th Century* (Stroud, UK: Sutton, 2003), 192.
12 Quoted in Hernon, *Britain's Forgotten Wars*, 193.
13 Kathryn Tidrick, *Empire and the English Character: The Illusion of Authority* (London: Tauris, 1992), 1.
14 Quoted in Hakim Adi, "West African Students in Britain, 1900–60: The Politics of Exile," in *Africans in Britain*, ed. David Killingray (Ilford, UK: F. Cass, 1994), 110.
15 Quoted in Parsons, *King Khama*, 56.
16 Quoted in Parsons, *King Khama*, 209.
17 Quoted in Neil Parsons, "The 'Victorian Internet' Reaches Halfway to Cairo: Cape Tanganyika Telegraphs, 1875–1926," in *The Social Life of Connectivity in Africa*, eds. Mirjam de Bruijn and Rijk van Dijk (New York: Palgrave Macmillan, 2012), 107.
18 Breyten Breytenbach, *Dog Heart: A Memoir* (New York: Harcourt Brace, 1999), 33.
19 Quoted in James Morris, *Farewell the Trumpets: An Imperial Retreat* (London: Faber and Faber, 1978), 66.
20 Quoted in Walter Arnstein, *Queen Victoria* (Basingstoke, UK: Palgrave Macmillan, 2003), 192.
21 Quoted in Paula Krebs, *Gender, Race, and the Writing of Empire: Public Discourse and the Boer War* (Cambridge: Cambridge University Press, 1999), 60.
22 Quoted in Krebs, *Gender, Race*, 63.
23 Quoted in Krebs, *Gender, Race*, 64.
24 Quoted in Krebs, *Gender, Race*, 66–67.
25 Krebs, *Gender, Race*, 55.
26 Quoted in Martin Meredith, *Diamonds, Gold, and War: The British, the Boers, and the Making of South Africa* (New York: Public Affairs, 2007), 430.

27 Meredith, *Diamonds, Gold, and War*, 494.
28 Peter Warwick, *Black People and the South African War, 1899–1902* (Cambridge: Cambridge University Press, 1983), 149.
29 Meredith, *Diamonds, Gold, and War*, 495, 466.

Bibliography

Adi, Hakim. "West African Students in Britain, 1900–60: The Politics of Exile." In *Africans in Britain*, edited by David Killingray, 107–28. Ilford, UK: F. Cass, 1994.

Adu Boahen, A., ed. *UNESCO General History of Africa*, Vol. VII: *Africa Under Colonial Domination, 1880–1935*. Berkeley: University of California Press, 1990.

Arnstein, Walter. *Queen Victoria*. Basingstoke, UK: Palgrave Macmillan, 2003.

Brendon, Piers. *The Decline and Fall of the British Empire, 1781–1997*. New York: Knopf, 2008.

Breytenbach, Breyten. *Dog Heart: A Memoir*. New York: Harcourt Brace, 1999.

Chanock, Martin. *Law, Custom and Social Order: The Colonial Experience in Malawi and Zambia*. Cambridge: Cambridge University Press, 1985.

Coombes, Annie E. *Reinventing Africa: Museums, Material Culture, and Popular Imagination in Late Victorian and Edwardian England*. New Haven, CT: Yale University Press, 1997.

Farwell, Byron. *Queen Victoria's Little Wars*. New York: Harper & Row, 1972.

Hernon, Ian. *Britain's Forgotten Wars: Colonial Campaigns of the 19th Century*. Stroud, UK: Sutton, 2003.

Krapf, Johann. *Travels, Researches and Missionary Labours in East Africa*. London: F. Cass, 1968 [1860].

Krebs, Paula. *Gender, Race, and the Writing of Empire: Public Discourse and the Boer War*. Cambridge: Cambridge University Press, 1999.

Lawrance, Benjamin, Emily Osborn, and Richard Roberts, eds. *Intermediaries, Interpreters, and Clerks: African Employees in the Making of Colonial Africa*. Madison: University of Wisconsin Press, 2006.

Lonsdale, John. "The Conquest State, 1895–1904." In *A Modern History of Kenya*, edited by William Ochieng', 6–34. Nairobi: Evans Brothers, 1989.

Matera, Marc, Misty L. Bastian, and Susan Kingsley Kent. *The Women's War of 1929: Gender and Violence in Colonial Nigeria*. Basingstoke, UK: Palgrave Macmillan, 2011.

Meinertzhagen, Richard. *Kenya Diary, 1902–1906*. London: Eland Books, 1983 [1957].

Meredith, Martin. *Diamonds, Gold, and War: The British, the Boers, and the Making of South Africa*. New York: Public Affairs, 2007.

Morris, James. *Farewell the Trumpets: An Imperial Retreat*. London: Faber and Faber, 1978.

Oliver, Roland, and Gervase Mathew, eds. *History of East Africa*, Vol. I. Oxford: Clarendon Press, 1963.

Osborne, Myles. *Ethnicity and Empire in Kenya: Loyalty and Martial Race among the Kamba, c. 1800 to the Present*. New York: Cambridge University Press, 2014.

Parsons, Neil. *King Khama, Emperor Joe, and the Great White Queen: Victorian Britain through African Eyes*. Chicago, IL: University of Chicago Press, 1998.

Parsons, Neil. "The 'Victorian Internet' Reaches Halfway to Cairo: Cape Tanganyika Telegraphs, 1875–1926." In *The Social Life of Connectivity in Africa*, edited by Mirjam de Bruijn and Rijk van Dijk, 95–121. New York: Palgrave Macmillan, 2012.

Ranger, Terence. "The Invention of Tradition in Colonial Africa." In *The Invention of Tradition*, edited by Eric Hobsbawm and Terence Ranger, 211–62. Cambridge: Cambridge University Press, 1983.

Reid, Richard. *Political Power in Pre-Colonial Buganda: Economy, Society & Warfare in the Nineteenth Century*. Oxford: James Currey, 2002.

Ross, Robert. *A Concise History of South Africa*, 2nd edn. Cambridge: Cambridge University Press, 2008.

Steinhart, Edward. *Conflict and Collaboration: The Kingdoms of Western Uganda, 1890–1907*. Princeton, NJ: Princeton University Press, 1977.

Thompson, Leonard. *A History of South Africa*, 4th edn. New Haven, CT: Yale University Press, 2014.

Tidrick, Kathryn. *Empire and the English Character: The Illusion of Authority*. London: Tauris, 1992.

Warwick, Peter. *Black People and the South African War, 1899–1902*. Cambridge: Cambridge University Press, 1983.

5 Africans in the white man's wars, 1914–1945

Six-year-old Ojebeta heard the drums sound a warning for her village in Ibuza in the interior of southeastern Nigeria. "There is a kind of death coming from across the salty waters," the gongman announced. "It is now coming to us. They call it Felenza. It is white man's death." Rumors about its sudden appearance circulated throughout the area – the British "were at war with their neighbors 'the Germanis'; and the latter fought the British by blowing poisonous gas into the air. When you breathed it in, you died." None of the villagers understood what any of that had to do with them; all they could do was watch helplessly as person after person fell victim to the disease.

The whole world was dying, it seemed to Ojebeta, the protagonist of Buchi Emecheta's 1977 novel *The Slave Girl*. She saw her father carried back to his hut one evening; he had died suddenly while working in his fields. Her oldest brother left the village to find work with the Europeans rather than wait for the felenza to find him, leaving his mother, his younger brother Okolie, and his sister behind. Ojebeta clung desperately to her mother over the next few days, fearful of the death all around her. And then one morning she awoke to the noise of her mother's friends and relatives crying loudly. Ojebeta's mother was dead: "taken away from her by the same felenza."

This spelled disaster for the young girl. "Why did she leave me behind with no one to look after me?" she protested to her aunt. In ordinary circumstances Ojebeta could have counted on close kin caring and providing for her just as they would their own children, but these were no ordinary times. Her feckless brother Okolie, unwilling to take responsibility for his younger sister and unencumbered by family ties that would have obligated him to do so, took her to Onitsha and sold her into slavery to a trader named Ma Palagada.[1]

The Slave Girl tells the story of Buchi Emecheta's mother, which the author learned as a young girl. The story traces the devastation of kinship and community ties wrought by the influenza epidemic that broke out worldwide in 1918 just before the Great War came to an end. We cannot claim the novel as historical "fact" (Emecheta claims that the flu appeared in 1916, for example) but we can see in it traces of the powerful influence the epidemic had on virtually all of Africa. Families and communities suffered its ravages, with sometimes entire villages succumbing to death. Emecheta's narrative represents the difficulties that peoples across the continent faced during and after the war, the scope of death brought by the epidemic – following as it did hard on the heels of the terrible mortality caused by the Great War – and its contribution to social disintegration and hardship among Africans.

The experiences of the Great War, followed just two decades later by a second European world war, spurred widespread discontent with British colonial rule. Africans came to feel that they had been betrayed. They fought and died in the thousands for Britain yet received little in return. Indeed, the hand of colonial rule fell more firmly than before during the interwar period as Britain consolidated its grip on the colonies. Officials meddled in social ordering and economies as never before, bringing even the most remote areas of the continent into their orbit.

The Great War

In August 1914 the tensions that had simmered in Europe for over two decades exploded into war. Rivalries, competition, disputes, jealousies, and conflicting national interests had driven the great powers to seek security and advantage in alliances. The Triple Alliance of Germany, Austria-Hungary, and Italy faced off against the Triple Entente of Britain, France, and Russia. Many of those tensions concerned Africa, where Germany, France, and Britain vied for control over territory; indeed, some historians have suggested that colonial disputes had acted as something of a safety valve in keeping warfare among European nations away from the European continent itself. By 1914 that safety valve no longer operated to reduce European hostility.

Germany's policy of *Weltpolitik*, which aimed to challenge British supremacy throughout the world, called for a vast buildup of its navy, and, importantly for our purposes, the stationing of a number of ships in all of its African colonies. Germany regarded the African continent as a point of vulnerability for Britain and France, in defense of which the allies would have to expend resources and men that they might otherwise utilize in Europe or Eurasia. As it turned out, the first shots fired by the British in the Great War came from the weapon of a sergeant-major in the Royal West African Frontier Force by the name of Alhaji Grunshi who was stationed in German Togoland.

Few British or German officials believed that the war would truly come to Africa in any significant way. Neither side seemed to have adequate supplies nor troops for any sort of prolonged engagement and in many cases British and German officers were friendly with one another, given that their territories often shared borders. Thus at the war's first naval engagement, which took place on Lake Nyasa (Malawi) on August 16, 1914, the British Captain Rhoades shelled the steamer *Hermann von Wissman,* leading its skipper (and his drinking companion) Captain Berndt to row out to Rhoades in a small boat screaming, "Gott for damn, Rhoades, vos you drunk?"[2]

The British had a variety of reasons for engaging in the African theater of war to the extent that they did. Defense of their shipping from German attacks originating from colonial ports required the presence of allied troops on land; and when the German commander Paul von Lettow-Vorbeck embarked on his multi-year dash around southern and eastern Africa attacking allied targets British troops were forced to follow. Beyond these purely defensive aims the conquest of additional African territory held significant attraction. Gaining German East Africa would place the Cape to Cairo route entirely in British hands; at the same time, in the minds of India Office officials, it would provide a destination for a great deal of Indian emigration.

Not all Britons, however, shared the view that fighting the Germans in Africa was a priority. In Kenya white settlers protested that the most important task for Europeans was not to fight one another but to secure control of Africans. Vastly outnumbered by blacks and insecure in their hold on the territory, whites feared that fighting among themselves would diminish their prestige in the eyes of Africans; moreover, enlisting Africans in the fight among Europeans would result in blacks killing whites and therefore threatening the fragile white supremacy on which their position was based. In the event these fears did not materialize: while Europeans certainly took part in the African campaigns of the Great War, their numbers were small and by far the majority of participants were Africans. In the short run the war had the effect of strengthening the cooperation of Africans with British colonial officials. In the longer term the extraordinary impact it had on the continent, second only to that of the slave trade in its dislocation of peoples, communities, societies, and economies, contributed to the demise of colonialism some 50 years later.

For those Africans living in the most remote areas, the Great War brought the colonial system into their lives in a meaningful way for the first time. Even as late as 1910 colonial administrators had yet to visit many of the villages that were situated far from the cities and towns of their colonies, in part due to a lack of easily passable roads. By 1918 few regions had gone untouched by the war and the conflict had pulled more than two million Africans directly into service. Most worked as carriers – or porters – serving the unrelenting supply needs of allied forces. Because the fighting took place in areas where roads, railways, and motorized vehicles were few and far between, artillery pieces, rations, and the other tools of war had to be shifted by hand by carriers. (Draft animals could not survive in many areas of fighting because of the presence of endemic trypanosomiasis.) Ten percent of those who saw service – over 200,000 – lost their lives, either killed in action or dying from disease or malnutrition in the horrific conditions under which they worked. Only a minority served as actual soldiers in the British armies – some 25,000 Africans from West Africa; 30,000 from Uganda, Nyasaland, and Kenya; and 2400 from Rhodesia.

Figure 5.1 Lieutenant Dimmer poses with African soldiers in front of a machine gun, c. 1917

Described as "volunteers" in official correspondence, carriers in sufficient numbers could only be obtained through intimidation, threats, and kidnapping. West Africans regarded carrier work with disdain even when it paid, characterizing it as "donkey work." They avoided it unless economic circumstances or physical force compelled them to comply, as was often the case during the war. As one western Nigerian official recounted in 1915,

> I have evidence that . . . men have invariably been compelled to serve as carriers . . . On all sides I hear of charges of extortion and oppression. . . . It is possible, also, that harsh treatment in the past may have caused an added distaste for such work. An English officer has recently told me in confidence that he has known of instances of carriers being put in prison for three or four days at a certain station to prevent them going away.[3]

The dangers and harsh treatment involved in military carrying rendered the work unattractive. Though British officials had used forced labor throughout sub-Saharan Africa in the early years of administration, it was never on the scale that war now required. British officials had to threaten chiefs to produce carriers for the Cameroonian and East African campaigns in order to achieve the requisite high numbers. Chiefs, in turn, forced their villagers to "enlist" as carriers, an abuse of their power that constituted perhaps the greatest grievance against the chief system. One southern Nigerian recruit, Nwose, told of his experience.

> We came back one night from our yam farm. The chief called us and handed us over to a Government messenger. I did not know where we were going to, but the chief and the messenger said that the white man had sent for us and so we must go. After three days we reached the white man's compound. Plenty of others had arrived from other villages far away. The white man wrote our names in a book, tied a brass number ticket around our neck, and gave each man a blanket and food. Then he told us that we were going to the great war to help the King's soldiers, who were preventing the Germans coming to our country and burning it. We left and marched far into the bush. The Government police led the way, and allowed no man to stop behind.[4]

Carriers faced difficult conditions and suffered harsh treatment at the hands of their masters. Wholly apart from their vulnerability to sniping by the enemy carriers experienced hardships of the most extreme kind. While soldiers wore uniforms and carried equipment issued by the British, carriers had no such protection from the elements until late in the war. They went barefoot throughout and received only a kernel sack for protection from the rains in the Cameroons and East Africa. Food was scarce – often no more than 1000 calories a day for a carrier who might have to trudge 15 miles with 60 pounds on his back – and disease was rampant among both troops and carriers, though the latter received the least attention in these matters. In the Cameroons half of the 14,000 carriers fell ill to leg and foot ulcers, respiratory and stomach ailments, malaria, and illnesses described as "debility" and "wasting." One British officer reported that carriers working in the flooded Rufiji valley in East Africa were attacked and killed or mutilated by crocodiles as they trod paths where the water was waist deep. Overworked, inadequately clothed and fed, lacking cooking pots and even blankets in many cases, carriers fell prey to disease in enormous numbers, a situation that prompted one Colonial Office member to remark, "Of course before the end of the East African campaign . . . the rate of mortality in East Africa only stopped short of a scandal because the people who suffered most were the carriers – and after all, who cares about native carriers?"[5] When serving in East Africa, the Southern Nigeria Carrier Corps suffered a death rate of 394 per 1000; after nine months 63 percent of its ranks had been lost to death, injury, or disease. The death rate for northern Nigerian carriers stood at 83 per 1000, while that of Sierra Leoneans was 174 per 1000. The conditions the Nigeria Regiment encountered in East Africa, where disease and starvation took a hideous toll, beggars the imagination. Lugard described carriers of the Nigeria Regiment as "a fine body of men"; upon their return in 1917, he lamented, "it is like a collection of half-broken skeletons."[6]

Those invalided out returned to little better conditions. Lugard admitted in 1917 that carriers – "obviously in a bad state of health" – who landed in Lagos found themselves "without definite care or supervision." He and others persuaded military officials that the British should build a camp for demobilized Nigerians but little progress was made. The acting commandant of the Nigeria Regiment, Colonel F. Jenkins, observed that "neither the roofs nor walls of the shelters erected afford any protection from the weather. It would be quite impossible to quarter any human beings least of all invalids in these shelters."[7] To add injury to injury, soldiers and carriers went without pay for months and months and often lost promised leave time or payment settlements. Troops did not receive the pensions, gratuities, and honors the British had promised them at the beginning of the conflict. One ex-private recalled that "the Government did not care about the families . . . did not even take care of living soldiers . . . The British could not be trusted."[8]

The Royal West African Frontier Force saw action in the Cameroons in 1914 and 1915, then traveled to East Africa in November 1916 to take part in action against the Germans there. Conditions in both the West and East African theaters wreaked havoc with troop movements. The rains in the East African Rufiji valley proved relentless, at one point flooding the entire area and washing out 120 miles of road within two days that had taken thousands of man-hours to build. With little functional wheeled transport available carriers took over responsibility for supplies. Twelve thousand of them – the number required to supply 3000 soldiers – struggled through crocodile- and lion-infested terrain to provide food and ammunition to the troops, who, for all the efforts of the carriers, received only 13 ounces of food a day. Fresh meat was unavailable so soldiers resorted to eating roots they dug out of the ground, along with animal carcasses whose consumption produced "disastrous results on many occasions." Men removed hides used to reinforce bridges and boiled them up in soup; and they ate "bush rat pie and monkey's brains on ration biscuits." Officers reported that February, March, and April 1917 were "black months" for the Nigeria Regiment, as their men were "terribly thin and wretched, till they became almost unfit to take the field in any active operations." "The hardships passed must be unparalleled in military operations of our time," wrote Captain W.D. Downes, "Our condition could not have been worse even if we had been in a siege."[9]

The loss of recruits to the military and carrier services produced severe difficulties for families and communities throughout Africa. Large-scale recruitment of carriers left a shortage of workers for industry and agriculture and the absence of men in the villages created greater responsibilities for women. This generated anxiety and anger within the local populations. In southeastern Nigeria, for instance, District Officer Edward Falk wrote from Owerri in 1919 that "relatives of men who have not come back from military expeditions or railway work invariably consider the chiefs who recruited the men to be guilty of a species of homicide or slave dealing."[10] For Igbo-speaking peoples the exploitation and disappearance of manpower for foreign military purposes suggested a darker cosmological design. Many believed that men who sold their services for warfare engaged in abominations against the earth. Colonial policies, whatever their rationale from the British perspective, appeared to spread ill-fortune indiscriminately throughout the land, prompting the outbreak of a series of rebellions against the agents of British rule in 1914 and 1915. The British suppressed these with considerable violence: in the so-called "Owerri massacre" in late 1914, for instance, they retaliated with the destruction of two towns and the killing of an undetermined number of people; in 1915, British officials, traders, and local police slaughtered 200 Igbo men who had rebelled against their forced labor assignments on the railroad, killing government workers and supervisors. In 1916 an Oujo rebellion against recruitment practices was savagely put down. The British carried out at least 12 counter-insurgency campaigns against the Igbo that year, during which they commonly burned houses and whole villages and beat elderly men who acted as village representatives.

In the final months of the Great War, influenza swept across the globe, compounding the miseries brought about by four years of warfare. The influenza pandemic of 1918–1919 killed at least 30 million – and perhaps as many as 100 million – people throughout the world. It proved more deadly than any other outbreak of disease since the Black Death in the fourteenth century, and it killed more people than any other single event of the twentieth century save World War II. George Newman, chief medical officer of Great Britain's Ministry of Health in 1918, called it "one of the great historic scourges of our time, a pestilence which affected the wellbeing of millions of men and women and destroyed more human lives in a few months than did the European war in five years." It appeared with explosive suddenness and "simply had its way. It came like a thief in the night and stole treasure."[11] Doctors estimated that 800 out of 1000 persons who came down with the flu contracted only a mild case; of the other 200 who were severely afflicted, some 80 percent of them died.

The virus – though doctors and scientists did not know that this was what caused the disease – arrived in Freetown on August 15, 1918, carried by 200 sick sailors who had traveled from Britain on board the naval ship H.M.S. *Mantua*. Within the space of two weeks local dockworkers had spread the flu into town. They also carried the flu on board other ships tied up at Freetown, which transported the virus to other ports along the African coast. The *Shango* carried the disease from Freetown to Accra in Gold Coast and on to Cape Coast; the S.S. *Bida* took it from Sierra Leone to Lagos in mid-September, from where it spread inland along the railway lines, bicycle and walking paths, and streams carrying canoes upriver. Troopships *Jaroslav* and *Veronej*, calling at Freetown, later transported 1300 troops from the South African Native Labour Contingent who had seen service in France to Cape Town. As these men made their way home they brought the virus into southern and central Africa. The illness devastated communities, killing people at the prime of their lives and breaking down social ties. It had such a powerful impact on Africans that many named age-grades after it; others referred for decades to the time before or after the influenza.

Africans respond to the Great War

The devastation of the Great War produced a variety of responses among African peoples. In many cases the war provided the impetus for the expression of longer-held dissatisfactions. Some of the easiest movements to identify are those we might label "political," but many others expressed their anger against British rule in ostensibly "religious" terms. Christianity in particular gave many peoples an opportunity to respond to the indignities of the colonial system. These movements were not "proto-nationalist" in content; they rarely aimed at achieving any sort of political "independence" from British control, though nationalist leaders in the 1940s and 1950s would hark back to them for inspiration, drawing a direct line from those who went before them.

On January 24, 1915, the Reverend John Chilembwe's usual Sunday service in Nyasaland's highlands was a little different. The location and timing were the same but the head of a British estate manager named W. J. Livingstone stuck high on a pole in the rafters was certainly out of the ordinary. Livingstone was one of several Europeans killed over the previous 24 hours in what became known as the "Chilembwe uprising." The fact that Livingstone could claim distant kinship to the great explorer and missionary – the very face of the benevolent British effort to bring "light" to Africans – made the attack all the more troubling to British authorities.

The rising grew out of long-standing discontent with land and labor policies in the Shire Highlands of Nyasaland. British farmers had grabbed up land here *before* the implementation of formal colonial administration. Livingstone managed the A. L. Bruce estates, one of the larger European properties that together comprised nearly one million acres by the 1880s. African workers, many of whom originated from outside Nyasaland, came to work on the European farms in exchange for a place to settle. They lived in poor conditions and Livingtone in particular had a reputation for beating his workers. British planters enjoyed something of an alliance with local Yao chiefs, Muslims who helped the planters procure labor. Chilembwe and his supporters on the other hand were Christian (as a Yao Christian, Chilembwe was something of a rarity). They were also mostly planters – competing with Britons for business – or plantation workers. Most were Nguru and had migrated from Mozambique; as such, they had weaker claims to land than Africans from the Nyasaland Protectorate and therefore had to accept whatever conditions for land residence and labor contracts the British planters demanded.

The Baptist missionary Joseph Booth had converted Chilembwe to Christianity during the 1890s. In 1897, in his twenties, Chilembwe traveled to the United States where he became a preacher with the American Negro Church and studied at the Virginia Theological Seminary in Lynchburg. There he became familiar with ideas of equal rights and appropriate protections for the treatment of individuals, especially in matters of land tenure. He preached these ideas at the Providence Industrial Mission he founded upon his return to Nyasaland. Before the outbreak of the Great War his teachings were in line with standard Baptist orthodoxy, but the circumstances of war altered them.

The Chilembwe uprising arose from grievances related to the war piled on top of pre-existing conditions. Onerous tax obligations, a scarcity of farmable land, and poor treatment of African workers on British farms, compounded by conscription for the war, hunger resulting from famine, and war-related economic distress ratcheted up discontent. Chilembwe had made a great effort to draw attention to these concerns in the months before the uprising. He published an article in the settler *Nyasaland Times* on November 26, 1914, demanding that Britons compensate Africans for their contributions to the war effort and the ills they suffered as a consequence. "We understand that we have been invited to shed our innocent blood in this world's war," he began. "A number of our people have already shed their blood, while some are crippled for life. . . . Will there be any good prospects for the natives after the end of the war? Shall we be recognised as anybody in the best interests of civilisation and Christianity after the great struggle is ended?"[12]

When it became clear to him that the answer was no, Chilembwe and his compatriots began to conspire. Chilembwe told his followers about African-American slaves who had risen up against their masters and spoke at length about the American Civil War. It appears that he did not genuinely believe the revolt could succeed; rather he and his men decided as one to "strike a blow and die."[13] Chilembwe thought that he would most likely become a martyr. He sent 200 men to procure guns and ammunition and then they attacked Livingstone. Chilembwe hoped that Africans in other districts would also rise up and support the movement but few did. It took only one platoon of the King's African Rifles to restore the peace. The ringleaders were caught the following week and hanged after quick trials; Chilembwe was shot and killed while trying to evade arrest. Nationalists would later remember Chilembwe's actions as the first blow struck against colonial rule in Nyasaland and today his portrait adorns the kwacha, the currency of Malawi.

It is important to remember, though, that the existence of the colonial system did not mean that African movements were by default direct responses to it. Many religious and social movements espoused alternative visions of community and social order that appealed to their followers but were only indirectly – or to a limited degree – related to the foreign presence (consider, for instance, Isaiah Shembe's Nazareth Baptist Church, founded in Natal in 1910). One of the most fascinating episodes in this regard was the Watchtower movement, as the Jehovah's Witnesses of the day identified themselves. The movement was notable for its geographical and chronological breadth: it ranged from the British territories of Nyasaland and Northern Rhodesia (Zambia) to the Belgian Congo and its three "outbreaks" took place during each of the first three decades of the twentieth century. The second outbreak of the Watchtower movement, occurring late in 1917, speaks directly to the experience of war and the unique way African peoples responded to its pressures.

The Great War caused dramatic social disorder in Northern Rhodesia. The need for labor to assist the war effort, which included road-building and cutting down trees, was keenly felt in the north. The government raised tax rates to force men into work in the wage labor economy, sometimes burning down the homes of those who refused. The colonial administration rewarded chiefs who recruited men to serve in the army, raising the limit of their already coercive powers. To make matters worse wartime grain requisitioning caused extreme hunger in many communities. The vulnerable and battered people of Northern Rhodesia, where mission Christianity of all denominations had taken hold deeply and broadly, were ready to listen to those who offered them solace. Because the different missionary churches had trained Africans to work as catechists a critical mass of them had the skills and learning to spread their ideas.

The movement appeared in Northern Rhodesia in the final months of 1917 when seven migrant laborers who had been expelled from a labor camp in Southern Rhodesia journeyed north to their homes. Led by a man named Sindano and his assistant Kanjale, the small group preached as they passed through the villages and towns of Northern Rhodesia, exhorting their listeners to receive baptism before the "end of days," which was nigh. Africans should not trust European missionaries, they urged, who were false prophets working against the interests of their congregants. The claim fell on keen ears for the missionaries had shown little sympathy to "backsliders" in the midst of war, driving many who transgressed from their congregations. Where missionaries required a two- to four-year training period before baptism could take place Watchtower preachers offered instant baptism. Baptism was the one and only ritual that would permit a person to enter heaven at the "end of days."

In 1918 the German commander von Lettow-Vorbeck burned several mission stations and buildings of the colonial administration, and then influenza settled upon the region, killing thousands. What appeared to be unmistakable signs of the end of days compelled thousands of worshippers to join the Watchtower movement. Watchtower thought derived inspiration from missionary teaching but it differed from conventional Christianity in important respects. Adherents believed that unbaptized people were *wasatani* – devils – and they looked to traditional remedies to protect themselves against them. Converts to the new ideas seemed to care little about the existing social order or the potential repercussions of their actions. They held church services in the forests outside the villages, drumming and singing and demonstrating no fear of the evil spirits that were meant to inhabit the forests at night. Children who converted rejected the authority of their parents; converted women refused to have sex with their unconverted husbands; and Watchtower followers dismissed the chiefs who claimed authority over them.

From the perspective of the colonial administration the Watchtower movement presented a difficult problem. Was it "anti-colonial" and "political" and therefore required a response? Certainly some aspects of it seemed to point in that direction. One French priest said he heard a Watchtower preacher telling villagers, "Africa for the Africans," and preachers apparently exhorted their followers to stop using European tools and implements. But adherents were also unquestioningly inspired by religious zeal and this made British colonial officers nervous. They had long been taught to avoid meddling in African "religion" or "superstition." But the movement could not be ignored. Convinced that the end of days was approaching, Watchtower converts began acting in ways that undermined colonial control. Soldiers deserted their posts; farmers stopped growing crops; villagers ignored the orders of chiefs and headmen; and workers refused the legal requirement to pay tax. Adherents went so far as to publicly show disrespect for district officials – even hitting one man named Draper. For officials who knew full well that their positions were based largely on the premise that they could command authority over entire districts by little more than the force of their personalities alone, such insolence threatened their ability to control the situation.

Open defiance of colonial rule could not be tolerated but officials understood that their authority would be utterly disregarded if they used force against the Watchtower movement. As Justice MacDonnell, involved in many Watchtower legal cases, noted later, we "realized the delicate and fragile nature of our hold over these people and at times we saw the abyss opening."[14] The British therefore took the extraordinary step of permitting Sindano to join his followers together in a village under the ostensible control of a government chief. (The community thrived, surviving into the 1950s.) The alternate vision of community espoused by Watchtower adherents acted as a powerful challenge to the state and Sindano won a sort of independence for his people. After the war African leaders would grow more confident and aware of the ways that they might challenge the tenuous hold of the British over them.

The mandate colonies and "trusteeship" in the interwar period

Many treatments of the British empire still identify the interwar period as the time when Britain's hold on its colonies began an inevitable decline. In fact during the years between World Wars I and II Britain's empire increased dramatically in size, reaching its territorial zenith; certainly no official, settler, politician, or member of the public held any notion that Britain might relinquish its lands within the next century or so.

Following the end of the Great War the delegates to the peace talks in Paris had to decide what to do with the colonies and territories held by now-defeated Germany and the Ottoman empire. American President Woodrow Wilson had declared the United States' commitment to the self-determination of nations when it entered the war, a sentiment that won significant popular support in Europe, much to the discomfiture of imperialists across the globe. Widespread acceptance of the principle meant that the victors could not simply seize Germany's colonies and the lands of the former Ottoman empire as spoils of war. In order to placate Wilson and bid for American friendship, British Prime Minister David Lloyd George bowed to his desire to create a mandate system under the newly created League of Nations through which the lands of their enemies would be administered as a "sacred trust of civilization." This proved to be little more than a smoke screen behind which Britain governed the mandated territories it received just as it did its own colonies. The Union of South Africa won German South-West Africa (today Namibia), while Britain gained part of German Togoland in West Africa (which was added to Gold Coast) and, more importantly, German East Africa, now renamed Tanganyika (today's Tanzania). This latter addition fulfilled Britain's long-held dream of controlling an unbroken chain of territories running from the Cape to Cairo.

The League of Nations body charged with overseeing the mandates, the Permanent Mandates Commission (PMC), sought to enforce the policy of "trusteeship" embedded in the article that established it. Mandate powers were obliged to pursue and maintain the "wellbeing and development" of peoples supposedly not yet able to adequately negotiate the conditions of the modern world. The concept of trusteeship differed little from earlier notions of Britain's "civilizing mission" or the "white man's burden," but it implicitly acknowledged that colonization would at some time in the future come to an end. Moreover, the job of the mandate powers was to prepare for that time by developing the economic, political, social, and cultural institutions that would make those colonies viable states in the future. The idea of trusteeship proved a useful counter to critics of colonialism at home, to whom apologists for empire could reply: "we are in (pick West Africa, East Africa) not to exploit the peoples and resources of the territories but to improve them." The reality of the situation never lived up to the rhetoric of trusteeship, for Britain's needs often conflicted with those of its colonies in the fraught years between the wars.

Britain emerged from the Great War victorious but broke. It had liquidated its overseas investments in order to pay for the war; lost overseas and colonial markets to the United States and Japan while occupied fighting Germany; was saddled with outdated machinery and plants throughout its industrial north; and as a result began to slip into depression as early as 1920. As demobilized service members returned home, unemployment levels rose: by 1921 one million Britons could not find work. Angry veterans and militant trade unionists appeared to be threatening revolution. In this heated and tense atmosphere the Colonial Office's scheme to pay for the resettlement of ex-servicemen and -women in the empire, no matter its great cost, looked like the best option to a government eager to establish security and social peace. Starting in January 1920 the first wave of what would be a total number of 86,000 emigrants left Britain's shores bound for the dominion or colony of their choice. Many landed in South Africa, Kenya, and Southern Rhodesia. Their departure did little to alleviate Britain's domestic economic problems but their arrival in Africa had a significant impact on the future of the white settler colonies.

Controlling Africans was one aspect of empire, certainly, but it was vital from the imperial perspective that colonies both continue to support the metropole financially and create their own strong economies. This proved difficult. Prior to the Great War Britain had virtually no coherent policy governing the economic administration of its colonies. Its aims were to see that colonial economies served to enhance Britain's domestic prosperity. To that end, colonial governors had worked to facilitate the growing and extraction of primary materials – foodstuffs, metals, and minerals – that were exported to feed a world market and supply Britain's and others' industrial needs. They had not viewed their mission as including any effort to stimulate the growth of industry itself in their colonies, as these would compete with

Britain's. This meant that most African economies depended upon one or two crop-growing or mining enterprises and lacked diversification.

The extraction of minerals and metals and the farming of cash crops for export had taken place at the expense of agriculture for local food production and had brought about increased proletarianization as farmers left the land to work for wages in the mines and on plantations. The officials and politicians who had shaped this process often had direct financial interests in the companies that benefitted, like the United Africa Company, Elder Dempster, Lever Brothers, and Cadbury Brothers. Bad working conditions – including poor rations, low wages, and insufficient housing – had led to frequent labor turnover, which Britons attributed to Africans' laziness. We should view some of their behavior as resistance to the indignities of the colonial system.

Now, however, with the war over British officials took a new approach. The difficulties of the postwar era compelled them to begin thinking about how Britain's colonial possessions ought to be ruled so as to meet the obligations of trusteeship on the one hand and assist Britain's recovery on the other. The incompatibility of these two aims ensured that neither succeeded. Truly enhancing the welfare of African subjects would have required careful improvement of local economies through diversification – encouraging small-scale peasant agriculture for domestic consumption rather than export and promoting local manufacture of secondary goods. These activities would have harmed Britain's domestic economy because its own goods would have no longer found the markets they had once enjoyed and unemployment at home would have increased. So British colonial officials turned to policies of "empire strengthening" aimed at developing infrastructure – railroads, roads, communications systems, factories, port facilities, and warehouses – that would enhance the production of and trade in the commodities that constituted most of Africa's economic exchanges with Britain. These measures, wrapped up in the Colonial Development Act of 1929, increased Africa's dependency on one or two export commodities, and as the depression became worldwide after 1929, the prices Africans could command for their products fell dramatically. Their economies and the standards of living they could support deteriorated concomitantly. In the 1930s depressed worldwide prices reduced living conditions for Africans even further. Prices for West African commodities such as cocoa and palm oil dropped by 60 to 70 percent, forcing down wages and inducing private companies to drive their workers harder. Africans faced terrible poverty and immiseration; they could barely live on their wages. Meanwhile at home the act had no impact on British unemployment levels.

Empire-strengthening projects cost large sums of money at the best of times and the Great Depression ensured that these sums were not forthcoming. Instead bureaucrats called for efficiencies in all areas of government. Nowhere did the need to economize appear as markedly as in the imperative to "make the colonies pay for themselves." Colonial administrators cut costs where they could but in most cases they balanced their books by increasing tax revenues. British authorities believed taxation to be a "moral tonic." Since Africans had to pay taxes in cash the system forced them to work to earn wages. Work increased the output of commodities that could be exported from the colonies; perhaps more importantly in the minds of British authorities, it instilled in purportedly work-shy Africans the civilized habits of industry and discipline.

But direct taxation – a levy imposed on a person or a piece of property as opposed to one placed on the sale or purchase of a product – was a concept with which many African peoples were unfamiliar. No indigenous Igbo term existed to express taxation as it is known in the west, for example. Nor did wage-earning yield enough cash to meet the ever-increasing demand of colonial authorities for additional revenue. Authorities implemented the first direct taxation in southeastern Nigeria in 1928. The tax amounted to five shillings per adult male. Although colonial officials judged it eminently fair Igbo men found such a sum difficult to pay. Most Igbo had limited access to British currency and colonial tax collectors would accept no local substitute – such as cowries, manillas (metal armlets), or brass rods – for hard currency. Although the British had introduced sterling to Igboland as the official currency as early as 1902, away from the cities it was rarely seen and people viewed it as somewhat useless.

Village men in southeastern Nigeria and elsewhere often had to borrow sterling from warrant chiefs at exorbitant rates of interest to pay the tax or were forced to pawn members of their families to get hold of the necessary cash. Most households suffered impoverishment with the imposition of direct taxation. Although taxation did not fall directly upon women, their minor children, or their property, many women were forced to contribute to men's tax payments. Widows – who often were called upon to help their unmarried sons pay their tax and who were more numerous after the influenza pandemic – and women with some access to outside currency owing to their involvement in trade found themselves particularly burdened.

Taxation was perhaps the most visible manifestation of British rule that took on a more prominent role in organizing the lives of Africans after the war. Before 1914 some remote villages and hamlets had never even received a visit from a district officer; now colonial governments began to meddle in every aspect of Africans' economic and political lives. This trend was somewhat limited in protectorates like Uganda or Bechuanaland where a small administrative staff was the limit of British influence. In colonies like Kenya and Southern Rhodesia, however, influential and vociferous white settlers demanded and won advantages for themselves that entailed greater and greater intrusion into the lives of African men and women by the colonial state. Usually this intervention involved land and almost always resulted in disadvantages for Africans.

Land stood at the heart of the colonial experience in white settler colonies from 1900 onward. In Southern Rhodesia the first Britons were those "pioneers" who had arrived with Rhodes. Disappointed by the failure to discover the "Second Rand" they turned to farming to cover their losses and make their futures. In Kenya Governor Sir Charles Eliot decided to invite Britons and some South Africans to the colony, backing a scheme in which settler farmers would provide the revenue to balance the colony's books. In both cases colonial governments passed laws that enabled the transfer of land from the African to the white settler population, though in Kenya the extent of this exchange was sometimes later exaggerated for political purposes. Initially the small number of settlers meant that they had a relatively minor impact on Africans: in 1907 the East Africa Protectorate could boast only 2000 settlers but by 1914 these whites had amassed 639,640 acres. Limited in number, they nevertheless cast larger-than-life shadows. Men like Lord Delamere or "Cape to Cairo" Grogan (who bore the distinction of being expelled from both Winchester College and Cambridge) procured vast farms and exerted pressure on the government to assist them in their dealings. Their well-publicized deeds played a role in expanding settlement in Kenya after the Great War. The Soldier Settlement Scheme made available 2.5 million acres at negligible cost to junior officers and their families.

During the interwar period governments in Kenya and Southern Rhodesia (which became self-governing in 1923) acted to consolidate their hold over the colonies. They passed a series of laws designed to ensure that the settlers remained profitable, often to the direct detriment of the African populations in the colonies. Perhaps the most significant step toward achieving this goal was the creation of the "native reserves." Areas designated exclusively for African habitation, the reserves often contained only marginal land. Ownership of private property on the reserves was banned, though in practice people commonly bought and sold land among themselves. In order to induce Africans to leave the reserves to find work on settler farms, authorities deliberately populated them with far more people than the land could support. Many did leave and made their homes on settler ranches where they provided labor or paid rent in exchange for a place to raise a family. Known as "squatters" in the Kenyan case, they would become important later in the Mau Mau uprising of the 1950s (see Chapter 6).

The Kenyan government formalized control over labor through the Native Authority Ordinance in 1912, a law permitting colonial authorities to compel Africans to perform "compulsory labor" without payment. Much of the colonial infrastructure was built by men conscripted under the ordinance. In the 1920s the development of the *kipande* – or pass – system expanded white control over labor. African migrant laborers had to carry passes that provided details of their employers and wages, enabling settlers or government agents to round up those who had deserted their contracts and punish them for doing so. It became more difficult for Africans to leave jobs and negotiate better salaries with their employers, as their employment details were written in the *kipande* for all to see.

Despite these restrictions and systemic disadvantages many African farmers continued to produce livestock and crops and some of them prospered. When the depression struck in 1929 the governments of Kenya and Southern Rhodesia acted to divert the wealth of these farmers to the white settlers. They did so by prohibiting Africans from growing lucrative cash crops – maize and tobacco in Southern Rhodesia and maize and coffee in Kenya. This practice ensured that only white settlers could produce the most profitable crops, striking directly at the wellbeing of middle-class African farmers and incurring their undying enmity.

Southern Rhodesia and Kenya also made liberal use of the notorious marketing board system that hurt Africans so badly. Take a Shona maize farmer living in eastern Southern Rhodesia as an example. When he harvested his maize he was legally obligated to sell the entirety of his crop to the government Maize Marketing Board at a price fixed by the board. The government then marked up the maize, sold it on the world market for a significantly higher price, and pumped those profits into instruments like credit, loans, fertilizers, and equipment for white settlers. Our Shona farmer's cattle-keeping neighbor faced the same discrimination. The government taxed cattle raised for domestic consumption – that is, African cattle – but did not tax cattle for export, the stock owned by Britons. It directed the resultant tax revenues to the settlers. The two control systems often overlapped. In Kenya in 1938 the government forced the Kamba to sell their cattle for one-quarter of their market value to a firm on the outskirts of Nairobi called Liebig's, a Southern Rhodesian company experienced in culling African "scrub cattle" from the Victoria and Gutu reserves in the southeastern region of its own country. The profits the company realized from the sale of the cattle on the world market provided funds for building a facility to chill settler beef for export. As one settler whose family raised cattle in Kamba areas at the time put it, Liebig's operated "solely for our benefit."[15]

Fighting back

The heavy weight of colonialism in the interwar period made it clear to all but the most oblivious that Africans were facing a system that viewed their interests as secondary at best. Africans responded to the situation in a variety of ways. Some formed political organizations to try to bring about change peacefully while others turned to violence to demonstrate their dissatisfaction. Many forms of resistance or adaptation involved far more subtle strategies. African women, young men, and Christians, in particular, sought to harness opportunities brought by colonialism to better themselves and their social positions and implement their own visions of community.

Throughout the colonies African intellectuals formed organizations to oppose different aspects of colonialism. In Gold Coast from 1918 and Nigeria from 1920 members of the legal, medical, and business professions joined together in the National Congress of British West Africa (NCBWA).

Its aims were largely conservative; the National Congress sought to improve voting rights for Africans in the colonies' governments but any suggestion that Africans might throw off the mantle of colonialism was still some years away. In Kenya Harry Thuku's East African Association, formed in 1921, sought to draw attention to high levels of unemployment and the poor housing inhabited by workers in Nairobi's slums. Thuku succeeded in winning support beyond his own ethnic group, the Kikuyu, but his career in government opposition ended in tragedy. On March 16, 1922, a crowd of 1000 people, "many with large sticks," gathered to protest his arrest at a Nairobi police station. The police opened fire, killing at least 20. Some of Kenya's white settlers holed up in the neighboring Norfolk Hotel found time between gin and tonics to join in the slaughter, emptying a number of rounds into the crowd without having to leave the comfort of the bar.

These political organizations were usually headed by the graduates of the early mission schools, though alumni of a few government schools such as Alliance High School in Kenya were also beginning to make their presence felt. Some leaders had attended the universities that were starting to spring up across the continent – Cairo University, Makerere College in Kampala, or Khartoum's Gordon Memorial College. Officials argued about the sort of education Africans should receive. Certainly some amount of bureaucratic training for lowly civil service positions was thought to be a good idea but many also viewed education as bringing potentially dangerous "new" ideas to Africans who were unprepared to properly understand them. They were not entirely wrong in their assessment, for across the continent men and a few women who had received education came to lead their communities. They were generally wealthy; because they could read and write they won government jobs, established successful businesses, and procured title deeds to land they owned wherever possible. Several decades later they would become the elites of Africa's newly independent nations. They came to occupy a sort of middle ground between colonizer and colonized: Europeans rarely accepted them and in many cases they were treated with suspicion by the average villager.

Because of the still-limited number of universities on the continent most Africans seeking higher education had to look abroad, to the United States or Britain. During the interwar period increasing numbers of mostly male students enrolled at Edinburgh, Oxford, Cambridge, and the colleges that comprised the University of London. In 1918 students residing in London formed two new black associations to help newcomers adjust to the environment they faced, one often marked by racism and hostility. Neither the Union of African Descent nor the African Progress Union (APU) started out with intentions of becoming political organizations, but the settings in which students found themselves made it difficult to sustain that position. By the mid-1920s unofficial color bars and racial discrimination prompted members of the associations to make changes. Establishing a residence for Africans and West Indians – a "home from home" that would eliminate the need to expose themselves to hostility from white landlords and provide a common social space – was a top priority, but it would be another decade before it was accomplished. In the meantime the APU joined forces with the NCBWA to lobby the Colonial Office for reforms. Africans in London also facilitated the interactions of various African groups. In 1920 NCBWA emissaries such as Herbert Macaulay traveled to London and, through the offices of the APU, met Sol Plaatje and Josiah Gumede, representatives of the South African Native National Congress, which became the African National Congress in later years.

In 1924 the British Empire Exhibition, a world's fair-type display of the products and peoples of Britain's imperial holdings, opened at Wembley in north London. Many of the depictions of colonial peoples offered up stereotypical images of savage cannibals, backward and superstitious sub-humans, and illiterate and unskilled "natives" whose future depended upon continued British overlordship. They enraged many Africans, chief amongst them Ladipo Solanke, a Yoruba man studying law at University College, London. He railed against the Wembley representations of Africans in a series of articles published in Britain and West Africa and was moved by its racism and prejudice to establish the West African Students' Union (WASU), arguably the most important African organization in Britain for the next 30 years, in 1925. In its first decade WASU enrolled men exclusively, but in the mid-1930s a number of African women began to join the union, including the first African women seeking degrees in Britain. WASU established a hostel for visiting Africans and people of African descent, insisting that its operations remain entirely independent of the Colonial Office or any other official entity so that its guests might live and work without interference. WASU's commitment to this principle made for some difficult days for the hostel, financially speaking, and sparked some debate among its members as to how to sustain the residence, but the staunchness of its commitment demonstrated to all that Africans could and must attend to their own affairs.

WASU engaged in a number of protests against policies and practices imposed in Britain's African colonies throughout the late 1920s and 1930s and its members spent many hours discussing and promoting pan-Africanism. Ideologically speaking, pan-Africanism raised a revolutionary suggestion – that people living on the African continent and those of African descent living elsewhere identify themselves and act as *Africans*, as opposed to members of political parties, ethnic groups, or any other component of identity. WASU delegates attended a number of congresses devoted to pan-Africanism in the 1920s and 1930s. This focus on a broad "Africanness" derived in part from the interests of its first formulators, men like Marcus Garvey and W.E.B. Du Bois who sought to broaden the struggle of African-Americans and Afro-Caribbeans to include all peoples of African heritage. In the case of African intellectuals and activists, the appeal of pan-Africanism reflected the reality of an imperialism that had created colonies that paid no attention to natural boundaries or social, ethnic, economic, cultural, or historical commonalities. Where Britons saw "Gold Coast" or "the Gambia,"

"Sierra Leone" or "Nigeria," West Africans saw states that either divided indigenous peoples from one another or lumped diverse groups into single units that made no sense. Pan-Africanism had numerous followers among Africans in Britain and on the continent during the interwar and postwar periods, many of whom were educated and relatively well-off, but it would not fare well after decolonization, when the colonies carved out by Britain in the 1880s and 1890s became national states with virtually no changes whatsoever to their boundaries. Only Kwame Nkrumah, the new president of Ghana, would continue to enthusiastically embrace pan-Africanism after independence.

Africans in Britain kept in close contact with colleagues at home in their efforts to improve the conditions of peoples living under British colonialism. Some of the most effective resistance to colonialism appeared in the guise of trade union formation and strike activity. These new organizations often had relatively low numbers of members but they articulated grievances effectively. Imperial officers often responded harshly to labor protests, in part as a result of paranoia about the possibilities of communism spreading to Africans. In Gold Coast in 1933, for instance, the conditions in the mines – where workers toiled seven days a week for low wages, lived in company housing, and purchased food sold by company agents at a jacked-up price – led miners to go on strike to demand the payment of wages they had earned but not received. The mine owners ordered their security to open fire on the strikers. Strikes also broke out in southern Nigeria in 1936 and in 1938 and 1939 in Sierra Leone. These events, in the wake of strike activity and mass protests in Kenya, Tanganyika, and Northern Rhodesia, alarmed officials sufficiently to compel them to rethink imperial policies and practices. A new model of colonial rule – sometimes referred to as "development," sometimes as "partnership" – appeared in the late 1930s to expand the concept of "trusteeship." It emphasized Britain's obligation to establish policies and practices that would make life better for colonial subjects, but in practice it differed little from earlier efforts.

The implementation of new development policies failed to improve the standard of living for most Africans, though some privileged groups did benefit from them. These changes were, to all intents and purposes, too little too late. By the late 1930s small groups of educated, "westernized" Africans, influenced by the intellectual currents of pan-Africanism emanating from the United States, the Caribbean, and London, had come to believe that social and economic reforms were simply not enough. Even reforms that would grant increased participation in the political arena and reduce segregation of Africans from Europeans – which were not in any event in the offing – did not go far enough for this new class of intellectuals. Men like the editor of the *West African Pilot*, Nnamdi Azikiwe, and Gold Coast teacher, Kwame Nkrumah, who might once have been satisfied with political reform under the auspices of British rule began to look for self-rule and independence from Britain entirely.

Much of this shift in thinking derived from Italy's invasion of Ethiopia in 1935 and especially from Britain's failure to speak out against it. Worse still, in 1938 Britain recognized Mussolini as the emperor of Ethiopia, an especially galling act given that the Italians had just deposed the iconic Haile Selassie. As the last remaining African territory free from foreign rule Ethiopia held a powerful symbolic place in the imaginations of educated Africans. The fall of this proud independent state to the modern weaponry of Italian fascists acted to stir quiescent and diverse strands of pan-Africanism and bind them into a single stream of radical anti-colonial thought. After the invasion of Ethiopia African intellectuals insisted that Britons could not be trusted to look after their welfare. Buttressed by West Indian and African organizations in London such as WASU, this new generation of western-educated urban Africans became anti-colonialists who in the years after World War II would lead the movements for decolonization and independence in their respective lands. For now their activities and impacts were limited to a very small group of people who shared their backgrounds and beliefs.

Despite their small numbers and even smaller influence on large masses of Africans, anti-colonial activists in London and Africa worried colonial officials. Britain sought to deal with the potential threat by resorting to the tried and true imperial tactic of divide and rule. Imperialists like Malcolm Hailey, whose 1938 *African Survey* stands as the apotheosis of development thought, urged that colonial officials identify "moderate" Africans and groom them for participation in governance. Co-opting "reasonable" Africans into government, the thinking went, would preserve British rule by driving a wedge between them and more radical agitators (and indeed the masses), thus undermining the anti-colonial movement. Hailey's policies went into effect during World War II.

Pan-Africanism might have commanded the attention of many educated Africans but it had to compete with other intellectual and cultural trends that cut against its grain. Ironically, the British understanding of "tribe" – and their use of the concept to organize and control peoples within the colonies – also gave African men and women a tool with which to challenge their subjugation. As one historian has described them, tribes were in many instances nothing more than "empty boxes" in the early colonial period; they existed in the minds of administrative officers, missionaries, and anthropologists, but only Africans could fill the boxes with the cultural material that would give genuine meaning to the notion of "tribe."[16] During the interwar period Africans of all ages, genders, and statuses across the continent began to debate the values and moral standards that should characterize their "tribes." They created distinct histories for themselves and argued about their "traditions" and "customs." Through this process they argued about what it meant to be a Kikuyu, or Ndebele, or Fulani. Their discussions produced, often, a powerful external manifestation that one historian has termed "political tribalism."[17] Astute leaders came to understand that they could utilize the notion of tribe to mobilize a large, seemingly united front to pressure colonial governments for benefits. Many of them did so, especially in the years following World War II.

It is important to recognize, however, that ethnic creation was not always a result of the colonial system. In certain cases the development of a broad sense of ethnic identity pre-dated it. The example of the Yoruba, who live in southwestern Nigeria, is instructive in this regard for thinking about the subtleties of ethnicity or "tribalism" in sub-Saharan Africa and particularly the intersection of Christianity with the process. Yoruba ethnogenesis – the process of creating an ethnic identity – came about in the mid- to late-nineteenth century and developed around several distinct strands of influence that constantly interacted with one another: Protestant missionaries, colonialism, and African (soon to be "Yoruba") cultural tropes. As the foremost historian of the Yoruba put it, "what it has meant to be Yoruba and what it has meant to be Christian have evolved in continuous interaction with one another."[18]

At the earliest stage in the process of "making Yoruba," the "African" and the "Christian" were inextricably linked, as we see in the figure of Samuel Crowther. In 1836 Crowther did not use the term "Yoruba"; yet seven years later he published his *Vocabulary of the Yoruba Language*. The Niger expedition of 1841 played a central role in effecting his transition. Crowther came to think of the upriver converts he made – as well as those people from the kingdom of Oyo, from whence he came – as "Yoruba." The converts themselves took this identity to distinguish themselves from others. The transformation occurred in large part through the translation of the Bible into Yoruba, which together with Crowther's grammar set the tone for the standardization of the language. Another reverend – Samuel Johnson – built a history for the Yoruba in a sweeping book he wrote at the end of the nineteenth century. He tied Yoruba culture to the distant past in the guise of the ancient civilization of Ife to give it legitimacy.

By the 1930s Yoruba cultural nationalists and other elite mission-educated leaders across the continent were responding to the colonial context by evoking ideas of ethnic "nations" (such as those mentioned in biblical texts) and demanding recognition for those nations from the British. Their efforts proved successful in some respects, such as when the British acknowledged the Yoruba as deserving representation in the legislative council, but they also had the effect of hampering the creation of a "national" Nigeria in the years after 1960, as we will see in Chapter 6. In central Kenya men and women who had graduated from the first generation of mission schools fused Kikuyu stories of origin with biblical stories of creation. The most widely read text of this sort in the Kikuyu language asserted that "*Ngai* [God, in Kikuyu] gave the Gikuyu [an alternative to "Kikuyu"] a good country that lacks neither food nor water or forests. It's therefore good for the Kikuyu to be praising *Ngai*, for He has been very generous to them." These sorts of stories flattened potential discord or disagreement between

Kikuyu clans, genders, or generations and postulated a shared joint history of the people.[19]

Women responded in a variety of ways to negotiate better lives for themselves under the colonial system. In some ways the experiences of African women under British rule were doubly difficult. Not only were they discriminated against based on race but also along lines of gender, owing to British conceptions of women's role in society. At times they acted against the terms of colonialism in the most dramatic of ways, as in one of the most famous episodes of female activism that took place in Nigeria in November and December of 1929.

In part in response to rumors that the British planned to extend taxation to women, a remarkable series of demonstrations, protests, risings, and riots involving tens of thousands of women took place in the southeastern region of the colony. Taxation constituted only one element in a whole list of injustices women suffered at the hands of colonial administrators and their native collaborators, but the suggestion that women might be compelled to pay taxes crystallized their many grievances and set off an uprising. The Aba Riots, as the British dubbed them, are known to their participants and to subsequent memory and historiography as the *Ogu Umunwaayi*, the Women's War. Women attacked many of the symbols of colonialism – Barclay's Bank, warehouses that stored palm oil products, native courts, European trading houses – but purposefully refrained from harming people. Their restraint did not prevent the British from using violence against them, however. In the space of three days in December, more than 50 women were killed by British troops.[20]

The women's actions in the *Ogu Umunwaayi* serve as a reminder that colonialism was far more than a black versus white struggle during the interwar period; it might also be thought of as a struggle between men and women brought about by the colonial system.[21] One of the techniques the women used during the uprising, for instance, was "sitting on a man": they humiliated their male relatives who failed to support the community, singing rude songs and sometimes beating them up physically, pressing into service an Igbo practice women had used since the nineteenth century.[22] The mechanisms of colonialism had allowed African men to impose new levels of restrictions on women (see Chapter 4) but they also gave women the ability to push back. Especially from the 1920s onward new roads, bus systems, and marketplaces allowed women to move easily throughout the colonies. Increased security allowed them to expand businesses ranging from prostitution to trading and to win autonomy from those who sought to curtail them. The experience of women in Gold Coast reveals much of the gendered negotiation and conflict that characterized social life in interwar colonial Africa.

Asante women living in the north of the territory at the forest's edge took advantage of the colony's new laws to make gains. British authorities had abolished pawnship (the indenturing of humans to pay off a debt) at the turn of the century, providing women with newfound freedom. They quickly utilized the laws to rid themselves of husbands who failed to live up to their duty to provide sustenance and care. As one woman put it, "If you are energetic and the man is not taking care of you, definitely you will divorce him and find another one."[23] Women had used this strategy in the years since 1900 and their daughters did the same when they became women in the 1920s. By this time, however, the stakes were higher owing to the burgeoning cocoa industry. By and large the industry had disadvantaged women, who did much of the physical labor as a result of their conjugal obligations but received pay only at their husbands' whim. Divorce enabled both rural and urban women to remove themselves from uneconomic situations and set up their own farms or businesses. (As one historian notes, "There was a much greater readiness [of officials] to grant divorces to African women in Africa than British women in Britain during the same period."[24])

Cities like Accra, Kumasi, and Sekondi-Takoradi attracted women. They became bakers, fish sellers, and petty traders, and in many cases provided domestic services like cooking or cleaning for young men who had left their villages to find fame and fortune. They also worked as prostitutes, harnessing the revered ability of women to produce children in exchange for financial gain. Such a violation of apparent customary practice frequently angered men, who expressed their outrage in the names they gave to the two suburbs in Sekondi-Takoradi where prostitutes worked, Nkontompo ("deceit") and Sikaduse ("under the money tree"). Women in the cities could decide for themselves whether or not to marry – as they were no longer subject to oversight from their male relatives – and they demanded financial advantages from their husbands in order to enter marital unions. Many earned more money than men because laborers' wages were low; men frequently found themselves going to their lovers and wives for loans and financial help. Men and women argued about their supposed relationship roles in song. "*Wo pe tam won pe ba*," went one song that attacked the materialism many men had come to believe city women exhibited; "You like cloth but you don't want children." Another waxed wistfully about the simplicity and purity of rural women: "Give me the Bush Girl."[25]

Men did not take these perceived slights lying down. In rural Asante between 1929 and 1933 chiefs *ordered* all women over the age of 15 who did not have husbands to find one forthwith. If an unmarried woman walked into a public area in town a gong rang to announce her arrival and she was detained. These extraordinary attempts to rein in women were common across the continent. In western Kenya chiefs sent men from their villages to the cities to round up and repatriate "out of control" women. By the late 1930s their efforts were relatively successful because they merged with the concerns of colonial officers about the dangers of immorality and unchecked migration to urban areas, where Africans, Britons feared, would become "detribalized" and detached from the secure bonds of tribe. But when war broke out again in 1939 restrictions became impractical, and men again found themselves depending on women to sustain their families.

A second "white man's war"

In 1939 Africans were asked once more to support Britain and its allies in a conflict that had little to do with them. By 1945 more than half a million had served under the Union Jack in World War II. African soldiers performed sterling service throughout and rates of desertion were low. Expressions of popular discontent in the colonies were few and far between, and where they did occur were muted. No one could deny that Africans had – once again – stepped forward to aid their colonial masters.

War came to sub-Saharan Africa in late 1940 following Mussolini's formal declaration of war against Britain. Britain had viewed Mussolini's conquest of Ethiopia in 1935 with alarm but the event did not hold sufficient importance for the Foreign Office to act. Mussolini, having already taken Eritrea and Italian Somaliland, viewed Italy's colonies in Africa as part of a new "Roman empire" to which he hoped to add Sudan and Kenya. In 1940 he sent Italian forces across Kenya's northern border. The King's African Rifles (KAR) of East Africa, in combination with troops drawn from West Africa and other allied units from the empire, were tasked with driving the Italians from the region. They did so rapidly, for the Italians put up only feeble resistance. The allies restored Haile Selassie to the throne as soon as they could, cognizant of the great symbolic significance he held for Africans and people of African descent around the world. Many African-Americans, Afro-Caribbeans, and Africans viewed the liberation of Ethiopia as a pan-Africanist victory in which black soldiers freed the iconic Ethiopia and restored its rightful ruler – the *Ras Tafari*, viewed by Rastafari as Jesus Christ in his Second Coming – to power in Africa's oldest empire.

Wherever the allies called upon them African troops distinguished themselves. In Madagascar in 1942 the KAR set the unofficial record for rapid deployment, with the 22nd East African Brigade moving 130 miles in a single day. Their sweep through territory held by Vichy France (the collaborationist regime that worked with the Nazis) led British authorities to conclude that African troops were "naturally" predisposed to fighting in jungle conditions, a reputation that resulted in their being assigned to Burma two years later. In 1944 troops drawn from practically every British colony in Africa formed a major part of General Slim's 14th Army, the force ordered to advance into central Burma. In 1945 it beat the onset of the monsoon season to capture Rangoon. Much of the fighting in 1944 and 1945 took place in heavy rains and featured some of the most difficult fighting conditions in the entire war, earning Burma the nickname the "Green Hell of Asia."

British officers who served with African soldiers abroad came to respect them greatly. In Burma they often noted that Africans seemed to have visual

Figure 5.2 Soldiers of the King's African Rifles served with distinction in Madagascar, c. 1942

and hearing abilities far surpassing those of Europeans, making them superior to European troops in jungle fighting. But though British officers noted the bravery of African soldiers they continued to believe that they were "dependent . . . on the initiative of the white man in times of crisis."[26] They assumed that the men could not fight without their officers. Back in barracks in Kenya or Southern Rhodesia white officers and blacks troops occupied separate quarters, as was the case in peacetime. They never lived close to one another and blacks were expected to remove their hats in the presence of whites. But at the front all races fought side by side. Major Michael Blundell recalled one difficult evening after taking fire from Italian artillery as his troops prepared for an assault on Gondar in Ethiopia. He returned to a make-shift camp with his men at 5 AM and counted them in. "As so often in withdrawals," he recounted,

> coys [companies] had become muddled up and the last six hours of the night I myself, the adjutant and OC (Officer Commanding) C Coy fought . . . and recced a trail as the rest of the battalion if left for a minute simply fell asleep on the ground. They lay in rows dead beat, Europeans, Africans all twisted up together. I learnt a lot about who had guts . . . [the next day] From 11 at night till 2 in the morning we just lay in single file along the track we had made, like corpses, asleep until the small waning moon should rise to help us.[27]

Men like Blundell became colonial officials and settler luminaries after the war. They had personally seen the bravery of the KAR and other African soldiers in difficult conditions but the comradeship of war never brought closer race relations in the colonies, where the system of racial segregation was too deeply entrenched.

The war also had a profound impact on those far from the battlefields. "Total war" required not just the fighting forces of the KAR, Royal West African Frontier Force, and Sudan Defence Force; it demanded tremendous amounts of civilian labor to provide raw materials ranging from food to tin to agricultural fertilizers to feed the apparatus of the war effort. Colonial officials instituted compulsory labor regulations, making it legal to force Africans to work in a variety of jobs. In Gold Coast, for instance, as many as 13,000 men at one point were involved in building roads and a railway line to transport bauxite (to make aluminum) from its source. The Public Works Department in Nigeria employed 55,000 people in 1942 to build roads, government facilities, and other wartime infrastructure. In Kenya over 10,000 men and women undertook compulsory labor in the sisal industry alone. White settlers benefitted from many of these regulations as they owned the industries that produced these and other vital products like beef, maize, and coffee. With thousands of African men absent – and drought and famine conditions common in many parts of sub-Saharan Africa during the war years – many families' farms became overgrown and unworkable. Women often resorted to black market trading to survive.

War often brings financial booms to certain sectors of the economy. Industry improves as new factories are built; harbors are rapidly constructed; transport facilities developed; and food-growing enterprises prosper from the demands upon their products. This proved not to be the case for the economies of Britain's colonies, which frequently struggled during wartime. Sierra Leone provides a clear case study of this phenomenon. In order to maintain space for "war goods" in the colony's ports and shipyards, imports were cut and luxury items became difficult to procure. The government artificially fixed the price for African-produced goods from the colony in order to allow British quartermasters to buy them more cheaply. At other times the Sierra Leone government gave up its cash reserves in interest-free loans to the metropole, and companies extracted minerals and raw materials more intensively than before in order to meet the needs of war. These damaging economic policies wrought political changes as well: the Sierra Leonean government squashed the fledgling independent labor union movement that had appeared in the interwar period.

Britain could count on support for the war effort from all of its sub-Saharan colonies with just one exception. As a dominion, South Africa enjoyed self-government, meaning that the decision about whether the country should join the war on the allied side rested with its politicians. By 1939 the United Party, headed by the Afrikaner nationalist J.B.M. Hertzog (see Chapter 6) and the former South African War general (but advocate of the merits of the British empire) Jan Smuts, dominated South African politics. Like most

Afrikaners Hertzog opposed supporting the British in the war, in large part owing to the indignities imposed on the Afrikaner population several decades earlier. He advocated neutrality, which was in fact a more moderate position than many others took, viewing South Africa and Nazi Germany as natural allies. But Smuts was able to sway the majority in the government to support the war on the allied side. A close friend of Winston Churchill, he was quickly made a member of the Imperial War Cabinet in London.

Even those South African whites who supported the war would only go so far, however. They opposed the possibility of African soldiers learning to use advanced weaponry. As a result the segregated branches of the non-white military – the Cape Coloured Corps, Malay Corps, and Native Military Corps – did not carry guns until February 1944. The recruitment of Africans into the army consequently fell short, for blacks hesitated to accept the low pay and discrimination they would encounter if they joined up. Even so 123,000 non-white South Africans served, their wartime participation contributing to a promising, if short-lived, opportunity for multiracialism: South Africa under the leadership of Smuts weakened its racialist laws after 1945 and the prime minister even considered abandoning the entire system of segregation

Figure 5.3 Children living in South Africa play cards, 1939. Black and white children knew little about racialized segregation until they entered primary school.

altogether. The moment didn't last, however. Smuts' support of Britain during the war gave a radicalized National Party the inspiration and opportunity to gain power in 1948, ushering in half a century of apartheid (see Chapter 6). Throughout the colonies the promises of wartime were quickly broken.

On August 3, 1941, four months before the Japanese attack on Pearl Harbor, President Franklin Roosevelt boarded the yacht *Potomac* for a two-week fishing holiday. The "fishing trip" was in fact a cover; six days later the president made his way below deck on the heavy cruiser U.S.S. *Augusta* off the coast of Newfoundland. Shortly afterwards, while the ship's band played "God Save the King," British Prime Minister Winston Churchill, cigar clenched in his teeth and right arm held aloft with his fingers spread in the "V for Victory" sign, stepped from a small boat onto the *Augusta*'s deck.

The secret meeting between Roosevelt and Churchill lasted four days, and by its end the two men had hammered out the text of a document known as the "Atlantic Charter." A statement of their vision of a "better future for the world" after the war, it called for lasting peace and improved living conditions and rights for all peoples. Most significantly the charter advocated "the right of all peoples to choose the form of government under which they will live; and . . . [the] wish to see sovereign rights and self government restored to those who have been forcibly deprived of them."[28] Churchill would later back off from the promises of the charter with regard to empire, asserting that "I have not become the King's First Minister in order to preside over the liquidation of the British Empire,"[29] but Roosevelt – particularly following a visit to the depressed, swampy Bathurst in the Gambia in 1943 – would become an "outspoken foe" of colonialism, a position followed by his successors who came to view the institution as anachronistic in the post-war world.[30]

Colonized peoples across the British empire were thrilled by the promises of the Atlantic Charter. They viewed them as a fair exchange for the sacrifices they had made for Britain in the two world wars. They eagerly anticipated vast changes in the colonies; the time had come when they would no longer be fobbed off by vague promises of better working conditions or political rights. The two world wars and their impact contributed mightily to the unwillingness of Africans to wait much longer for colonialism to end, as we will see in the next chapter. They had helped break down the loyalties of rural peoples to their traditional conservative rulers; moved large numbers of people from rural areas to urban centers; demanded the building of roads and railways; and developed a cash economy through the exploitation of local resources. By 1945 rural villages were connected to the wider world, road networks enabled residents to move cheaply and easily to capital cities, and newspapers and radios brought news of happenings elsewhere around the globe to their metaphorical doorsteps. The Africans of 1945 bore little resemblance to their counterparts of just a decade earlier.

Notes

1 Buchi Emecheta, *The Slave Girl: A Novel* (New York: G. Braziller, 1977), 25–29.
2 Quoted in Edward Paice, *Tip and Run: The Untold Tragedy of the Great War in Africa* (London: Weidenfeld and Nicolson, 2007), 20.
3 Quoted in David Killingray and James K. Matthews, "Beasts of Burden: British West African Carriers in the First World War," *Canadian Journal of African Studies* 13 (1979), 13.
4 Quoted in Killingray and Matthews, "Beasts," 14.
5 Quoted in Killingray and Matthews, "Beasts," 17.
6 Quoted in Peter B. Clarke, *West Africans at War, 1914–18, 1939–45: Colonial Propaganda and its Cultural Aftermath* (London: Ethnographica, 1986), 13.
7 Quoted in Killingray and Matthews, "Beasts," 19–20.
8 Quoted in James K. Matthews, "World War I and the Rise of African Nationalism: Nigerian Veterans as Catalysts of Change," *Journal of Modern African Studies* 20 (1982), 501.
9 W.D. Downes, *With the Nigerians in German East Africa* (London: Methuen, 1919), 89–91.
10 Quoted in A.E. Afigbo, *The Warrant Chiefs: Indirect Rule in Southeastern Nigeria* (London: Longman, 1972), 273–74.
11 Great Britain, Ministry of Health, *Report on the Pandemic of Influenza, 1918–19* (London: His Majesty's Stationery Office, 1920–21), iv, xiv, 69.
12 Quoted in Robert Rotberg, *The Rise of Nationalism in Central Africa: The Making of Malawi and Zambia, 1873–1964* (Cambridge, MA: Harvard University Press, 1965), 82.
13 Quoted in Rotberg, *Rise*, 84.
14 Quoted in Karen Fields, *Revival and Rebellion in Colonial Central Africa* (Princeton, NJ: Princeton University Press, 1985), 160.
15 Quoted in Myles Osborne, *Ethnicity and Empire in Kenya: Loyalty and Martial Race among the Kamba, c. 1800 to the Present* (New York: Cambridge University Press, 2014), 108.
16 Terence Ranger, "The Invention of Tradition Revisited," in *Legitimacy and the State in Twentieth-Century Africa: Essays in Honour of A.H.M. Kirk-Greene*, eds. Terence Ranger and Olufemi Vaughan (Basingstoke, UK: Macmillan, 1993), 84.
17 John Lonsdale, "The Moral Economy of Mau Mau: Wealth, Poverty, and Civic Virtue in Kikuyu Political Thought," in *Unhappy Valley: Conflict in Kenya and Africa*, Book II: *Violence and Ethnicity*, eds. Bruce Berman and John Lonsdale (London: James Currey, 1992), 315–504.
18 J.D.Y. Peel, *Religious Encounter and the Making of the Yoruba* (Bloomington: Indiana University Press, 2000), 279.
19 Derek Peterson, *Creative Writing: Translation, Bookkeeping, and the Work of Imagination in Colonial Kenya* (Athens: Ohio University Press, 2004), 97–98.
20 See Marc Matera, Misty L. Bastian, and Susan Kingsley Kent, *The Women's War of 1929: Gender and Violence in Colonial Nigeria* (Basingstoke, UK: Palgrave Macmillan, 2011), Chapter 3.
21 Consider also the "circumcision crisis" in Kenya in 1929. Lynn Thomas, *Politics of the Womb: Women, Reproduction, and the State in Kenya* (Berkeley: University of California Press, 2003).
22 Judith van Allen, "'Sitting on a Man': Colonialism and the Lost Political Institutions of Igbo Women," *Canadian Journal of African Studies* 6 (1972): 165–81.
23 Quoted in Jean Allman and Victoria Tashjian, *"I Will Not Eat Stone": A Women's History of Colonial Asante* (Portsmouth, NH: Heinemann, 2000), 136.

24 Diana Jeater, "The British Empire and African Women," in *Black Experience and the Empire*, eds. Philip Morgan and Sean Hawkins (Oxford: Oxford University Press, 2004), 238.

25 Emmanuel Akyeampong, "'*Wo pe tam won pe ba*': ('You Like Cloth but You Don't Want Children'): Urbanization, Individualism, and Gender Relations in Colonial Ghana, c. 1900–39," in *Africa's Urban Past*, eds. David Anderson and Richard Rathbone (Portsmouth, NH: Heinemann, 2000), 224–28.

26 K.C. Gandar Dower, *Into Madagascar* (New York: Penguin Books, 1943), 41.

27 Michael Blundell, *A Love Affair with the Sun: A Memoir of Seventy Years in Kenya* (Nairobi: Kenway Publications, 1994), 67.

28 "The Atlantic Charter," August 14, 1941, accessed December 15, 2014, www.nato.int/cps/en/natolive/official_texts_16912.htm.

29 "Mr. Churchill on Our One Aim," *The Guardian*, November 11, 1942.

30 Donald Wright, "'That Hell-Hole Of Yours,'" *American Heritage* 46 (1995): 47–53.

Bibliography

Afigbo, A.E. *The Warrant Chiefs: Indirect Rule in Southeastern Nigeria*. London: Longman, 1972.

Akyeampong, Emmanuel. "'*Wo pe tam won pe ba*': ('You Like Cloth but You Don't Want Children'): Urbanization, Individualism, and Gender Relations in Colonial Ghana, c. 1900–39." In *Africa's Urban Past*, edited by David Anderson and Richard Rathbone, 222–34. Portsmouth, NH: Heinemann, 2000.

Allman, Jean, and Victoria Tashjian. *"I Will Not Eat Stone": A Women's History of Colonial Asante*. Portsmouth, NH: Heinemann, 2000.

Blundell, Michael. *A Love Affair with the Sun: A Memoir of Seventy Years in Kenya*. Nairobi: Kenway Publications, 1994.

Bush, Barbara. *Imperialism, Race and Resistance: Africa and Britain, 1919–1945*. London: Routledge, 1999.

Carotenuto, Matthew. "Repatriation in Colonial Kenya: African Institutions and Gendered Violence." *International Journal of African Historical Studies* 45 (2012): 9–28.

Clarke, Peter B. *West Africans at War, 1914–18, 1939–45: Colonial Propaganda and its Cultural Aftermath*. London: Ethnographica, 1986.

Downes, W.D. *With the Nigerians in German East Africa*. London: Methuen, 1919.

Emecheta, Buchi. *The Slave Girl: A Novel*. New York: G. Braziller, 1977.

Fields, Karen. *Revival and Rebellion in Colonial Central Africa*. Princeton, NJ: Princeton University Press, 1985.

Gandar Dower, K.C. *Into Madagascar*. New York: Penguin Books, 1943.

Great Britain, Ministry of Health. *Report on the Pandemic of Influenza, 1918–19*. London: His Majesty's Stationery Office, 1920–21.

Havinden, Michael, and David Meredith. *Colonialism and Development: Britain and its Tropical Colonies, 1850–1960*. London: Routledge, 1993.

Jeater, Diana. "The British Empire and African Women." In *Black Experience and the Empire*, edited by Philip Morgan and Sean Hawkins, 228–56. Oxford: Oxford University Press, 2004.

Killingray, David. "Labour Mobilisation in British Colonial Africa for the War Effort, 1939–46." In *Africa and the Second World War*, edited by David Killingray and Richard Rathbone, 68–96. Basingstoke, UK: Macmillan, 1986.

Killingray, David, and James K. Matthews. "Beasts of Burden: British West African Carriers in the First World War." *Canadian Journal of African Studies* 13 (1979): 6–23.

Killingray, David, with Martin Plaut. *Fighting for Britain: African Soldiers in the Second World War*. Woodbridge, UK: James Currey, 2010.

Lonsdale, John. "The Moral Economy of Mau Mau: Wealth, Poverty, and Civic Virtue in Kikuyu Political Thought." In *Unhappy Valley: Conflict in Kenya and Africa*, Book II: *Violence and Ethnicity*, edited by Bruce Berman and John Lonsdale, 315–504. London: James Currey, 1992.

Matera, Marc. *Black London: The Imperial Metropolis and Decolonization in the Twentieth Century*. Berkeley: University of California Press, 2015.

Matera, Marc, Misty L. Bastian, and Susan Kingsley Kent. *The Women's War of 1929: Gender and Violence in Colonial Nigeria*. Basingstoke, UK: Palgrave Macmillan, 2011.

Matthews, James K. "World War I and the Rise of African Nationalism: Nigerian Veterans as Catalysts of Change." *Journal of Modern African Studies* 20 (1982): 493–502.

Morton, H.V. *Atlantic Meeting*. London: Methuen & Co., 1943.

Ochieng', William, ed. *A Modern History of Kenya, 1895–1980*. Nairobi: Evans Brothers, 1989.

Osborne, Myles. *Ethnicity and Empire in Kenya: Loyalty and Martial Race among the Kamba, c. 1800 to the Present*. New York: Cambridge University Press, 2014.

Paice, Edward. *Tip and Run: The Untold Tragedy of the Great War in Africa*. London: Weidenfeld and Nicolson, 2007.

Pedersen, Susan. "Settler Colonialism at the Bar of the League of Nations." In *Settler Colonialism in the Twentieth Century: Projects, Practices, Legacies*, edited by Susan Pedersen and Caroline Elkins, 113–36. New York: Routledge, 2005.

Peel, J.D.Y. *Religious Encounter and the Making of the Yoruba*. Bloomington: Indiana University Press, 2000.

Peterson, Derek. *Creative Writing: Translation, Bookkeeping, and the Work of Imagination in Colonial Kenya*. Athens: Ohio University Press, 2004.

Ranger, Terence. "The Invention of Tradition Revisited." In *Legitimacy and the State in Twentieth-Century Africa: Essays in Honour of A.H.M. Kirk-Greene*, edited by Terence Ranger and Olufemi Vaughan, 62–111. Basingstoke, UK: Macmillan, 1993.

Robinson, David. "The Atlantic Charter Meeting: An Eyewitness Account." In *The Atlantic Charter*, edited by Douglas Brinkley and David Facey-Crowther, 173–88. New York: St. Martin's Press, 1994.

Rotberg, Robert. *The Rise of Nationalism in Central Africa: The Making of Malawi and Zambia, 1873–1964*. Cambridge, MA: Harvard University Press, 1965.

Sekgoma, Gilbert. "The Second World War and the Sierra Leone Economy: Labour Employment and Utilisation." In *Africa and the Second World War*, edited by David Killingray and Richard Rathbone, 232–57. Basingstoke, UK: Macmillan, 1986.

Shepperson, George, and Thomas Price. *Independent African: John Chilembwe and the Origins, Settings, and Significance of the Nyasaland Native Rising of 1915*. Edinburgh: University Press, 1958.

Shutt, Allison. "The Settlers' Cattle Complex: The Etiquette of Culling Cattle in Colonial Zimbabwe, 1938." *Journal of African History* 43 (2002): 263–86.

Strachan, Hew. *The First World War in Africa*. Oxford: Oxford University Press, 2004.

Thomas, Lynn. *Politics of the Womb: Women, Reproduction, and the State in Kenya*. Berkeley: University of California Press, 2003.

van Allen, Judith. "'Sitting on a Man': Colonialism and the Lost Political Institutions of Igbo Women." *Canadian Journal of African Studies* 6 (1972): 165–81.

White, Landeg. "'Tribes' and the Aftermath of the Chilembwe Uprising." *African Affairs* 83 (1984): 511–41.

Wright, Donald. "'That Hell-Hole Of Yours.'" *American Heritage* 46 (1995): 47–53.

6 The road to independence, 1945–1960

In October 1956 Seretse Khama – grandson and heir to the throne of the Chief Khama we met in Chapter 4 – returned to his home in the protectorate of Bechuanaland after six years of exile in Great Britain. He had been forced from his homeland not by his people, the Bangwato, but by the British government acting at the behest of the governments of South Africa and Southern Rhodesia.

While a student in London preparing himself to become *kgosi*, or king, Khama had married a white woman, Ruth Williams, in 1948. Their marriage – and the warm and deep-seated acceptance it met with among the Bangwato – threatened the very foundations upon which white supremacy rested. In the supercharged atmosphere of the Cold War, with North Korea threatening South Korea and the Soviet Union and United States conducting nuclear tests and building their arsenals of atomic weapons, British officials felt they could not afford to alienate the apartheid government of South Africa, whose uranium supplies Britain needed so badly for its own nuclear stockpile. To the dismay and outrage of peoples all over the colonized world as well as many Britons of all parties at home, the Labour government of Clement Attlee declared that Seretse and Ruth Khama would not be permitted to return to Bechuanaland for a minimum of five years and that the governance of the Bangwato would be transferred from native authorities to a British administrator.

The sheer hypocrisy of this action shocked observers. Colonial officials and government ministers lied shamelessly to parliament, their African subjects, and British citizens alike in order to cover up their perfidy. Khama's accession to the throne as *kgosi*, they insisted, would foment discontent and even civil war among the people of Bechuanaland. Knowing full well that this was not the case, they concocted a series of official reports designed to buttress their arguments. No, they argued, Seretse was not fit to be *kgosi*, nor did the Bangwato want him to be – statements directly contrary to the findings of the government's own commission of inquiry. No, neither South Africa nor Southern Rhodesia had made any request of the British government to ensure that Seretse did not return – a bald-faced lie engaged in by the highest governmental officials in southern Africa and London. No, they said, this was not British complicity in the enforcement of a color bar but rather a measure designed to ensure greater democratic participation in the administration of Bechuanaland.

But by 1956, when Khama petitioned the British government to return to his homeland, circumstances had changed to such an extent that Britain could no longer deny him. Widespread anti-colonial agitation throughout Africa; reports of British atrocities committed against Mau Mau rebels in Kenya; and the spanking delivered by the United States when Britain and France attempted to assert their imperial prerogative in Egypt – all these made it impossible for Britain to refuse Khama's request to repatriate himself. He and his wife returned to Bechuanaland to wild acclaim. Upon their arrival Khama set about reforming his kingdom and those of neighboring regions in the protectorate, creating the institutions and laws that would underpin the independent republic of Botswana in 1966. Botswana's experience was in many ways typical of those of many of Britain's African colonies. The "wind of change" was in the air and it had originated in the upheavals of World War II.

Disruptions of war and urbanization in Africa

In October 1945, just two months after the war in the Pacific came to its dramatic end, delegates to the fifth Pan-African Congress convened in Manchester. Boasting a line-up that included many of the luminaries who would lead Britain's colonies to independence in the 1950s and 1960s, the organization declared "the right of all Colonial peoples to control their own destiny. All Colonies must be free from foreign imperialist control, whether political or economic."[1] Delegates hoped that the throwing off of imperial rule would occur peacefully but they were prepared, they warned, to use violence if necessary to achieve their ends. The intellectuals had little means of backing up what some of them meant to be a threat, for back home in places like Nigeria, Gold Coast, and Nyasaland, few political parties existed that had the ability to organize the grievances of African peoples against their British overlords, nor – had they wanted to – could they yet access the arms to back up such a claim.

During the post-war period, a wide range of peoples and organizations pressed their visions for the futures of African nations and, on a smaller scale, for their communities at home. In places like Nigeria, Gold Coast, and Northern Rhodesia, activists often worked through unions, which existed in large part as a consequence of the demands placed on the colonies during World War II. In these areas unions possessed the organizational clout to put pressure on colonial authorities. In other British colonies such as Kenya and Southern Rhodesia unions were less powerful, but urban labor leaders were still able to mobilize migrant workers against employers and colonial officials. In addition, marginalized groups like peasants or women expressed views that did not necessarily align with nationalist political parties. World

War II had ushered in the process of transforming anti-colonialism from the writings and protests of a few western-educated urban elites to a diverse spectrum of approaches and interest groups that ranged from peasant women to cocoa farmers to urban youth.

The British were perhaps most deeply concerned about those Africans who had served under the Union Jack during World War II. Veterans had come to feel overwhelmingly that the British had betrayed them. They claimed that they had been promised permits to start businesses, pensions, education, land, and other benefits, but across the board their expectations were disappointed. The words of Karigo Muchai, who had worked as a driver in the King's African Rifles, are worth quoting at length because they represent the experiences and feelings of many. "We Africans were told over and over again that we were fighting for our country and democracy," he pointed out,

> and that when the war was over we would be rewarded for the sacrifices we were making. . . . I was only trying to be given a small piece of land somewhere and to be treated a little more decently by the Kenya Government and white settlers . . . These hopes and dreams of mine were quickly crushed on my return home. The army talk was false propaganda intended only to get Africans like me to risk our lives for Britain and the white settlers of Kenya. . . . The life I returned to was exactly the same as the one I left four years earlier: no land, no job, no representation and no dignity.[2]

The British expected Africans to return to working in the fields, content with the lot they had had before the war; they were mistaken, however, as the war had changed these men profoundly. Like many veterans Waruhiu Itote – who later became a leader of Mau Mau during the 1950s – had become a "worldly" man through his service in Burma and Ceylon (Sri Lanka). He struck up friendships with West Africans and Indians and discussed the Haitian Revolution with African-American soldiers. He simply could not readjust to the discriminatory laws of colonial Kenya when he returned home, which privileged white skin above all else. The Kenyan satirist and novelist Binyavanga Wainaina succinctly if scatologically described the situation faced by the returning soldiers: they had "met and [seen] people from all over. . . . They saw them shit; they saw them die. They saw them sing. They . . . found no mathematical principle to account for their designated roles back home."[3]

Wartime service had afforded hundreds of thousands of Africans a standard of living they had not known before. They had become accustomed to it and expected it to improve further once they returned home. Men in the armed forces had learned skills they planned to put to use in peacetime employment at war's end, but they were disappointed. Tens of thousands of army drivers could find no employment upon their return and those

Africans who had served in non-fighting units – where they had learned to read, write, and keep accounts – won the plum jobs, much to the dismay of the soldiers. Pent-up frustration and resentment over insults, assaults, and deprivations administered by colonial officials erupted in protest in virtually all of Britain's imperial holdings. Across the continent men like Muchai and Itote flocked to ex-servicemen's organizations and unions to protest against the grievances they felt. The Gold Coast Legion, for example, represented some 36,000 African ex-servicemen in 1948; the more radical Ex-Servicemen's Union boasted a membership of 6650 that same year. In Nigeria fully one-third of the 110,000 Nigerians who had signed up for war service could not find work in 1947. "The brave new world they had fought for," lamented Mokwugo Okoye, a close associate of Nigeria's first president, Nnamdi Azikiwe, and himself a veteran, "had easily faded into a rotten world of unemployment and frustration."[4]

Strikes and demonstrations, often featuring veterans wearing their uniforms but including many more civilian men and women, broke out in cities across the continent, frequently resulting in widespread violence. In Southern Rhodesia in 1945; South Africa in 1946; Mombasa and Dar es Salaam in East Africa in 1947; Gold Coast and Southern Rhodesia again in 1948 – in all these places and more mass actions against employers and colonial authorities posed profound challenges to British rule. British officials also watched goings-on in French colonies warily, aware that a "French problem" might quickly become their own. In November 1944, for instance, French regulars massacred 35 African troops who were protesting the conditions of their service at Camp de Thiaroye in Senegal; the episode provided the inspiration for several burgeoning nationalist movements in French West Africa. In many rural areas, too, where traditional chiefly authority prevailed under the colonial doctrine of indirect rule, returning veterans refused to bow to chiefs they no longer respected nor even recognized. The Burma Boys of Sierra Leone, for instance, so-called for their military service in South Asia against the Japanese, led demonstrations against the Kissi chief Kai-Tungu between 1948 and 1950, even going so far as to use their jungle training to protect a trade in illegal diamonds they had begun. As we have seen, protests against colonial regimes had occurred during the interwar period as well but now Britain possessed neither the resources – nor, ultimately, the will – to bring to bear the kind of force necessary to curb the challenge to its rule.

For many veterans the absence of jobs and the tedium of life in the rural areas impelled them to head for cities to find work and excitement. They earned higher wages in cities and could purchase goods like books and clothes to which they had become used. In doing so these veterans joined a wave of migrants across Africa who had arrived in cities during the 1930s and 1940s to find their fortunes. Some had fled the overcrowded reserves where the iron fist of government-appointed chiefs offered few prospects. Others had come to find work in the mining industry on the Rand in South

Africa or the Copperbelt in Northern Rhodesia and lived in the cities that sprung up around these industrial centers. In Nigeria many workers from all areas traveled to the cities but maintained their hold on land back in the rural areas.

Many women, too, arrived in the burgeoning urban centers like Lagos, Nairobi, and Accra. Some traveled with or for husbands. In her novel *The Joys of Motherhood*, Buchi Emecheta provides a stark depiction of the kinds of lives they might find there. Her protagonist, the Igbo woman Nnu Ego, travels to Lagos to meet a man to whom her family has arranged a marriage. The husband is weak-willed and a poor provider so she is forced to sell anything she can find – like matches – on the street in order to support her children. But many others came to view the city as a place of great opportunity and traveled there independently to find their fortunes. In Nairobi increasing levels of crime threatened skilled, well-off male workers, but women were largely left alone. Single women moved into areas like Pumwani and Shauri Moyo to avoid violent husbands and rural associations that sought to control them. They came from all parts of Kenya and established themselves as prostitutes. With regulated, established customer bases, they enriched themselves, often earning enough to buy houses. Many chose to keep their levels of earnings quiet from their customers or relatives, whom they feared would be jealous of their success. One woman called Masaba summed up the advantages the city could bring: "At home, every minute would have to be accounted for, I would either have to be working in the farm, or looking after the children, or cooking, and there was always someone to tell me what to do. Here my time is my own."[5]

The level of urbanization in the 1940s was staggering. In 1938 Lagos had around 65,000 residents. A decade-and-a-half later that figure had jumped to 267,000. Colonial governments struggled to provide infrastructure – especially housing and roads – to keep pace with the expansion but town-planning was often hasty and involved bulldozing "slum" areas. Urban planning acted as a vital exercise of colonial control. As one historian put it, "it emphasized difference and hierarchy."[6] The segregated spaces of the city sought to replicate the social ordering colonial officials believed was best for Africans and Britons. Officials often justified segregation on the basis of "hygiene," building corridors and buffer zones between spaces designated as African and those set apart for Europeans and prohibiting Africans from remaining in white areas except temporarily. Little had changed since Lugard had laid down the ground rules in 1922. As he put it, "We have learnt that malarial germs – and . . . those of yellow-fever also – are present in the blood of natives . . . and their dark huts and insanitary surroundings foster mosquitos. . . . Doctors, therefore, urge that Europeans should not sleep in proximity to natives, in order to avoid infection."[7] In the early twentieth century the British built a suburb named "Hill Station" above Freetown, the capital of Sierra Leone. African workers could serve Europeans there during the day but had to leave at night. In Gold Coast, the

Gambia, and Lagos, officials made concerted efforts to separate the African from the European population; in Mombasa they added a third area for "Arab" inhabitants. Europeans never spoke of the visits European men undertook to their African "girlfriends."

It would be a mistake to view sections of cities where Africans lived as depressed and gray, with their inhabitants crushed and ground under the colonial boot. Tight proximity provided the impetus for a vibrant social life. Take Malay Camp, a suburb of Johannesburg where many gold miners lived. Peter Abrahams set his classic novel *Mine Boy*, published in 1946, here and though a fictional account, Abrahams himself grew up in a similar neighboring suburb called Vrededorp. On Saturdays, a "national half holiday for the black citizens of Johannesburg,"

> the men in the streets spoke in loud voices and took out their purses and counted their money for others to see. And they wore their best and most colourful clothes. Red shirts and green shirts and yellow shirts and pink shirts. . . . Young women . . . [too] were dressed in the ways of white folk, only more colourfully. . . . [They would] meet on street corners and talk at the top of their voices. And there would be much laughter and fun-making. . . . [Men and women] would go to drink. . . . Or they would just walk. Or they would go to the Bioscope [cinema]. . . . [L]ife would move slowly and excitedly.[8]

South Africa's townships produced an extraordinary outpouring of music and culture. In Alexandra, for instance, an area to the north of Johannesburg's city center, Hugh Masekela, the famous jazz musician we met in Chapter 3, recollected how "gramophones blared out the music of township Kwela bands, pennywhistle combos, male and female trios and quartets, famous singers from home and abroad, gospel choirs and American swing bands." Street corners and shebeens (informal bars) served as sites for innovation and the sharing of tunes and songs. Some areas became associated with specific artists but many produced community songs to which a musician, singer, or regular citizen of the township added a bar or verse here or there. Trends began on street corners and spread into the rest of South Africa. Some of the musical creations became famous. Zakes Nkosi, for instance, created "African Jazz," mixing the American version with a traditional type of music from the township called "marabi." Every day and long into the night on weekends Alexandra rocked; sound emanated from every corner. Alexandra could be dangerous, as its fedora-clad, suited *tsotsis* (gangsters) roamed the streets, but danger made life exciting. Nelson Mandela remembered that "in spite of the hellish aspects of life . . . [it] was also a kind of heaven" where no government bureaucrats would bother you.[9] Other townships too – whether in Cape Town, Port Elizabeth, Pretoria, or Sophiatown (the "'Greenwich Village' of music, poetry, politics, and crime," in Bernard Magubane's words) – pulsed with sound and debate.[10]

Colonial welfare and development

World War II had a profound impact on the way Britain thought about its empire. In the first place, the massive logistical project of mobilizing the continent and its people for war impressed upon authorities just how inadequate their administration of the colonies had been. Second, if Africa was to play the role Britons hoped it would in assisting the mother country's economic recovery after 1945, colonial authorities would have to pay far greater attention to governance and the provision of resources to African peoples. And third, Britain needed a new approach to justify its control over a continent in which its overrule was viewed as anachronistic in the United States, Soviet Union, and among intellectuals in the colonies. As the under-secretary of state for the colonies Sir Charles Jeffries explained, it was "a matter of the highest political importance" that Britain show "unassailable justification for its claim that it acts as a beneficial trustee for its subject peoples."[11] Gone were any mentions of "natives" needing civilization; the way forward, as colonial officials now saw it, was through "local government" by and for Africans in "partnership" with Britain.

These lofty – but ultimately incompatible – aspirations informed British colonial policy in the postwar years, as notions of "development" and "welfare" in the colonies increasingly infused official thinking. The Colonial Development and Welfare Acts of 1940 and 1945 sought to improve the standards of living of Africans by investing in projects that would bring better and more hygienic housing, provide education and health care, increase the yields of harvests, and establish a manufacturing sector that would produce commodities then unavailable owing to the disruptions of war and inflationary pressures. Officials believed that a new class of better-housed, better-treated workers would produce a more efficient workforce and minimize the likelihood of discontent.

These aspirations for Africa, however, conflicted with Britain's domestic needs, which not surprisingly (given that Britons voted in elections and Africans did not) prevailed over the apparently altruistic aims of development. For at the end of the war Britain faced a dire economic situation. Its traditional industrial strengths in ship-building, coal production, and textile manufacturing could not compete on the world market any longer. Shortages of the most basic commodities – food, clothing, fuel for heat and for transport – reduced Britons to standing in long queues in order to purchase rationed staples such as bread, milk, and lard. Meat was rarely available. Politicians in the Exchequer and the Colonial Office looked to the empire to help offset Britain's impoverishment, to provide the resources and raw materials necessary to get the country back on its feet. Moreover, when the war ended the United States had discontinued its Lend-Lease aid to Britain, leaving the country with the additional problem of a crippling balance of payments. Britain looked to the foodstuffs and minerals that Africa could produce as one of the most effective ways to reduce this debt. By selling those commodities on the world market Britain could earn the dollars it needed to lessen its deteriorating financial situation.

These levels of production would require substantial economic development in the colonies, necessitating an unreachable level of assistance. The sum eventually hit upon by officials – £120 million to be split among the colonies over ten years – did a little to stimulate economic growth but not enough to meet the goals of the Welfare and Development Acts. Most of the aid went to social rather than economic development: educational initiatives, especially, received a generous portion of the amount, with health care coming second. But it wasn't merely a shortfall in funds that rendered the program irrelevant. Administrators in the African colonies did not share the outlook of their superiors in the Colonial Office. However much the notion of economic development and welfare might have overtaken people in the metropole, colonial governors remained wedded to earlier concepts of empire, especially those put forth by Frederick Lugard in *The Dual Mandate*, authored in 1922. Britain, Lugard had declared, had two responsibilities when it came to governing its colonial possessions. The first was to ensure that the valuable resources Africa possessed were made available to the industrialized nations that needed them at reasonable prices; the second was to protect native peoples from exploitation by Europeans and to ensure that the consequences of rapid economic development did not destroy their traditional societies and cultures. This latter mandate militated against policies that would promote rapid economic or social development; consequently, the conventional practice of having colonies produce primary goods like food and minerals – rather than manufacture secondary products – remained in place.

After 1945 the hand of colonialism fell more heavily on African peoples, a result of the new arrival of Europeans whose actions and activities constituted what is sometimes described as the "second colonial occupation." British settlers by the thousands arrived in Kenya and Southern Rhodesia after the war, desperate to escape the gloom of a Britain still under wartime rationing. Like their predecessors they viewed the colonial government as a guarantor of their livelihoods and expected it to provide cheap labor, loans, and land. These benefits could only come at the expense of African business, production, and land use. They were joined by a variety of scientists and experts who sought to "solve" the pressing agricultural problems British observers believed Africa faced – soil erosion, land degradation, and overstocking. Since the 1930s experts had prophesied doom for African land; now, full of confidence in their scientific knowledge, more descended upon the continent to "fix" Africa.

Sukumaland, a semi-arid region of northwestern and western Tanganyika inhabited by the colony's largest ethnic group, the Sukuma, offers a representative picture of the experience of colonial development in the 1940s. Every colony had a region that was supposedly in "dire" need of assistance; in Tanganyika, it was Sukumaland. Development officials had two aims for the area: first, to "stabilize" and regularize agriculture in the region and second, to increase the efficiency of the production of cattle and the important cash crop, cotton. Measures introduced to achieve these ends drastically altered the daily lives of Sukuma peoples. Some were removed from their farms and shifted to areas thought to be more productive. Others had their cattle culled because the stock numbers rose above the purported carrying capacity of the land. Britons' confidence in their scientific techniques – and belief in the backwardness of African agriculture – meant that they barely consulted Sukuma in the process of "improvement." Their extreme, poorly worked-out methods imposed in the 1940s failed to increase the productivity of the land and served to accomplish little more than irritating the population.

The Sukuma example, like others from across the continent, revealed two clear truths. First, officials learned that they could not impose development practices "from above" upon their African charges; second, they found themselves forced to take into account African strategies for production. Development, they came to appreciate, had to be the product of negotiation, not some neatly organized and imposed colonial project. Thus in the 1950s colonial officials pressed Sukuma farmers to produce cotton at increased levels to take advantage of high prices on the world market. The farmers achieved these goals but did so in the ways they thought best. They broke new land for farming, ignoring officials' instructions that they increase the productivity of existing cotton fields, and used traditional forms of labor recruitment instead of paying cash wages. Sukuma elites also independently created a system of cooperatives to assist their capacity to grow and market their cotton, something they believed would allow them to squeeze out Asian traders who sought to compete with them. They persuaded many rural producers to back their cause. Eventually development officials grabbed onto their coat-tails and belatedly provided funds and assistance to support the cooperatives. In other areas where Britons failed to listen to local farmers, rural opposition to government-enforced development schemes ultimately provided the basis for a grassroots movement that sought to drive out the colonial power in the late 1950s.

The gendered aspects of colonial development caused problems in many communities. Many strategies were based on officials' assumption that men should be the exclusive targets of their schemes. In the Northern Province of Zambia, for example, officials had long worried about citimene – "slash and burn" – agriculture, a technique in which trees and bushes are cut and then burned before the start of the rainy season in an effort to release nitrogen into the soil. Citimene was used as a part of a system of shifting cultivation, but officials viewed this technique as destructive for the soil. Their conviction on this score had two important repercussions in the 1940s and 1950s. First, officials failed to notice – and therefore support with development assistance – the "village gardens" and other projects that women undertook in order to sustain their families in the absence of migrant men; second, when they decided to provide funds to stimulate the production of small-scale farmers, the loans and facilities they provided went exclusively to men who had chosen to remain at home and not migrate for work.

Ironically, in some areas colonial development programs provided a catalyst for those who sought self-government from Britain. We'll see this in Mau Mau below, but first let's stay with our Sukuma example from Tanganyika for a moment. In the late 1940s and early 1950s even villages far from population centers felt the intrusive hand of officials in their daily lives. These earnest white men insisted, for example, that people dig terraces on their farms to help prevent erosion, a task that required immense physical labor. They told Africans to grow certain crops at certain times in certain ways and then taxed their products heavily; they forced pastoralists to destock their cattle when their numbers grew too high. These demands carried the force of the colony's legal system. Failure to comply could result in fines or imprisonment.

The shared experience of these onerous aspects of development provided the common ground on the basis of which protest movements against the colonial state could form. They arose in Sukumaland earlier than in other parts of the colony because colonial development was more focused there. Educated businessmen, teachers, and migrant workers capitalized on the upsurge of resentment among farmers to establish the Sukuma Union. After 1950 the union began to collect testimonies of people's dissatisfaction with colonial development and presented them to the government, going around the chiefs to make their case. They did so because they saw the chiefs as government stooges and regarded them as responsible for the troubles faced by the Sukuma.

The Sukuma Union and other small ethnically-based organizations soon incorporated themselves into the colony-wide Tanganyika African National Union (TANU) that drove Tanganyika to independence in 1961. TANU's origins were deeply embedded in rural grassroots groups and it built on the anger felt by people like the Sukuma toward colonial meddling. Moreover, TANU reminds us that nationalist movements were not the exclusive preserve of educated men. TANU leader Julius Nyerere might have served as the first president of Tanzania but arguably the most prominent activist within the organization was Bibi Titi Mohamed, a Muslim woman of little education who, along with her female compatriots, held dances in towns throughout the colony, building links among women to help expand the movement. Because women held no roles in colonial governance they could participate in TANU without fear of losing their jobs. British administrators rarely viewed these women as a threat, allowing them to act with far greater freedom than men. Women were not just concerned with ending colonial rule; they also argued that systems of compulsory labor and "traditions" that subjugated women to male authority had to be renegotiated.

Initial steps toward self-government

By the late 1940s the Colonial Office had begun to think differently about Britain's relationship to its empire. Foreseeing a day, far down the road, when African colonies might become self-governing imperial officials began to plan how a slow and gradual transfer of power might take place. In the past British colonialism had been made possible by the cooperation of traditional chiefs, but now their control over their peoples was eroding fast under the influence of world wars, urbanization, education, and upstart organizations like TANU. Officials therefore realized that if Britain was to succeed in introducing gradual political change, it would have to enlist the educated African elites. And they, it turned out, could only be brought on board if Britain agreed to the reforms they demanded.

Gold Coast provides a prime example of this process. In 1946 Governor Alan Burns adopted a new constitution for the colony that made elective 18 of the 30 seats on his legislative council. Manipulating the electoral process to their own ends, traditional chiefs appointed most of the new African members of the council, a result that frustrated many reformers. The new constitution thus provided only a small step toward self-government and it certainly did not satisfy educated Africans, who under the leadership of Joseph Danquah formed the United Gold Coast Convention (UGCC) to demand "self-Government in the shortest time possible." Kwame Nkrumah, recently arrived from London having spent a decade in the United States, brought with him a call to "throw the Europeans out of Africa" and became secretary of the organization.[12] Nkrumah set about organizing boycotts of European products and strikes in key industries. In February 1948 in Accra 2000 strikers – including former servicemen who had not been able to find work – marched to protest economic conditions in the colony. When the police confronted them a full-scale riot broke out, with tens of thousands of people taking to the streets to burn automobiles, attack Britons, and force open the gates of the local prison, from which the prisoners happily fled. The violence spread to other towns, forcing the governor to declare a state of emergency and arrest Nkrumah and Danquah. Two years later Nkrumah – ousted from the UGCC for being too radical and now leader of the Convention People's Party (CPP) – called for a general strike that virtually shut down the government. Trains didn't run, stores failed to open, and firms could not conduct business. Once again the British threw Nkrumah and his allies in jail.

In the 1950 elections for municipal office the CPP won the vast majority of votes. The following year it took 35 of the 38 seats in the elections for the legislative council. Fearing riots and violence, the governor released Nkrumah and his associates from prison and appointed him "leader of government business." The British changed this prosaic and unexciting title to prime minister in 1952. Colonial officials in London and Accra feared the rapid pace at which governmental change was taking place, but they could do little to slow it down. In 1954 the CPP won a general election, delivering the governor an all-African cabinet. Independence was around the corner.

Nigeria followed Gold Coast toward independence. But in a country as populous and divided as Nigeria – by topography, environment, climate, ethnicity, religion, language, culture, and social and political systems – unity proved difficult to forge. Wartime leaders such as Herbert Macaulay, Nnamdi Azikiwe, and Obafemi Awolowo – all southerners – had faced the herculean task of organizing more than 400 linguistic groups into a meaningful union to which all could subscribe. Azikiwe established the National Council of Nigeria and the Cameroons (NCNC) in 1944, an umbrella organization that pulled together a variety of self-help, regional, ethnic, and women's organizations. Though it claimed to act as a pan-Nigerian movement, Lagos was its power base and the majority of its members came from the southern parts of the colony. The NCNC effectively took advantage of strikes and protests against deteriorating standards of living that followed the end of the war, helping compel British authorities to incorporate educated Nigerians into governmental and administrative positions.

But the transition toward self-government was marked by increasing regional division. The Richards constitution in 1947, for instance – the first genuine effort to transfer some political authority away from the British – created three houses of assembly in the west, east, and north. The move was agonizing for Azikiwe, who went back and forth about it: as two historians put it, "regional legislatures marked a step backward from . . . pan-Nigerian goals. . . . On the other hand, nearly everyone recognized that . . . Nigeria was an extremely diverse place, and a single unitary government was unlikely to please many people for very long."[13] Regional jealousies began to arise among nationalist leaders. Awolowo was primarily interested in building a powerful Yoruba ethnic movement and he drew strong lines against the Igbo Azikiwe to limit what he viewed as potential Igbo domination of the country. In the Muslim north the conservative Northern People's Congress (NPC) dragged its feet over independence negotiations, fearing southern domination. In Nigeria's first general election Awolowo's Action Group (largely Yoruba) took the west, Azikiwe the east (largely Igbo, via the NCNC), and Alhaji Tafawa Balewa and the NPC the largely Muslim (and Hausa) north. This was particularly threatening to the remaining hundreds of ethnic groups who feared they would be squeezed out by these larger regional and ethnic blocs.

The British determined that only a decentralized federation that gave regional governments a great deal of autonomy would work in these circumstances, something that suited a large proportion of Nigerian political leaders. In 1954 they developed a constitution that gave the Nigerian federal parliament only limited powers over the provincial regimes. Jurisdiction over customs, defense, foreign affairs, policing, monetary policy, and immigration fell to the federal government but all other areas became the responsibility of authorities in the provinces. It would come into effect on October 1, 1960, creating the independent nation of Nigeria.

In south-central Africa no calls for self-government or independence could begin without the dismantling of the Central African Federation. Created for the benefit of European capital and loathed by Africans, the Federation had brought the three territories of Southern and Northern Rhodesia and Nyasaland into a semi-autonomous economic and political union in 1953. The creation of the Federation was driven by Southern Rhodesia's settlers, who had expanded in number from 80,500 in 1945 to 223,000 in 1960. (The African population rose from 1,640,000 to 2,830,000 in the same period.) The settlers hoped that the Federation could become a British dominion like South Africa, a practically autonomous nation with full control over its foreign policy and economy. Reflecting Southern Rhodesia's dominance of the Federation, the federal capital was placed at Salisbury (now Harare). Sir Godfrey Huggins resigned his 20-year position as Southern Rhodesia's prime minster to take the same post in the Federation.

The Federation was created to bolster the economic and political power of settlers in central Africa, by far the largest number of whom lived in Southern Rhodesia. As we saw in Chapter 5, the entire economy of Southern Rhodesia after the Great War was designed to benefit settlers to the detriment of Africans. In the settler imagination the Federation would extend this dominance for decades by harnessing the wealth of Northern Rhodesia's copper mines, adding a "labour reserve" in Nyasaland, and combining them with Southern Rhodesia's farming and industrial sectors. Federation could facilitate the improvement of transport facilities and help build a more modern infrastructure, a vital concern for all industries. One of the most visible manifestations of this new union, the vast dam on Lake Kariba, brought hydro-electric power to both Rhodesias, including the all-important copper mines in the north. The profits from the copper mines enabled the economy of the Federation to grow at a rate of more than 10 percent a year between 1946 and 1956, shoring up Southern Rhodesia's somewhat flagging financial sector.

African intellectuals in the Rhodesias and Nyasaland knew that dominion status for the Federation would constitute a powerful step toward the consolidation and formalization of white dominance over the region. In 1957 Joshua Nkomo founded the African National Congress (later the Zimbabwe African People's Union) to prevent that from happening. Nkomo's prominence came from his background as a trade unionist. He had been among the strikers on Southern Rhodesia's railways in 1945 and helped to lead a vast general strike in April 1948 that had paralyzed much of the country. He faced an uphill battle now, for Southern Rhodesia's settlers held too tight a grip on the colony for a genuine expression of African political grievances.

In Northern Rhodesia, however, the situation was different. Its settler population was significant – 65,000 in 1955 – but comparatively weak compared to its neighbor across the Zambezi to the south. Kenneth Kaunda quickly emerged during the 1950s as the most radical African politician in the colony and spent much of the decade opposing the policies of Northern

Rhodesia's senior settler politician, Roy Welensky, who took over the premiership of the Federation in 1956. Unlike the more moderate Harry Nkumbula, who was willing to tolerate limited African representation in the protectorate's legislative council, Kaunda refused anything but full equality for Africans. He publicly criticized Nkumbula as weak, his attacks doing a disservice to a series of deeply thought-out, liberal-democratic notions that Nkumbula envisioned for Zambia's future. In Nyasaland Dr. Hastings Banda shared Kaunda's radicalism. Both men attacked the Federation, denounced the color bar against Africans, and demanded independence. The two leaders visited Accra in December 1958 to attend Nkrumah's first pan-Africanist summit; Banda returned to Nyasaland crying "Kwacha!" – "The Dawn!" As we'll see in the next chapter, Nyasaland would gain its independence in the next few years.

More than anywhere else in British Africa, communism was starting to play an important role in the geo-politics of the Federation, something we will explore further in Chapter 7. For many British officials the threat of communism lurked around every corner. One Southern Rhodesian blamed its purported spread on migrant workers in South Africa, claiming in 1948 that most of the "Bolshevist. . . propaganda comes into this country from the South. Natives of this district habitually serve at least one term of employment in the Union [of South Africa], and return with much ill feeling against the white man's Government."[14] Officials suspected Nkomo, who had received his schooling in South Africa, of holding communist views, and Kaunda's leftward leanings were well known. The presence or absence of links with communist powers would shape European and American policy toward Africa for the next three decades.

Mau Mau

No movement on the African continent held broader significance than the guerrilla war that exploded in Kenya during the 1950s. It seemed a clear and straightforward battle of black versus white, of dreadlocked fighters in the forests of central Kenya conducting a campaign against British troops. The simplicity of this understanding proved attractive across the developing world; it inspired black politicians in the Caribbean and in New York City, where Malcolm X called for a "Mau Mau in Harlem." But the truth of the situation was far more complex, highlighting the reality of almost all anti-colonial struggles. They were never as clear as "black" and "white." The impact of colonialism over the previous half-century had been uneven and had created class distinctions among Africans. Many educated, wealthy Africans had prospered under British rule and they were as much the targets of anger – and often even more so – as colonial officials.

Mau Mau erupted among the Kikuyu of central Kenya, the colony's most populous ethnic group. At its roots lay a multitude of social problems created and exacerbated by the colonial system over the previous half-century.

Most of the problems revolved around land, a fundamental element within Kikuyu culture. The importance of land cannot be overstated: one was not considered a man in his own right without owning a piece of ground. Since the 1920s Kenya's native reserves had become progressively more crowded as two generations of fathers had subdivided their property among their sons, reducing the size of plots with each successive generation. As this had taken place wealthy and educated Kikuyu had proved adept at gathering up small pieces of land to add to their burgeoning property portfolios. Poor people lacking land had left the reserves and taken up residence on the vast European farms of Kenya's "White Highlands," where they worked for the settlers in exchange for a place to live. By the 1940s many of these "squatters" had been residents of European farms for more than two decades.

As in Southern Rhodesia Kenya's settlers had prospered during the war. Colonies had produced food and other products considered vital for the war effort. Kenya, as we saw in Chapter 5, passed legislation in 1942 that compelled Africans to work for free in war-related enterprises, the majority of which were owned by settlers. Settlers became so prosperous that in the mid- to late 1940s they were able to buy tractors and mechanized farming equipment, significantly reducing the need for squatters, whom they drove from their farms. When the squatters returned "home" to the reserves – places from which many had been absent for more than 20 years – they were told by residents there in no uncertain terms that they had forfeited any claims to land. They had few options. Some might find a scrap of land to work; others might take up employment on the land of their wealthier brethren; but the majority ended up in Nairobi. There they built temporary shelters in the ever-expanding slums where they tried to eke out a living. In these urban wastelands the movement that became Mau Mau brewed among discontented, disenfranchised, poor Kikuyu who had no realistic means of establishing livelihoods. Members of "the movement" – only later would it earn the moniker "Mau Mau" – began meeting in secret and administering oaths to bind themselves together. They were united by a vision of a renewed, ordered Kikuyu society in which the inequalities they faced no longer existed.

In 1952 Mau Mau activists in Nairobi and central Kenya began murdering individuals they believed had betrayed their people. Their victims were known as "loyalists," Kikuyu perceived to be "loyal" to the colonial government and who had often become wealthy from years of association with it. For much of 1952 the colony's governor Sir Philip Mitchell did little to stem the violence, both because he was ill and because he did not want to end his career ingloriously. When his replacement, Evelyn Baring, arrived in October 1952 the state of lawlessness into which parts of the colony's center had descended horrified him. In one of his first public engagements upon his arrival in the colony, Baring attended the funeral of one of the government's most prominent loyalist chiefs. Mau Mau warriors had killed Waruhiu wa Kung'u in broad daylight in his Hudson town car on October 7, 1952, demonstrating that the government could not protect even its most important supporters.

With Mau Mau's power on the rise Baring declared a state of emergency on October 20, 1952. The emergency gave the government extra-legal powers to clamp down on potential dissent; Baring's administration also used the decree to silence the vibrant African press. The government immediately rounded up 183 men it believed were the "ringleaders" of the organization, including Jomo Kenyatta. The arrest of wealthy intellectuals like Kenyatta demonstrated how little the government understood about Mau Mau: its members were poor, disenfranchised Kikuyu, not wealthy elites like Kenyatta.

Between late 1952 and mid-1954 Mau Mau fighters operating from bases in the two forests of central Kenya fought a series of running engagements with British troops and their loyalist allies, the Kenya Regiment (comprised of settlers), Kenya Police, King's African Rifles, and Home Guard. Led by three men who had fought under the Union Jack during World War II, Dedan Kimathi, Stanley Mathenge, and Waruhiu Itote, Mau Mau raids were highly organized. They typically took place at night. Gangs left the forest under cover of darkness to carry out their missions, which usually involved attacking a Home Guard post or raiding a police station for ammunition

Figure 6.1 Suspected Mau Mau held for interrogation in Kenya, December 1952
© Hulton-Deutsch Collection/Corbis

before melting back into the deep, heavily wooded forests where government forces could not track them. They enjoyed great success against better-equipped and -armed troops. Occasionally they carried out raids against isolated white settler farms, forays that led to hysterical pronouncements in the British and colonial press about blacks slaughtering whites, but settlers were rarely their targets. Only 36 settlers died during the period Mau Mau operated as opposed to more than 20,000 Kikuyu who lost their lives at the hands of the rebels. The British hanged 1090 "terrorists" at the gallows in the most extensive use of capital punishment in British imperial history.

Unable to rapidly defeat Mau Mau the British employed tactics last used in the South African War half a century earlier. They built an extensive system of "detention and rehabilitation" camps – concentration camps – in which more than 80,000 suspected Mau Mau were held. British staff and loyalists carried out torture – including rape, castration, and murder – in the camps, actions that would later become the subject of a landmark legal case (see Epilogue). That such behavior was possible less than a decade after the defeat of Nazi Germany was extraordinary; the fact that the victims were Africans and not whites was likely a factor, as was Britain's immense effort to depict the Mau Mau incursions as little more than a "crime wave." Had they deemed this a "war" or part of a "civil conflict," protections of prisoners under the United Nations Declaration of Human Rights would have applied. But even in these restrictive and appalling conditions Mau Mau fought back. Detainees smuggled letters out of the camps to sympathetic members of parliament in Britain and appealed to the colony's laws to demand better treatment. Some wrote to their families back home and by doing so claimed a measure of domestic control amidst the chaos.

Kenyans who sided with the government won extraordinary advantages during the 1950s. We see evidence of this in the "villagization" process imposed by British authorities. In order to cut off Mau Mau's logistical channels the British enclosed Kikuyu villages in barbed wire and imposed a curfew on them. As many as a million Kikuyu lived in these villages, in which the Home Guard and other loyalists enjoyed a practically unrestricted hand. At the end of the emergency, men returned home from the detention camps to find their wives pregnant, land seized, and cattle gone, but they had no recourse against the loyalists who had stolen their livelihoods and dishonored their wives. Colonial development and welfare programs, too, offered great benefits to those who remained "loyal." The Swynnerton Plan – the largest program of its kind in post-war Africa – was created to reward those loyal to the government. While those who sided with Mau Mau could expect to have their land confiscated, those who opposed the movement received agricultural assistance, loans, and voting rights.

But a second category of people actually received the lion's share of colonial development funding in Kenya (and future research may show the same in other colonies), East Africa's premier "martial race," the Kamba. The concept of "martial races" had appeared in British India in the mid-nineteenth century, purporting to describe people with an apparent "in-built" aptitude for warfare. Britons attributed to them qualities they associated with manliness, a perception that was reinforced in many cases when these peoples put up resistance to British troops in the late nineteenth or early twentieth centuries. As befit a martial race, the Kamba made up the highest proportion of the Kenyan army and police throughout the 1940s and 1950s. The unbalanced ethnic proportions of these institutions presented an opportunity: Kamba chiefs, veterans, and other leaders, aware of the pivotal position they enjoyed in any conflict in Kenya, leveraged their "historic loyalty" to the crown to win greater and greater rewards for their service. During this period and especially once the Mau Mau uprising was underway, they received more than half of the colony's development and welfare funding despite comprising less than 12 percent of its population.

The British won the military war against Mau Mau in late 1954, though the emergency lasted until December 1959. By that time, following revelations of brutality committed against detainees by colonial forces, Britons at home had raised difficult questions about the conduct of the army and about torture and killings in the detention camps. Despite white settler opposition, the Colonial Office moved toward reform, issuing two constitutions in the 1950s that provided for greater African (and Indian) representation on the legislative council. For many this did not go far enough and they continued to demand "one man, one vote." The pathway to independence was negotiated between British politicians and African leaders at several conferences at Lancaster House in London during the early 1960s. Despite numerous wranglings, the process resulted in Jomo Kenyatta leading the Kenya African National Union political party to independence in 1963.

The crisis in Suez

If in 1955 you had asked a settler in Kenya's White Highlands or a colonial official in the Bechuanaland Protectorate when Britain's African colonies might become independent, he or she would have probably answered, "not within 50 years." The more progressive might have replied "1975" or "1980." For at that time the empire *seemed* on solid footing. The very next year, however, a crisis over the Suez canal transformed that perception, demoralizing the British, galvanizing Africans, and ushering in the era of genuine decolonization.

In 1952 a number of young Egyptian army officers overthrew their ruler, King Farouk, whom they regarded as an ineffectual guardian of their nation's interests and a toady of the British government. At that time British armed forces occupied only the canal zone of Egypt, having withdrawn from the rest of the country in 1947. For Colonel Gamal Abdel Nasser and his fellow Free Officers (as they called themselves), the very presence of the British in what they regarded as a "state within the state" served as a reminder of their nation's servile status. Its weakness had been exposed in

1948, when Israeli forces readily turned back Egypt's invading army; again in 1955 the Egyptian army could not repel Israel's incursion into Gaza. In order to build up his country's military might and restore its dignity, Nasser approached the western powers for arms but was rebuffed. He turned then to the Soviet Union for support, a move that in the context of the Cold War alarmed Britain and the United States sufficiently to lead them to offer monetary assistance for the construction of the Aswan Dam on the Nile river. When Nasser accepted Soviet aid as well, the United States and Britain backed out of the deal.

On July 26, 1956, Nasser delivered a speech to 250,000 Egyptians gathered in Liberation Square in Alexandria, which was picked up and broadcast across North Africa and the Middle East. He denounced the efforts of the western powers to return Egypt to a position of financial subservience – "imperialism without soldiers," he called it – and then announced that Egyptian soldiers were at that very moment seizing control of the Suez canal from the French and British consortium that owned and ran it. Egyptian nationalization of the canal would enable the country to collect the transport fees ships had to pay to travel through it, thus replacing the funds that the Americans and British had promised – and then revoked – to build the Aswan Dam. By this action, Nasser could also restore national dignity and pride.

Figure 6.2 Nasser blocks the Suez canal, 1956

The seizure of the canal infuriated the British and the French, who resolved to regain their property, as they saw it, and to teach Egypt a humbling – and crippling – lesson in the process. Britain's prime minister, Anthony Eden, had to tread carefully, however, aware that the British public would not countenance a bald act of aggression. When the French and the Israelis proposed a subterfuge that would provide cover, Eden jumped at it. The plan called for the Israeli army to invade across the Sinai peninsula, at which point Britain and France would mobilize their forces to "protect" the canal, as an earlier British treaty with Egypt allowed, interpose themselves between the Israelis and the Egyptians, and overthrow Nasser. They would then return the canal to British and French possession.

At the end of October Israel crossed into Egypt and soon had the Egyptian army on the run back toward the canal to defend it. France launched its military initiative, as the plan called for, forcing Britain to do the same, though it was not ready yet to do so owing to disagreements among British military planners and politicians about how to proceed with the invasion. At the United Nations Britain's ambassador vetoed a cease-fire that the Security Council endeavored to impose, making it clear to most of the world that Britain's intentions were not honorable at all and that it was simply looking to recapture the canal. At this stage American distress over the situation blossomed into an all-out effort to ensure that Britain would not succeed, lest its actions send African and Asian colonies pressing for independence into the arms of the welcoming Soviets. President Eisenhower ordered the US Treasury Department to call in Britain's debts, forcing the chancellor of the Exchequer, Harold Macmillan, to plead with his prime minister, "We must stop, we must stop, or we will have no dollars left by the end of the week."[15] Faced with financial collapse at the hand of its erstwhile ally – with whom it enjoyed a "special relationship" – Britain had to back down and call off its invasion of the canal zone.

The outcome of the Suez crisis reflected a profound and dramatic shift in the balance of power throughout the world. World War II had dealt a death blow to the British empire, though most did not yet know it. But the writing was on the wall: many of the Arab states that Britain had obtained at the end of the Great War gained their independence when Britain relinquished its "mandates" after World War II ended. India, which the British could no longer govern, won independence in 1947 along with Pakistan, the two new countries having separated along religious and sectarian lines as part of Britain's extrication from South Asia. By the end of World War II British might had diminished to the point where it could no longer claim to be a great power. Instead it found itself in a world dominated by two superpowers, the United States and the Soviet Union, each of which espoused – at least publicly – a pronounced anti-colonialism. The Cold War and decolonization were closely linked with one another, developments in each affecting, if not determining, the other.

At the same time events that involved Egypt were happening at breakneck speed in Sudan. Since the interwar period the Egyptians and British had jointly administered Sudan as two entities. The southern regions, with a higher proportion of Christians and those practicing traditional beliefs, seemed to the British to be a different thing entirely from the north, which was largely Muslim and apparently "Arab." As Sudan moved toward independence in 1956, it became increasingly unified, leading southerners to believe that they were likely to lose out economically and politically to the north once Sudan was free. They rebelled, commencing a half-century of fighting between north and south. A period of peace between 1972 and 1983 interrupted the struggle for a while, but with new militias and motives appearing and receding over the years conflict persisted, most recently manifesting itself as the war in Darfur.

Publicly humiliated before much of the world by the Suez crisis, many Britons regarded this disaster as signaling the end of empire altogether. One official called the Suez fiasco the "psychological watershed, the moment when it became apparent that Britain was no longer capable of being a great imperial power."[16] For his part Nasser gained extraordinary prestige across the colonized world. He had stood up to the once-great imperial power and won. His revolt against the British demonstrated that the teeth of the mighty imperial behemoth had been pulled.

The Suez crisis marked a crucial moment for Seretse Khama and his wife Ruth, whose story of exile opened this chapter. In August 1956, right in the middle of the showdown over Suez, Khama approached the Colonial Office to request permission to return to Bechuanaland. Beset on all sides by anticolonialist pressures, the colonial secretary felt it diplomatic to approve the *kgosi*'s request, on the condition that Khama renounce his royal title and return as a private citizen. As Khama had offered this compromise years earlier it was easy for him to accept these terms, and in September it was announced to the Bangwato that Khama's exile would come to an end. Ruth and Seretse Khama arrived home in October 1956 to enormous crowds of jubilant well-wishers. Khama told his people that he had given up his claim to be *kgosi* so that Bechuanaland might be united and governed not by kings or chiefs but by councils of good men.

In 1957 Khama helped establish the democratically elected Bangwato Tribal Council that would administer his former kingdom, and a few years later he and other important men from across the Bechuanaland Protectorate proposed to colonial authorities that they create a legislative assembly to govern all of the people of the protectorate, white and black, though with veto power given to the British. A legislative council comprised of ten representatives appointed by colonial officials, and ten Africans, ten whites, and one Asian elected by voters across Bechuanaland would operate like a cabinet government. In the 1961 elections for the assembly, Seretse Khama won twice as many votes as any other nominee, elevating him to the legislative council. "Democratic development," he declared, "is much better than being a Chief" (though in actuality the "customary" authority of chiefs has played an important role in providing stability in the modern nation's political system).[17] Independence was a few years off still but Khama's commitment to democratic rule was winning him recognition across the entirety of Bechuanaland, soon to be known as Botswana. Those of you who have read Alexander McCall Smith's series about the Number 1 Ladies' Detective Agency will recall Mma Ramotswe, the protagonist, referring frequently to the wise men who founded her country, one of the only African nations that has enjoyed continuous democratic governance since independence. She had Seretse Khama in mind when making these comments.

The winds of change

On March 5, 1957, the former British colony of Gold Coast, now named Ghana, won its independence with Kwame Nkrumah at its head. The arrival of this momentous day in the history of Britain's relationship with Africa galvanized colonized peoples all over the world. Nkrumah invigorated its symbolic meaning the following year when he held the All African People's Congress in Accra. He exhorted all Africans to do what Ghana had done – seize their universal right to self-government and establish sovereign rule in their own nations. His clarion call resonated across the continent. For Britons Ghanaian independence made crystal clear that holding on to their African colonies was no longer in the cards. Colonial officers might debate matters of timing or the readiness of particular African colonies to move toward independence but the fact that independence *would* come in the very near future had been unambiguously established.

This realization found expression in the "wind of change" speech delivered by Britain's Conservative prime minister Harold Macmillan in February 1960. Venturing to Cape Town to celebrate the 50th anniversary of the Union of South Africa, he shocked his audience when he announced that a "wind of change is blowing through this continent, and whether we like it or not, this growth of national consciousness is a political fact. We must all accept it as a fact, and our national policies must take account of it."[18] The "wind of change" speech acknowledged what had been evident for a few years, and reflected an understanding, however reluctantly arrived at, that little could be done to preserve the British empire.

But just over six weeks later, 1000 miles to the northeast of Cape Town, the "wind of change" was blowing in the opposite direction. It swept a sobering and finally inescapable reality into the understandings of South Africa's non-white population. At a town called Sharpeville just south of Johannesburg police opened fire on several thousand black protesters who had gathered to protest the country's racist pass laws. They killed 67 and wounded 186.

Scholars today usually think of the twentieth-century history of South Africa in two phases. The first, beginning with the creation of the Union of South Africa in 1910 under an Afrikaner government, initiated "segregation." The second phase saw the imposition of apartheid from 1948 until around 1990. Much of the legislation that restricted African rights appeared under the Afrikaner nationalist J.B.M. Hertzog, prime minster of South Africa from 1924 to 1939. Since the Great War Hertzog had pressed for the rights of Afrikaners and angrily denounced his opponent, Jan Smuts, who believed that the investment power and capital of British mine owners and industrialists was vital for South Africa's survival. When Smuts took South Africa into the Great War on the allied side Hertzog – and many Afrikaners – viewed it as a betrayal of those who had died fighting the British in the South African War. His ability to whip up strong feeling over this issue proved crucial to Hertzog's victory over Smuts in the 1924 elections. Hertzog did all he could to promote the interests of Afrikaners, who soon came to constitute more than 50 percent of the white electorate. He formalized Afrikaans as one of South Africa's two official languages (along with English, and replacing Dutch).

The 1930s saw the mobilization of a variety of cultural symbols designed to create pride in an Afrikaner identity. The process of building "Afrikanerness" mirrored precisely the same dynamics as we saw at work among the Yoruba in Chapter 5. It involved creating the cultural material that would bind people together within their own "tribe" (some, indeed, refer to Afrikaners as the "white tribe" of Africa). Though Hertzog's power was based in large part upon such efforts, he was not directly responsible for some of the more prominent expressions of cultural nationalism. He benefitted from the work of D.F. Malan's more radical "Purified National Party" and a cultural/economic organization called the Broederbund. In 1938, for instance, thousands of Afrikaners reenacted the Great Trek of the 1830s and celebrated the battle of Blood River (see Chapter 1). The event was the culmination of several decades of work by men like Gustav Preller, who had sought to create and popularize the trek story, worked hard to earn legitimacy for the Afrikaans language, and built the foundations for Afrikaner history. (Today you can see the story of the trek commemorated in the frieze at the Voortrekker Monument outside Pretoria that was dedicated in 1949, and in a life-size replica of the Boer *laager* cast in bronze near Newcastle in Kwa-Zulu Natal). Blood River, in particular, gained a deeply religious symbolism. The Afrikaners were said to have made a covenant with God that day that gave divine consent for their settlement in the interior of southern Africa. Afrikaners in the 1930s celebrated the anniversary as the "Day of the Vow."

But the wheels of history do not turn on cultural symbols alone. Material conditions play an important part and Hertzog's policies had a strong economic angle to them. He viewed government as an instrument with which to promote Afrikaner interests over those of English-speaking whites and non-whites. For many Afrikaans-speakers in the 1920s lived in poverty; known as "Poor Whites," they came to depend entirely on the government for jobs that legally paid them more than Africans. Skilled jobs went only to whites, unskilled jobs to blacks, and semi-skilled jobs to Indians or Coloureds. Poor

Whites' dependence on Hertzog's vision practically guaranteed him their votes. White farmers enjoyed access to low-interest loans or credit to assist them in becoming productive and they paid low tariffs to move their products from their farms to markets. Blacks had none of these advantages. After 1920 white miners never received less than ten times the pay earned by their black counterparts. Hertzog justified the disparity by claiming that "barbarous and undeveloped peoples" needed little to live on.[19] A complex system of passes and permits ensured that African labor was siphoned to precisely where it was needed, whether in urban or rural areas.

Thus the government progressively (if haphazardly at times) eroded the rights of non-whites in South Africa over the first half of the twentieth century. This halting process changed dramatically after 1948, when Malan, a Dutch Reformed Church minister, won a surprising victory in the elections of that year. His defeat of the global statesman Jan Smuts surprised many observers and was a response to Smuts' decision to take South Africa into a second world war on the British side. Malan instituted the formalized segregationist system called apartheid. Often translated as "separateness" – and given colloquial expression as "apart"/"hate" – apartheid divided the population of South Africa in virtually every way along the lines of race. Its principal architect, Hendrik Verwoerd, minister of native affairs in Malan's government, presented a striking figure. Tall and blond, his charismatic personality enabled him to peddle the apartheid message with remarkable skill. Apartheid, the smiling, genial minister explained in 1961, "has been misunderstood so often . . . it could just as easily, and perhaps much better be described as a policy of good neighborliness, accepting that there are differences between people . . . You have to acknowledge them . . . at the same time, you can live together, aid one another, and that can best be done when you act as good neighbors always do."[20]

The structural backbone of apartheid – the Population Registration Act of 1950 – brought a rigidity to the oddly fluid and not legally defined notions of race that had governed South African society previously. The act stipulated that every citizen of the nation would be classified by race, as either a "white person, a coloured person, or a Native." (Indians would come to comprise a fourth group.) Its provisions served to construct "jackal-proof fencing" between races, asserted one politician in the senate. But because no biological "standards" existed that could separate people "scientifically" social criteria came into play. More "civilized" people were more likely to end up as "coloured" or "white." Additional legislation in 1949 and 1950 reflected the social basis of racial categories. The Mixed Marriages Act of 1949, which outlawed marriage between men and women of different racial groups, noted that "racial appearance and social habits" were important considerations. Indignities under apartheid multiplied: officials used the "pencil test" to determine whether people's hair was so tightly curled that they might be considered "black." If not, he or she might earn the designation "coloured." Bureaucrats sitting on Race Classification Boards in Johannesburg came up with guidelines asserting that "a soccer player is a Native, a rugby player is a Coloured" to assist them in their work.[21]

The Population Registration Act was the basis for tearing families apart, brother from sister, parent from child, and husband from wife. The Groups Area Act of 1950 magnified the social dislocation, stipulating that different racial groups had to live in different areas, a process begun by the Native Lands Act of 1913 (see Chapter 4). Whites rarely had to move from the lush suburbs they inhabited but coloureds and blacks did. The "removals" became notorious, as when Cape Town's District 6 was designated a "white" area in 1968 and 60,000 blacks and coloureds lost their homes. (*District 9*, the 2009 independent film that cast aliens in the role of township residents, drew its inspiration from this particular removal.) Much of District 6 remains uninhabited today, a blank space on the canvas of Cape Town viewed from the top of Table Mountain. In Sophiatown, outside Johannesburg, another 60,000 blacks lost their homes and property to bulldozers making room for the white suburb of Triomf. An Anglican priest named Trevor Huddleston watched the process unfold. "On the broad belt of grass between the European suburb of Westdene and Sophiatown (we called that strip 'the Colour Bar')," he recalled, "a whole fleet of army lorries was drawn up. . . . Lining the whole street were thousands of police, both white and black. . . . All this, to effect a slum-clearance scheme which would be of lasting benefit to the 'natives.'"[22]

Founded in 1912, the African National Congress (ANC) led the African response to segregation and apartheid. Known initially as the South African Native National Congress (until 1923), the ANC attracted a significant proportion of the educated, Christian elites who spent their evenings reading poetry, writing letters, and discussing political voting patterns, sometimes with white liberals who shared their views. For many years scholars assumed that these "top hat-wearing" elites had struggled to relate to the workers and poorer Africans that comprised the bulk of the nation, but recent research shows that in fact ANC leaders sought to represent and support workers' activities, viewing them as a crucial part of the ANC's mission, and attempted to minimize the importance of class distinction that could have divided black nationalists. Other organizations for other "racial" groups – the South African Indian Congress (SAIC), formed in 1923, and the African Political Organization, established in 1902 for coloured people – also tried to protest segregation and discrimination, as did the Industrial and Commercial Workers Union of Clements Kadalie, which occasionally put enough strikers on the streets to effect major disruptions of important government industries. Ignored by Hertzog's government, the organizations saw only limited success.

Malan's victory in 1948 galvanized African opposition to the white government of South Africa. Malan had run his campaign on the Afrikaans slogan *Die kaffer op sy plek* – "the nigger in his place."[23] The moment provided final incontrovertible proof that the ANC's moderate approach in the pre-war years had utterly failed. As workmen put up signs in parks, on beaches, and at public toilets reading "Net blankes" – "Whites Only" – youthful members of the ANC became increasingly angry. Such future luminaries as Nelson Mandela, Oliver Tambo, and Walter Sisulu mobilized the ANC Youth League, formed in 1944, to protest these actions. Mandela never held views as radical as some of his colleagues, for whom Marcus Garvey's slogan, "African for Africans," resonated. (Some of them, indeed, would form a rival group, the Pan-Africanist Congress – PAC – in 1959.) But everyone agreed that a more active approach than the old ANC had espoused was vital. With young firebrands in its vanguard, Chief Albert Luthuli lent the ANC Youth League a steady hand as the organization's guide.

Inspired by Mohandas Gandhi's non-violent resistance to the British in India, the ANC and SAIC instituted the Defiance Campaign in 1952. It is important to pause here to draw attention to the role Indians played in South African history; too often it is overlooked, a tremendous error in a country where half a million Indians lived in 1960 and where Gandhi, living and practicing law between 1893 and 1914, first carried out his program of civil disobedience. South Africa's Indian community actively participated in the Defiance Campaign just as it did in many other movements throughout the entirety of the anti-apartheid struggle. Like blacks and coloureds, Indians joined the effort to openly and flagrantly defy the nation's racialist laws. A "Whites Only" park in Port Elizabeth, for example, might find itself "invaded" by hundreds of black, coloured, and Indian families during a Sunday lunchtime. The campaign sought to overburden the police and judicial systems of the country; jail time became a badge of honor, especially in the eastern Cape where much of the opposition was centered. In 1955 the SAIC joined the ANC and South African Coloured People's Organisation to make arguably the most enduring and significant statement of purpose against apartheid. At the Congress of the People, 3000 delegates crafted and issued a short statement called the Freedom Charter, a document espousing the groups' vision for a multi-racial nation. "South Africa belongs to all who live in it," it declared.[24]

Black and coloured women played a central and determinative role in the struggle for a free South Africa. They had become especially visible during the 1940s as wartime austerity, manifested in food shortages and rising rents, had disproportionately affected them. Women were especially quick to take up placards and organize boycotts whenever their hold over beer-brewing – one of their few profitable sources of income – was attacked. Frequently their activism crossed color lines. They participated in multiracial trade union initiatives, and in March 1947 they marched side-by-side with white, Indian, and Chinese women "demanding freedom and equality" on International Women's Day. Their activism reached a new level with the formation of the ANC Women's League (ANCWL) in 1948, when the ANC recognized full formal rights for its female members. Building on the legacy of earlier leaders like Charlotte Maxeke and her Bantu Women's League, the ANCWL played a particularly important role in the Defiance Campaign of 1952 after the government decided to apply pass laws to women as well as men. Women believed the laws threatened their homes. As Alice Kunene put it, "The Pass Laws means the death of our children. The oppression of the Pass Laws is going to bring destruction to our homes." By July 1956 50,000 women had taken part in 38 separate pass law protests across the country in a process that culminated on International Women's Day in Pretoria. Outside the Union Buildings – the seat of the government – as many as 20,000 women gathered from across the nation. They wrote and signed notes to Prime Minister Johannes Strijdom, then stood in "perfect silence for half an hour, before breaking into a triumphant rendition of the ANC anthem [and South Africa's national anthem today], 'Nkosi sikeleli Afrika': 'God bless Africa.'" One of the songs written to commemorate the protest declared, "Strijdom, you have tampered with the women, You have struck a rock."[25]

Townships like Alexandra and Sophiatown were hotbeds for opposition. Demonstrations and political events occurred regularly despite government orders, and in the 1950s Alexandra's residents participated in a series of famous bus boycotts. To protest price increases on government buses, they commonly walked upward of ten miles each way to get to work. Music played an important role in the anti-apartheid movement. Vuyisile Mini, a labor union member and singer from the Transkei, wrote one of the enduring songs of the 1950s. Titled *Pasopa Verwoerd*, it offered an upbeat and cheerful rhythm accompanied by clapping and tapping of feet. The catchy tune belied its stark warning: "Watch out Verwoerd, the black man is coming." *Pasopa Verwoerd* and many other anti-apartheid songs were deliberately written and sung in Afrikaans. Their singers wanted the police and apologists for apartheid to know precisely what they were singing. But other songs in Xhosa or Zulu were incomprehensible to most whites. Conveying deep meanings that were invisible in their English or Afrikaans translations, these vernacular songs offered a way to take pride in African languages.

When Harold Macmillan arrived in Cape Town in February 1960, the excitement among South Africa's non-white population was palpable. New African nations were appearing every year; in March, the Kenyan Tom Mboya became the first African to grace the cover of *Time* magazine. In South Africa's townships people sang "Free in '63," viewing the end of white rule as just around the corner. But the optimism of the moment gave way to despair on March 21, as television cameras captured the slaughter of unarmed men and women by Transvaal police. The "Sharpeville Massacre" stands as the pivotal event dividing the century into two periods. It marked the culmination of 50 years of Afrikaner governance, during which time African negotiation with and resistance against the state had failed. It also denoted the moment when the ANC and PAC embarked upon armed resistance to the government through their militant wings, Umkhonto we Sizwe and Poqo, respectively. So symbolic did Sharpeville become for anti-apartheid crusaders that in 1995 the new South African government chose the date of the massacre for the start of the Truth and Reconciliation Commission's investigations into the evils of the apartheid system.

Decolonization in Africa occurred far more quickly than the British – or anyone – could have imagined. Even the most optimistic of African anti-colonialists did not envision anything like the pace at which the continent was freed. Britons imagined that another 50 years would pass before the colonies achieved the level of modernization necessary to secure self-government. As it turned out the process took less than 15 years for many of Britain's African colonies, an acceleration that no one had anticipated. The changes in African societies wrought by two world wars, a worldwide depression, and extensive migration to urban areas confronted British authorities with a situation unlike any they had faced before.

In the end, post-World War II economic development schemes did not yield sufficient revenues to make it possible for Britain to continue to govern its colonies on the cheap. Moreover, as population growth within the British colonies increased as a consequence of the technological improvements in

Figure 6.3 Africans and Britons protest apartheid at South Africa House in London, 1956

medicine and hygiene we saw taking place in the late nineteenth century, the metropole simply could not provide sufficient numbers of Britons to police and administer the huge and often discontented populations under their power. Indirect rule had always counted on systems of traditional authority that required few European staff, but dramatic changes in African societies had undermined those systems over the previous decades. Following World War II Britain simply lacked the resources and the political will to engage in the kinds of violence and punitive actions that would have been required. Workers, business and professional leaders, teachers, and peasant farmers would soon combine with prominent leaders like Jomo Kenyatta and Kwame Nkrumah to herald the final days of the red-painted map of Africa.

Notes

1 Quoted in R.D. Pearce, *The Turning Point in Africa: British Colonial Policy, 1938–48* (London: Cass, 1982), 136.
2 Quoted in David Killingray with Martin Plaut, *Fighting for Britain: African Soldiers in the Second World War* (Woodbridge, UK: James Currey, 2010), 221.
3 Binyavanga Wainaina, *One Day I Will Write About This Place: A Memoir* (Minneapolis, MN: Graywolf Press, 2011), 252.
4 Quoted in Killingray with Plaut, *Fighting for Britain*, 218, 221.
5 Quoted in Luise White, *The Comforts of Home: Prostitution in Colonial Nairobi* (Chicago, IL: University of Chicago Press, 1990), Chapter 8.
6 Andreas Eckert, "Urbanization in Colonial & Post-Colonial West Africa," in *Themes in West Africa's History*, ed. Emmanuel Akyeampong (Oxford: James Currey, 2006), 213.
7 Frederick Lugard, *The Dual Mandate in British Tropical Africa*, 5th edn. (Hamden, CT: Archon Books, 1965 [1922]), 148.
8 Peter Abrahams, *Mine Boy* (Oxford: Heinemann, 1946), 13–15.
9 Nelson Mandela, *Long Walk to Freedom: The Autobiography of Nelson Mandela* (Boston, MA: Little, Brown, 1994).
10 Bernard Magubane, note in book jacket of Don Mattera, *Sophiatown: Coming of Age in South Africa* (Boston, MA: Beacon Press, 1987). The explosion of music and culture was not, of course, restricted to South Africa. On Ghana see, for instance, Nate Plageman, *Highlife Saturday Night: Popular Music and Social Change in Urban Ghana* (Bloomington: Indiana University Press, 2013) and on Zambia, Jan-Bart Gewald, Marja Hinfelaar, and Giacomo Macola, eds., *Living the End of Empire: Politics and Society in Late Colonial Zambia* (Boston, MA: Brill, 2011).
11 Quoted in Joanna Lewis, *Empire State-Building: War and Welfare in Kenya, 1925–52* (Athens: Ohio University Press, 2000), 35.
12 Quoted in Piers Brendon, *The Decline and Fall of the British Empire, 1781–1997* (New York: Knopf, 2008), 523.
13 Toyin Falola and Matthew Heaton, *A History of Nigeria* (Cambridge: Cambridge University Press, 2008), 149.
14 Quoted in Terence Ranger, *Peasant Consciousness and Guerilla War in Zimbabwe: A Comparative Study* (London: James Currey, 1985), 121.
15 Quoted in Brendon, *Decline and Fall*, 501.
16 Quoted in Brendon, *Decline and Fall*, 504.
17 Quoted in Susan Williams, *The Colour Bar: The Triumph of Seretse Khama and His Nation* (London: Allen Lane, 2006), 306.

18 Quoted in "Macmillan Speaks of 'wind of change' in Africa," *BBC News*, February 3, 1960.
19 Leonard Thompson, *A History of South Africa*, 4th edn. (New Haven, CT: Yale University Press, 2014), 168.
20 "Hendrik Verwoerd Defines Apartheid," March 4, 1961, accessed July 14, 2014, www.youtube.com/watch?v=vPCln9czoys.
21 Deborah Posel, "Race as Common Sense: Racial Classification in Twentieth-Century South Africa," *African Studies Review* 44 (2001), 106.
22 Quoted in John Williams, *From the South African Past: Narratives, Documents, and Debates* (Boston, MA: Houghton Mifflin, 1997), 278.
23 Mandela, *Long Walk*, 104.
24 "The Freedom Charter," June 26, 1955, accessed December 15, 2014, www.anc.org.za/show.php?id=72.
25 Cherryl Walker, *Women and Resistance in South Africa* (London: Onyx Press, 1982), 189–201.

Bibliography

Abrahams, Peter. *Mine Boy*. Oxford: Heinemann, 1946.

Anderson, David. *Histories of the Hanged: The Dirty War in Kenya and the End of Empire*. New York: W.W. Norton, 2005.

Bonner, Philip, and Noor Nieftagodien. *Alexandra: A History*. Johannesburg: Witwatersrand University Press, 2008.

Brendon, Piers. *The Decline and Fall of the British Empire, 1781–1997*. New York: Knopf, 2008.

Eckert, Andreas. "Urbanization in Colonial & Post-Colonial West Africa." In *Themes in West Africa's History*, edited by Emmanuel Akyeampong, 208–23. Oxford: James Currey, 2006.

Elkins, Caroline. *Imperial Reckoning: The Untold Story of Britain's Gulag in Kenya*. New York: Henry Holt, 2005.

Falola, Toyin, and Matthew Heaton. *A History of Nigeria*. Cambridge: Cambridge University Press, 2008.

Geiger, Susan. *TANU Women: Gender and Culture in the Making of Tanganyikan Nationalism, 1955–1965*. Portsmouth, NH: Heinemann, 1997.

Gewald, Jan-Bart, Marja Hinfelaar, and Giacomo Macola, eds. *Living the End of Empire: Politics and Society in Late Colonial Zambia*. Boston, MA: Brill, 2011.

Gutkind, Peter, Robin Cohen, and Jean Copans, eds. *African Labor History*. Beverly Hills, CA: Sage Publications, 1978.

Havinden, Michael, and David Meredith. *Colonialism and Development: Britain and its Tropical Colonies, 1850–1960*. London: Routledge, 1993.

"Hendrik Verwoerd Defines Apartheid." March 4, 1961. Accessed July 14, 2014, www.youtube.com/watch?v=vPCln9czoys.

Hofmeyr, Isabel. "Popularizing History: The Case of Gustav Preller." *Journal of African History* 29 (1988): 521–35.

Killingray, David, with Martin Plaut. *Fighting for Britain: African Soldiers in the Second World War*. Woodbridge, UK: James Currey, 2010.

Lewis, Joanna. *Empire State-Building: War and Welfare in Kenya, 1925–52*. Athens: Ohio University Press, 2000.

Limb, Peter. *The ANC's Early Years: Nation, Class and Place in South Africa before 1940*. Pretoria: Unisa Press, 2010.

Lugard, Frederick. *The Dual Mandate in British Tropical Africa*, 5th edn. Hamden, CT: Archon Books, 1965 [1922].
Magubane, Bernard. Note in book jacket. In *Sophiatown: Coming of Age in South Africa* by Don Mattera. Boston, MA: Beacon Press, 1987.
Mandela, Nelson. *Long Walk to Freedom: The Autobiography of Nelson Mandela*. Boston, MA: Little, Brown, 1994.
Moore, Henrietta, and Megan Vaughan. "Cutting Down Trees: Women, Nutrition and Agricultural Change in the Northern Province of Zambia, 1920–1986." *African Affairs* 86 (1987): 523–40.
Osborne, Myles. "Controlling Development: 'Martial Race' and Empire in Kenya, 1945–59." *Journal of Imperial and Commonwealth History* 42 (2014): 464–85.
Osborne, Myles, ed. *The Life and Times of General China: Mau Mau and the End of Empire in Kenya*. Princeton, NJ: Markus Wiener Publishers, 2015.
Pearce, R. D. *The Turning Point in Africa: British Colonial Policy, 1938–48*. London: Cass, 1982.
Peterson, Derek. "The Intellectual Lives of Mau Mau Detainees." *Journal of African History* 49 (2008): 73–91.
Plageman, Nate. *Highlife Saturday Night: Popular Music and Social Change in Urban Ghana*. Bloomington: Indiana University Press, 2013.
Posel, Deborah. "Race as Common Sense: Racial Classification in Twentieth-Century South Africa." *African Studies Review* 44 (2001): 87–113.
Ranger, Terence. *Peasant Consciousness and Guerilla War in Zimbabwe: A Comparative Study*. London: James Currey, 1985.
Schuknecht, Rohland. *British Colonial Development Policy after the Second World War: The Case of Sukumaland, Tanganyika*. Berlin: Global Book Marketing, 2010.
Stockwell, Sarah, and L. J. Butler, eds. *The Wind of Change: Harold Macmillan and British Decolonization*. Basingstoke, UK: Palgrave Macmillan, 2013.
Thompson, Leonard. *A History of South Africa*, 4th edn. New Haven, CT: Yale University Press, 2014.
Wainaina, Binyavanga. *One Day I Will Write About This Place: A Memoir*. Minneapolis, MN: Graywolf Press, 2011.
Walker, Cherryl. *Women and Resistance in South Africa*. London: Onyx Press, 1982.
White, Luise. *The Comforts of Home: Prostitution in Colonial Nairobi*. Chicago, IL: University of Chicago Press, 1990.
Williams, John. *From the South African Past: Narratives, Documents, and Debates*. Boston, MA: Houghton Mifflin, 1997.
Williams, Susan. *The Colour Bar: The Triumph of Seretse Khama and His Nation*. London: Allen Lane, 2006.
Wills, A. J. *An Introduction to the History of Central Africa: Zambia, Malawi, and Zimbabwe*, 4th edn. New York: Oxford University Press, 1985.

7 Independence for Africans and Britons, 1960s–1970s

On the night of September 30, 1960, some 40,000 Nigerians gathered at the racecourse in Lagos, eager to witness the passage of their country from colony to independent nation. A few minutes before midnight the British governor-general and the prime minister, Alhaji Sir Abubakar Tafawa Balewa, both dressed in white, marched to a platform. As the clock approached midnight they watched in silence as the Union Jack was lowered and, at the stroke of twelve, the new green and white Nigerian flag raised in its place. Fireworks burst into the sky, filling it with bright, crackling color; bands played, spectators sang "God Save the Queen," and then followed it up with the new Nigerian national anthem. "Nigeria we hail thee,/ Our own dear native land,/ Though tribe and tongue may differ,/ In brotherhood we stand,/ Nigerians all, and proud to serve/ Our sovereign Motherland," roared the crowds, belting out the lyrics written for the occasion by a British woman living in Nigeria, Lilian Jean Williams. In Lagos throngs of people greeted the event with dancing and cheering in the streets as they listened to the anthem play out on radios; ships in the harbor blew their horns and set off their sirens.

Prime Minister Balewa, of the Northern People's Congress, stepped to the microphone and lauded the "full and open consultation . . . between representatives of all the various interests in Nigeria" in the country's constitutional achievement, arrived at "without bitterness or bloodshed." But he tempered the joy of the occasion with a warning to his fellow citizens, telling them that however jubilant they felt now at independence – and however gratified they should be by their accomplishment – they faced "grave international issues" that had arisen in recent months. He was referring in particular to the Sharpeville massacre in South Africa and the crisis in Congo.[1]

Margery Perham, an Oxford don and longtime Africa hand, watched the independence ceremonies with mixed emotions. At the lowering of the Union Jack, she confided, she "felt a wholly unexpected, almost physical shock." She lamented "what it was that was being brought to an end." But as the Nigerian flag ran up the flagpole and "the assembled Nigerians of all the regions and tribes saluted it with unmeasured pride and hope," her dismay turned into something else, a cautious optimism that "the incalculable force of energy and pride . . . harnessed behind the new nation" would send it off on what she regarded as the "right" direction.[2]

Amidst the excited singing and dancing of the ecstatic crowds, another British spectator sounded a sour note, highlighting a feature of the independence ceremonies that would play out divisively and disastrously over the next several years. A journalist for *The Guardian* observed that the prime minister had not invited two of the most prominent Nigerian nationalists, Nnamdi Azikiwe, the Igbo leader of the National Council of Nigerian Citizens, and Chief Obafemi Awolowo, the Yoruba leader of the Action Group, to join him on the platform for the flag raising. His failure to do so, asserted the reporter, "will long rankle as a mark against him." More substantively, he noted, Balewa had decided to keep the portfolio of foreign minister for himself rather than offer it to one of the coalition members of his government.[3]

These flag-raising ceremonies symbolized the passage into new nationhood for Britain's African colonies in the 1960s. Initially, there was unrestrained joy for and pride in the freedom and independence won by the people of new nations and great hopes for these united, sovereign states. But the promises of independence soon faded. Many of the structural political and economic problems of the colonial state handicapped the new nations, and inexperienced leadership exacerbated their difficulties. Many nations remained dependent on British input and assistance, and intellectuals on the continent and beyond quickly realized that hosting glorious ceremonies of independence was a far cry from economic, political, and cultural independence. In many areas the simmering pressures of regional differences and ethnic tensions alluded to by *The Guardian*'s reporter came back to haunt the new nations. These divisions would prove to be one of the most lasting legacies of the colonial system. Within half a decade in Nigeria, Ghana, and elsewhere, observers came to temper the optimism of those heady independence day celebrations, realizing that their new nations had extraordinarily difficult paths ahead of them. But initially, there was no dampening the excitement that spread like wildfire across the continent.

The "year of Africa"

The year 1960 was often described as the "Year of Africa." Seventeen nations across the continent gained independence from their colonial masters, following in the footsteps of Ghana. This was no sudden jump to a new era but the product of a long process of hard-fought battles since World War II (see Chapter 6). In 1961 in East Africa, Julius Nyerere's Tanganyika threw off colonial rule, something that surprised many observers who viewed the country's lack of educational facilities and economic resources as hindrances. Uganda gained independence in 1962 in an agreement that created an uneasy power-sharing alliance between the Uganda People's Congress and the *kabaka* (king) of Buganda. Buganda's prominence under the

British would soon become a source of conflict in the new nation. Kenya followed in 1963 after several years of political wrangling between Britain, Kenyan settlers, and the two major African political parties. Settlers' fears about the "horned" figure of Jomo Kenyatta proved unfounded, as he quickly guaranteed their place in the new nation's future, silencing those who suggested he redistribute land from whites to blacks. Finally, Zanzibar became independent the same year before joining Tanganyika in 1964 to form the nation of Tanzania. In West Africa, as we have seen, Ghana and Nigeria had became independent in 1957 and 1960, respectively. They were followed by Sierra Leone in 1961 and The Gambia in 1965.

In southern Africa independence was inextricably linked to the demise of the Central African Federation. African nationalist politicians like Kenneth Kaunda, "Old Harry" Nkumbula in Northern Rhodesia, and Hastings Banda in Nyasaland feared the replacement of the Federation with informal white settler domination. They demanded constitutional change – "one man, one vote" – and spent the later years of the 1950s leading widespread campaigns of civil disobedience that resulted in their detention. But the roll toward independence was unstoppable; as Kaunda put it, "they have banned the great name of Zambia but the greater name of *freedom now* is spiritual."[4] In 1963 the Federation was wound down and both Northern Rhodesia and Nyasaland gained their independence in 1964 as Zambia and Malawi, respectively. Only Southern Rhodesia remained steadfast in its resistance to majority rule. Finally, the protectorate of Bechuanaland – where little more than half a million people lived – came into existence as Botswana in 1966, under its president, Seretse Khama. Lesotho followed the same year and Swaziland in 1968.

A mood of extraordinary optimism infected Africa's inhabitants. Ghana, for instance, seemed to thrive under the leadership of the charismatic Nkrumah. Even before 1957 the granting of partial self-government to Ghana's black majority meant that Nkrumah had a measure of control over development projects. He focused on building roads, highways, schools, and medical facilities. Nkrumah regarded schools and free education as crucial elements in Ghana's future success, as they would allow Africans to throw off the mental shackles of colonialism. Short of that independence would be meaningless. After 1957 he increased the scope of his aims, establishing Ghana Airways and a shipping company called the Black Star Line, named after a firm started in 1918 by the Jamaican pan-Africanist Marcus Garvey. Nkrumah's biggest and most prestigious project, the Akosombo Dam, built in the early 1960s, created the vast Lake Volta and was soon providing more than half of the country's power.

Everybody seemed to feel good about their economic prospects. In Nigeria Shell had discovered oil in the late 1950s and by the time of independence production and export were underway. In Botswana Seretse Khama's government had the tremendous fortune to preside over the discovery of one of the world's largest deposits of diamonds a year after the British departed.

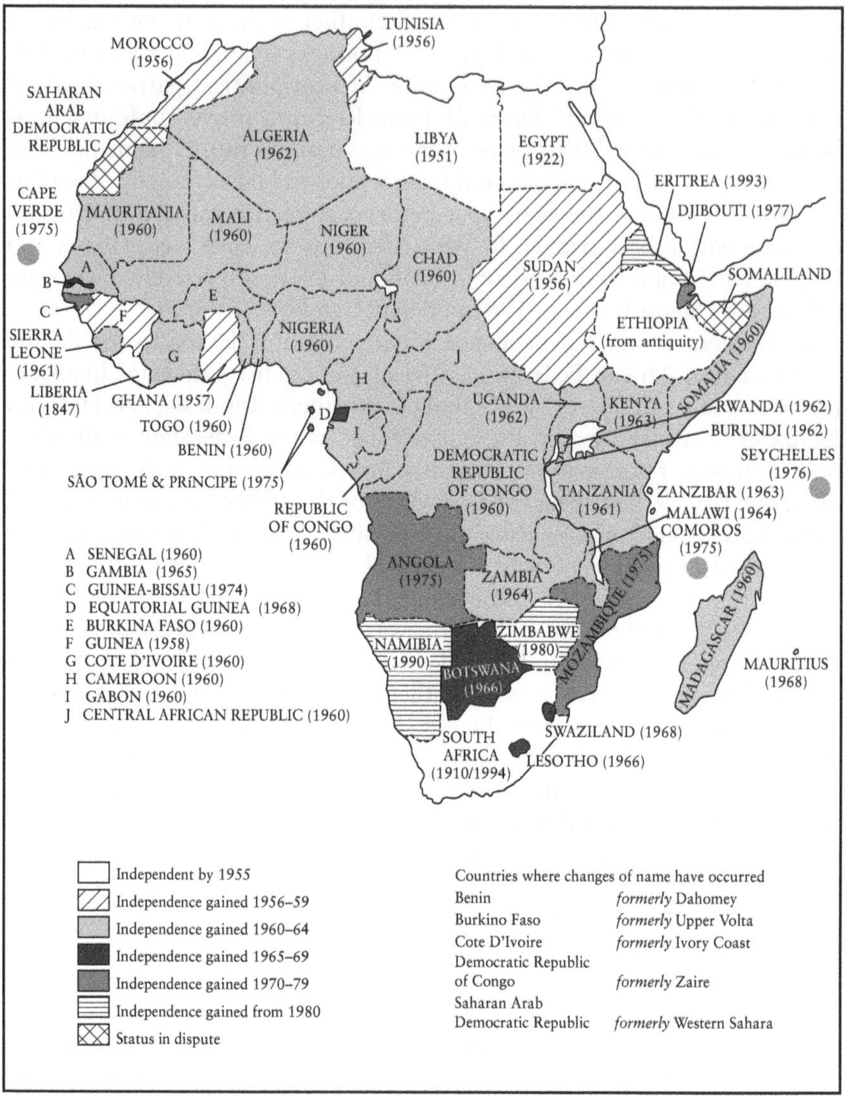

Map 7.1 Decolonization
© *A History of Africa* by J. D. Fage and W. Tordoff, p. 464 (Routledge, 2002).

Located in the center of the country, the mines stimulated economic successes in other parts of the economy and helped solidify Khama's government in the minds of Botswana's people. In Kenya the economy grew rapidly at an annual rate of 3.2 percent during the 1960s. Across sub-Saharan Africa, life expectancy was increasing, infant mortality dropping, and more and more children attended school. In 1960 an average of 54.4 of 100 men and 32 of 100 women attended school. A decade later the figures had increased to 62.3/100 and 42.8/100, respectively. In 1962 30 percent of the men and 10 percent of the women in Kenya could read; in Zambia in 1963 the equivalent numbers for male and female literacy reached 53 percent and 30 percent. Eight years later the figures had risen to 56 percent in the case of Kenyan men and 26 percent for Kenyan women, and 64 percent and 32 percent for men and women in Zambia. The spirit of excitement about Africa extended abroad as well. Universities in the United States and Britain came to offer African history as a course of study for the first time. Graduate students in the United States, Britain, and Africa worked collaboratively to begin unpacking the enormously complex and diverse history of the continent. They are the professors emeriti of today, having passed the mantle onto their students who now hold senior faculty positions at universities across the United States, Europe, and Africa.

From the British perspective African economic growth could only be an advantage if Britain could maintain close relationships with its former colonies. Officials hoped that the British commonwealth, formed in 1949 in its modern manifestation, would serve that end, facilitating the creation of beneficial trade relationships between Britain and its partners. Nkrumah, for one, shared the vision the British had for these relationships and he brought Ghana into the commonwealth at independence in 1957. Though he spoke widely and at length about pan-Africanism and a "United States of Africa" (a proposed political union with himself at the helm), it was quickly apparent that his vision had little chance of success and he therefore became a useful trading partner for Britain. In the 1960s every former British territory entered the commonwealth at independence with the exception of the tiny region of British Somaliland. It became part of the Somali Republic in 1960.

Cold War calculations

The mood of optimism was – at least initially – bolstered by what many African leaders and intellectuals viewed as tremendous advantages that might accrue from the Cold War. The Soviet Union and United States were falling over one another to provide loans, trade deals, arms, and technical assistance to new African states. Africa's first generation of presidents was faced with a choice: which side to join? Some intellectuals like Nyerere had strong sympathies with socialist systems of government, which they believed were more "African" in their communal use of facilities. Nyerere, indeed, won vast funds from China to build the "Tanzam" railway to Zambia. Others like Kenyatta were firmly of the view that capitalist alliance with Britain (and Europe) would be more beneficial.

There was a third path, too, along which men like Nkrumah and Kaunda strode. Nkrumah skillfully played the capitalist western states off against the communist powers. Despite Ghana's membership in the commonwealth and its close economic ties to Britain, Nkrumah sought out and received funds from the Soviet Union and sent Ghanaian students there to study.

Kaunda also took the "middle ground," but in a different way, espousing a policy of non-alignment. Kaunda stated that Zambia would accept aid from anyone provided that it did not tie his nation into "political and economic commitments" that could embroil it in the Cold War struggle. As his foreign minister put it, "We all know that where two elephants meet to fight, the elephants do not suffer but the shrubs under the feet of the elephants suffer." This meant refusing even the hand of friendship from the United States when necessary.[5]

As the 1960s progressed it became increasingly clear that Africa was a pawn on the chessboard that was the Cold War conflict at large. The continent became the site for proxy wars that pitted the two superpowers against one another, most prominently in places like Angola and Mozambique but drawing nations across the continent into the superpowers' orbit. It is, indeed, difficult to understand the period of decolonization and independence in isolation from the Cold War, which informed and complicated all relationships between former colony and colonial master from the 1950s onward. The British formulated policy toward Africa during the 1960s and 1970s with the Cold War always in mind.

The dynamics of the Cold War are perhaps most clearly illustrated in a colony that the British never controlled. British actions in Congo in the 1960s – an area entirely beyond its sovereignty and apparent influence – demonstrate both the importance of Cold War considerations in formulating British policy and the lengths to which British agents were willing to go to support their nation's interests. In September 1961 United Nations Secretary General Dag Hammarskjöld was murdered on his way to negotiate a truce between forces contesting power in Congo. His plane was shot down over Northern Rhodesia, probably by agents employed by the US Central Intelligence Agency and Britain's MI-6. In one of the starkest examples of the direct connection between decolonization and Cold War politics, the United States and Britain refused to allow the mineral-rich Congo to fall into the hands of Africans who had sought assistance from the Soviet Union to protect their new democratic nation.

Congo had won its independence from Belgium on June 30, 1960, and its people elected Patrice Lumumba, the leader of the nationalist movement, as prime minister. On July 4 the new national army mutinied against their still-present Belgian officers, setting off a panic among Europeans and providing Belgium with an excuse to reassert control over its misbehaving former colony. The following week the province of Katanga, which held more than 60 percent of the country's natural resources in vast stores of copper, uranium, tin, manganese, diamonds, and cobalt, seceded from Congo, probably at the behest of the European corporations that mined the region. Moïse Tshombe, who declared himself president of an independent Katanga, enjoyed the support of the Belgian troops in the area and the corporations that had amassed incredible wealth from its mining concessions, the Belgian company Union Minière du Haut Katanga, and the British firm

Tanganyika Concessions, which had close ties with the Rhodesian Trust and the British South Africa Company.

Faced with the collapse of his country, which could not survive without the mineral wealth of Katanga, Lumumba approached the United Nations for assistance in ridding Congo of Belgian troops and recovering the wayward province. The UN Security Council, with both the United States and the Soviet Union in support but Britain abstaining, passed Resolution 143, insisting that Belgium remove its troops from Congo and authorizing UN forces to help out until the Congo government could handle the situation on its own. Some 3500 UN troops were dispatched to the country.

In early August another Congolese province, South Kasai, where the bulk of Congo's diamonds came from, also declared its independence. Despairing that the UN would not be able to do what was necessary to keep his country intact and defend its democracy, Lumumba turned to the Soviet Union for military aid. Soviet arms, equipment, and advisors soon arrived, alarming officials in the United States and Britain. CIA director Allen Dulles cabled his station chief in Congo that "the removal [of Lumumba] must be an urgent and prime objective . . . this should be a high priority of our covert action." In London similar thinking led a senior member of the Foreign Office to recommend one of two solutions to the "Lumumba problem." The second one called for ousting him from power; but the first, noted the official, "is the simple one of ensuring Lumumba's removal from the scene by killing him."[6] In the end both options were employed, though we do not know precisely who orchestrated them. On September 14, 1960, Joseph-Desiré Mobutu, a young colonel in the Congolese army on the US payroll, staged a coup and took control of the country. In January 1961 Mobutu's army arrested Lumumba and two other members of the elected government and murdered them. Outraged, UN delegates protested loudly that the prime minister and his government had not been protected and demanded redress. The Security Council responded by passing a stronger resolution demanding that all foreign troops and advisors leave Congo and empowering UN forces, now raised to 15,000 in number, to do what was necessary to restore order in Congo and avert civil war. The UN troops arrived in June 1961; in September, without informing his superiors, the head of the UN forces ordered them to invade and occupy Katanga, setting up a showdown with Tshombe and his western-backed troops.

The white settler government of the Central African Federation watched these developments with grave apprehension. Katanga province shared a 2000-mile border with Northern Rhodesia, a good portion of it aligning with the copperbelt region that provided much of the Federation's wealth. The Federation prime minister, Roy Welensky, regarded Katanga as an effective bulwark against anti-colonial and pan-Africanist movements to the north, telling British Prime Minister Harold Macmillan in January 1961, "we have always pinned our hopes on the survival of a strong and friendly regime in the Katanga." He feared that a UN overthrow of Tshombe would put his government in danger. "The alternatives are too frightful to contemplate," he warned.[7] With the approval of the British high commissioner in Salisbury, Welensky sent troops and air support to the town of Ndola, six miles from the Katanga border, on September 13.

The presence of UN troops in Katanga infuriated the governments of the United States and Britain, which demanded their removal. Hammarskjöld – who had not been privy to the UN commander's decision to invade the province – determined to prevent what Welensky predicted would be a third world war. He arranged through the British government to meet with Katanga leader Tshombe in Ndola to hold talks designed to bring about a cease-fire.

Hammarskjöld never made it. His plane was shot down short of the Ndola airport; when investigators reached it they found that the secretary general had received a bullet to the head. The timing of the shot and the identity of the shooter remain a mystery. The aborting of his mission in this horrific way rebounded entirely to Tshombe's advantage: a cease-fire was indeed put in place but with it came a guarantee that the UN would not interfere in Katanga any longer. This meant, in practice, that the commercial interests behind the Katanga secession benefitted as well, companies that included on their boards of directors the marquess of Salisbury; Lord Clitheroe, the former chair of the Conservative party; Lord Selborne, a cousin of Salisbury's, and Captain Charles Waterhouse, chairman of Tanganyika Concessions. Loosely known as the "Katanga Lobby," these influential men and others fought to preserve white rule in Africa and successfully pressured the British government to look after their interests. In public Macmillan distanced himself from the Katanga Lobby but certain members of his government behind the scenes rejoiced in the failure of Hammarskjöld's mission. As Secretary of State for Air Julian Amery – a former MI-6 operative – put it, "the prosperity of our people rests really on the oil in the Persian Gulf, the rubber and tin of Malaya, and the gold, copper and precious metals of south and central Africa. As long as we can realize the investments we have there; as long as we trade with this part of the world, we shall be prosperous." Should those holdings fall into the hands of those former colonies that were gaining their independence from Britain or other European powers, Amery warned, "we would lose the lot."[8]

These sorts of actions were powerful, direct interventions in the politics of African states, but perhaps the more insidious and long-lasting effects came in the form of foreign aid. Britain and other foreign powers came to use aid as one of the most effective tools in the battle of the Cold War powers for the allegiance of new African nations. It did not matter how badly a ruler behaved as long as his – and it was in every case a he – government professed its fidelity to one side or the other. The United States and Britain, among other western powers, provided monetary and military support to some of the most brutal dictators in Africa in return for loyalty and, not incidentally, unhindered access to much-needed minerals and other raw materials. From

Mobutu Sese Seko in Congo to Idi Amin in Uganda, to name but two, the western powers frequently bankrolled corruption and despotism in African states in their struggle against communism. Despite its propaganda efforts to portray the capitalist nations as the sources of all that was evil in the world, the Soviet Union did the same.

New coups, old constraints

The impact of the Cold War, along with economic and political realities, finally became inescapable by 1966. That was the year that Africa's most prominent figurehead, Kwame Nkrumah, was unceremoniously deposed from his position as president of Ghana in a military coup. It was also the year that Africa's most populous nation, Nigeria, began its descent into the chaos of civil war. The roots of these difficulties lay in the structures of colonialism that made successful governance all but impossible. In some cases they were magnified by inept leadership among African presidents and ruling classes. People came to view the heady days of the early 1960s as a chimera, a time when optimism and excitement had disguised the realities of the difficult conditions new states faced. While some countries continued to win relative success – Botswana and Zambia among them – they were the exception rather than the rule.

For the economic structures of the colonial state, British or otherwise, had been designed to benefit the metropole. This dynamic had produced narrow, brittle economies focused on the export of raw materials to Britain. The former colonies lacked manufacturing sectors, leaving them with little diversity of production to help them counteract periods of economic downturn. Moreover, infrastructure had been designed to serve Britain: railway lines and roads ran between areas of production and coastal regions in order to export produce as quickly as possible. There had been no effort to connect market towns or trading centers in the rural areas, which meant that the average villager wanting to go 20 miles to the north of his or her home on public transport often had to ride six or seven hours into the capital, then catch a connecting vehicle the same distance to his or her destination. Placing a telephone call to London from Nairobi was simple, cheap, and efficient; placing one from Nairobi to Dar es Salaam was fraught with difficulties. African economies were so tied to Europe that whenever the latter was in an economic depression Africans had to cut the prices of goods they sold; when things picked back up again Africans had to buy more expensive manufactured goods from Europe. In other words, the new African nations inherited the economies created by colonial development schemes, most of which had not worked while the British were in charge and did not work any better once they ceded power. New African leaders had to absorb and pay for the huge bureaucratic apparatus put in place during the "second colonial occupation" of the postwar period while at the same time trying to live up to the intense hopes of people who now believed the state belonged to them.

Perhaps the cruelest part of the downturn was that in the early 1960s economic success seemed not just possible but certain. African countries had received high prices for their goods on the world market, thereby disguising the degree to which their economies were warped. The majority of colonies had poorly diversified economic portfolios: most earned money from one product, like copper in Zambia or cocoa in Ghana. Any collapse in world prices, as occurred in both cases, proved disastrous. In Ghana the state did not act to invest in and support its cocoa farmers, underestimating their importance; instead it remained extractive, behaving in the same way the colonial state had. It left in place the high tariffs and taxes and notorious marketing boards imposed by the British. Cocoa farmers responded to these attempts to shackle them in just the way they had in colonial times: they protested by carrying out "go-slows" or "holdups" to slow cocoa production or traded cocoa illegally – beyond government oversight – across international borders.

To make matters worse, Ghana and the other new nations across Africa lacked a competent class of bureaucrats to administer their governments. Even in the mid-1950s Britain had not anticipated African nations becoming independent for several more decades and had trained few men and women to work in high levels of government. The transition to independence had occurred hastily, giving little time for a careful handover of governing structures. Lacking an established bureaucracy African political leaders turned to their friends and family members, producing cronyism, corruption, and gross mismanagement of state resources. Financial mismanagement could easily destroy hard-won gains. As the Ghanaian journalist and later political appointee Tawia Adamafio warned, corruption was a "howling monster threatening to wreck the whole nation."[9]

Ghana's finances, in particular, were in an appalling state. Nkrumah borrowed with little regard to the payments the country was incurring, building up a national debt of £184 million by 1963 and £349 million a year later. Government agencies overstaffed with Nkrumah's friends and relatives and other assorted allies underperformed dramatically while lining their pockets handsomely by skimming a routine "fee" of 10 percent from the top of every government contract. Ghana Airways, for example, existed almost entirely on the basis of government largesse. Planes filled with politicians and their families flew to locations such as Cairo and Moscow on tickets paid for by the government. One journalist described a scene typical of Nkrumah's way of doing business, in which a shady European salesman had convinced the president to sign on to some cockamamie project. "Nkrumah had his pen in his hand ready to sign over a contract for more than £1 million," recounts one expert, when one of his advisors interrupted the transaction. "Shall I just look it over, Mr President?" the man asked. "He carefully took the document away and that day saved the exchequer £1 million. The more ambitious the project that was put forward, the more likely it was to gain approval."[10]

While Ghana's government signed on to ever-larger prestige projects the common people struggled. Improved health care and medical treatment delivered in the 1940s had meant that Africa's population was increasing rapidly, but access to land or jobs became progressively more difficult. Nkrumah's decision to privilege urban and infrastructure projects – "modernization," as he described it – required heavy borrowing, and rural areas were ignored. The government taxed farmers more heavily and gave scant regard to their living conditions. With the construction of the Akosombo Dam, hundreds of villages were flooded; Nkrumah barely seemed to notice. Many villagers and struggling city dwellers came to feel that their president spent so much time playing the role of international statesman that he forgot about his people at home. As the nation began to crumble Nkrumah took increasingly drastic actions to maintain his hold on power, detaining opponents on a whim and changing the law as it suited him. In a 1964 referendum in which he asked his people whether Ghana should become a one-party state vote-fixing was so blatant that in some cases ballot boxes did not even have a slot for "no" votes. According to government figures 2,773,900 people voted for a one-party system and 2452 against in an election with a 96 percent turnout. This kind of despotism rankled. In 1966, while traveling in Beijing, Nkrumah was overthrown in a military coup. People cheered in the streets.

In Nigeria a coup followed by a counter-coup in 1966 destabilized the uneasy power-sharing federal system that had sought to provide an ethnic and regional balance. This arrangement, so effusively hailed by the prime minister during his independence day speech, hinged on the ability of profoundly diverse peoples to subordinate their local and regional identities and desires to an untried and untrusted national unity. This proved impossible. Balewa's Northern People's Congress (NPC) dominated the federal apparatus before 1966, but the NPC, as well as Awolowo's Action Group (AG), and Azikiwe's National Council of Nigerian Citizens constantly feared losing power to their rivals. Each took steps at both the regional and national level to assert and/or consolidate his party's power. Over the next few years relations between the parties deteriorated badly, leaving the federal government almost powerless in face of increasingly strong regional governments. Elections in 1964 and 1965 displayed some of the most egregiously corrupt practices anyone could remember seeing, prompting five majors in the Nigerian army to stage the coup of January 15, 1966, in order, they claimed, to end the divisiveness and corruption that plagued the country. They arrested all of the regional heads of government and killed Prime Minister Balewa, two other regional premiers, and a number of military officers in the northern region.

Regional fears of domination only increased, however, as the commanding officer of the army, Major General John Aguiyi-Ironsi, an Igbo, took control of the regime and acted in ways that led northerners and westerners to believe that he favored the eastern region where Igbos far outnumbered other peoples. At the end of July 1966 northern military men led a coup against Ironsi, setting up a young lieutenant colonel, Yakubu Gowon, as the commander of the army and the new head of state. A great deal of violence ensued, much of it directed against Igbo people. Some 80,000 to 100,000 easterners died in a series of massacres, provoking reprisals against northerners living in eastern Nigeria. The bloodletting convinced the military governor of the eastern region, Lieutenant Colonel Emeka Ojukwu, that Igbo peoples could not live safely within a federal Nigeria. Ojukwu exhorted Igbos living in northern Nigeria to return home to the east, similarly urging northerners to leave the eastern region. Huge numbers of people followed his advice, resulting in significant population transfers during late 1966 and early 1967.

In March 1967 Ojukwu went further, announcing that the eastern regional government would assume the responsibilities of federal departments and for revenues. This amounted to a declaration of secession on the part of the eastern region, now styled Biafra, from Nigeria. The federal government could not allow such an action to stand for a number of reasons. First, it would embolden other regions to take similar steps, resulting in a collection of fragmented and hostile states – in short, no nation. Equally important from the perspective of Gowon's government, Biafra possessed two-thirds of the known oil reserves in Nigeria. The federal government's response to Ojukwu's declaration was severe. It implemented a naval blockade of the Biafran coast and sealed its borders, preventing much food from entering the region. The resulting inflation sent food prices skyrocketing; a chicken that cost 15 shillings before the war cost £30 (600 shillings) by its end. Hundreds of thousands of Igbo people starved to death, adding to the numbers of those lost in the physical fighting. Estimates of those killed before the fighting came to an end in 1970 range between one million and three million people. On January 12, 1970, Biafra surrendered and was "reincorporated" into Nigeria.

The civil war presented Britain with a dilemma. Its chief concern was the oil resources in the east in which it had great interest, but to back one side or the other meant ruining diplomatic relations with a party that might end up in control of the oilfields. This was especially true because the outcome of the war was not initially evident. Biafra won some success in the conflict's early days. Britain therefore chose to sit back and wait until the likely victor became apparent, as did the United States. Britain's inaction frustrated the federal government in Nigeria, which turned to the Soviet Union for assistance. The Soviets gladly complied by providing arms and military advisers to assist the government side. As the fighting neared an end and it became clearer that the federal government would prevail, Britain finally threw its support behind the government. But as scholars delve more deeply into recently released Foreign and Commonwealth Office files, we will have a better understanding of what role the British government played in the outcome of the conflict.

When the war ended the Nigerian military government under Gowon moved quickly to consolidate its control of the country. Gowon rearranged the nation's system of states, adding a series of smaller entities in an effort to weaken regional blocs. In many ways the military became the single institution that could plausibly claim to be national in scope and it strove to impose unity and order on the diverse peoples of Nigeria. It did so, however, while maintaining the practices of corruption and incompetence in administration that had marked the civilian government in earlier years. The military government differed from the civilian one in its ability to sustain itself in power, largely by the use or threat of force. The army grew exponentially during the Biafran civil war, increasing from 10,000 soldiers in 1966 to 270,000 in 1970; its share of the national budget increased from 0.2 percent in 1961 to 6 percent at the end of the decade. Nigeria's oil wealth, which made it the wealthiest country on the continent apart from South Africa in the 1970s, provided the resources to keep the military in power, enriching a tiny sector of the population and leaving the vast number of Nigerians impoverished.

In Kenya elites acted to consolidate their political power by maintaining colonial economic structures and the colonial state's focus on the politics of ethnicity. The fledgling nation was led by Jomo Kenyatta, whose political agenda favored his own people, the Kikuyu. He increased their numbers in the army, gave contracts to Kikuyu businessmen, and ensured that the country's second most populous ethnic group – the Luo from western Kenya – went without new roads or development funds. The system of what we might call "ethnic politics" grew out of the colonial experience of the 1950s, when colonial officials, fearful of nationalist movements, had permitted only the formation of ethnic parties.

Kenya's political elites did not tolerate challenges to their authority. As one historian put it, once they gained power, they "kicked away" the ladders "before others . . . could climb them."[11] Their unwillingness to share the political spoils of independence gave rise to political dynasties. Kenyatta's son Uhuru, to give just one prominent example, serves as the nation's current president, and Raila Odinga, the son of Kenya's first vice president, Oginga Odinga, held the post of prime minister between 2008 and 2013. In the 1960s Kenyatta cited the need for nation-building as justification for squashing any political opposition, turning Kenya into a de facto one-party state after 1966. Competition would "damage" attempts to create unity among Kenyans, he argued. In this he was not alone. Banda, Kaunda, and Milton Obote in Uganda did the same thing.

By the mid- to late 1960s Kenyan intellectuals and common people alike had come to realize that little had changed in the years since the British gave up their imperial rule in 1963. By 1966 Oginga Odinga had fallen out with Kenyatta and formed a short-lived socialist party called the Kenya People's Union (which Kenyatta would soon crush). The following year Odinga published *Not Yet Uhuru* (*uhuru* means "independence"), a scathing indictment of those who had betrayed the struggle for freedom. "[I]t suits the ambitions of the self-seeking politicians to divert our people from the real freedom aims," he wrote, arguing that Kenya was a neo-colonial state. He directly attacked Kenyatta's "acquisition of large farms."[12] In 1969 he was arrested and put in detention, a common fate for those who voiced dissent but safer than six feet below ground, where a number of opposition politicians who spoke against Kenyatta ended up.

Other dissidents expressed their opinions through literature. The literary corpus of Ngugi wa Thiong'o, arguably Africa's most prominent intellectual, reflected his growing disillusionment. In 1964 he published the classic *Weep Not, Child*, in which he recounted the story of Mau Mau and its brutal suppression by the British. Kenyatta appears as a heroic figure. By 1977, with the publication of *Petals of Blood*, Ngugi's views had changed. He depicted Kenya as a nation in which little had altered since the end of colonial rule. Black faces had simply taken over from white; the poor had been forced into degraded jobs like prostitution; those who had fought in Mau Mau were ignored as inconvenient reminders of the past.

The upheavals that characterized Nigeria and Ghana – and to an extent, Kenya – in 1966 were mirrored in Uganda the same year, where long-standing ethnic divisions and hostility burst out in conflict. As we saw in Chapter 4, the British had historically favored the kingdom of Buganda since the time of Lugard, regarding the Ganda as an industrious people – the "Japanese of Africa," as famed explorer and administrator Sir Harry Johnston described them.[13] This favoritism was reflected in the wide-ranging political authority given to the *kabaka* of Buganda at independence in 1962. Not surprisingly this preferential treatment angered most of the rest of the country. In 1966 Prime Minister Obote staged a coup to take executive control of Uganda, suspending the constitution and arresting those who protested his actions. He stripped Buganda of its power, formally ending the system of traditional kingdoms, and sent government troops under his newly appointed commander, Idi Amin, to raid the *kabaka*'s palace and send him into exile in London. With the support of Amin and the army, Obote established one-party rule, eliminated his rivals, and led the country into dictatorship. His rule depended heavily on the military and in order to keep it loyal he lavished state resources on its members until they operated virtually independently of him. As the military grew more powerful, Amin became more and more autonomous of Obote.

Over the next four years Obote made himself progressively more obnoxious to his former British rulers and the British commercial interests that had remained in Uganda after independence. In what became known as the "Move to the Left Strategy," Obote nationalized some 85 British corporations, seizing up to 60 percent of each company for the state. On the international stage he lambasted Britain for its decision to provide arms to apartheid South Africa, causing consternation in London with his efforts to stir up the African members of the commonwealth and the newly developed Organisation of African Unity over the issue. British antipathy toward

Obote had reached such great heights that when army commander Idi Amin (with whom Obote had fallen out) overthrew him in January 1971 while he was in Singapore, Britons issued nary a protest. In fact they welcomed the new regime, thinking they had in Amin a man who could be reasoned with.

Idi Amin had proved himself in the colonial military, rising through the ranks of the King's African Rifles, which he joined in 1946. He hailed from the north of Uganda, the area where the British believed the country's "martial races" lived. Tall, strong, not particularly bright, and uneducated, he was exactly what British recruiters sought in their draftees. Amin fought against Mau Mau in Kenya in the early 1950s, thereby proving his loyalty to the British crown and ultimately earning a promotion to sergeant. As "Africanization" of the army and the civil service proceeded during the years prior to independence, Amin became first a platoon commander and then a captain. During a revolt of indigenous officers seeking greater advancement in 1964 he remained loyal and helped to put down the mutineers, gaining the respect and admiration of both soldiers and British officers within the King's African Rifles. Amin's popularity with Ugandans and Britons alike enabled him to overthrow Obote with little or no resistance. Britain's major newspapers – *The Times*, *The Guardian*, and the *Daily Telegraph* – editorialized rapturously about the new era that had

Figure 7.1 Fourteen Europeans pledge their allegiance to the Ugandan army in front of President Idi Amin, September 1975

dawned in Uganda; the government recognized his regime and Queen Elizabeth lunched with him when he visited London in July.

For two years Amin presented himself as a man of peace and reconciliation at home and abroad by releasing men and women whom Obote had jailed. He established a permanent secretary for religious affairs who was charged with easing relations between Christians and Muslims and, most importantly for many Ugandans, he brought home the body of the exiled *kabaka* for reburial. Behind the scenes, however, Amin carried out a brutal policy of murder in the army ranks against those soldiers belonging to the ethnic groups favored by Obote. In a series of four campaigns in 1971 and 1972 Amin's loyalists massacred Acholi and Lango soldiers and officers. Because of a press blackout few reports of the bloodshed made their way out of the barracks. Those that did were pooh-poohed by western diplomats in Kampala.

Amin's disastrous and deadly policies moved into the open soon enough as his behavior became increasingly erratic. He proclaimed himself His Excellency President for Life, Field Marshal Al Hadji Doctor Idi Amin, VC, DSO, MC, Lord of All the Beasts of the Earth and Fishes of the Sea, and Conqueror of the British Empire in Africa in General and Uganda in Particular (and periodically claimed to be the king of Scotland as well). In the spring of 1972, after he could not obtain the arms he wanted from either Britain or Israel, he expelled Israelis from Uganda and turned to Muammar Gaddafi of Libya for military and economic support. He then threw out the Asian population too – some 50,000 people, over half of whom were Ugandan citizens, and seized their property. This act did huge damage to Uganda's economy but it also created difficulties for Britain, for most of the exiles ended up there, as Amin well knew would be the case. His aim, he later asserted, had been to teach "the British a lesson they would never forget."[14] But these actions paled in comparison to the outrages he and his followers committed against Ugandans over the following seven years. They included the destruction and dispossession of property; indiscriminate harassment, humiliation, assault, and rape at the hands of untouchable soldiers and police; and the mass slaughter by "killer squads" of anyone and everyone Amin construed as his rival or foe. Politicians, Christian and other religious leaders, military officers, and ordinary citizens lost their rights, their dignity, their livelihoods, and their lives by the thousands before the country was liberated from the "Butcher of Uganda" in 1979 by Tanzanian troops after Amin crossed the border into their country to punish enemies who had fled his wrath.

Neo-colonialism and the global 1970s

In 1973 Africa's fragile economic and political independence was dealt a crushing blow by global events. In October, in response to the United States' support of Israel in the Yom Kippur war, Arab oil-producing states halted the sale of petroleum products to the United States, Britain, Canada, the Netherlands, and Japan, bringing about a 400 percent increase in the price of oil on the global market. Almost immediately world economies fell into deep recession. Increased oil costs drove up the price of food, as many African countries had begun to mechanize their agricultural practices, and in any case relied on mechanized transport to move their goods to market. At the same time countries that purchased agricultural commodities from Africa could not now afford what they had paid in the past, thus lowering the price African farmers could command for their products. The curious phenomenon of inflation and recession – or stagflation, as those in the United States called it – ensued. In Ghana, for example, inflation stood at 3 percent in 1970; it increased to 30 percent in 1975 and skyrocketed to 116 percent two years later. Gross domestic product on the other hand fell by 12 percent between 1973 and 1975.

The oil embargo also had another direct effect on the economies of African nations. Arab oil-producing states deposited their vast earnings in banks around the world. These banks, bursting with cash, sought outlets for it. The combination of low interest rates and slack rules regulating money-lending meant that even the poorest of countries – even those with little or no chance of paying back loans – could borrow what they wished at interest rates that floated according to the volume of money in supply. Because there was so much cash in circulation interest rates stayed low, some even fell into the negative range, and money flooded into the coffers of many African states, providing extraordinary temptations for those rulers who thought to use it for corrupt and dictatorial purposes. Countries like Zambia – which was also struggling with a major decline in world copper prices, a product on which it was dependent – had little choice but to borrow.

In 1979 another oil crisis brought on by war between Iran and Iraq wracked the global economy. This time, however, the central bankers of the world responded by tightening up the supply of available money and raising interest rates. Those countries that had borrowed at very low rates now found themselves owing much higher amounts, and many of them simply could not pay the increased debts. Between 1975 and 1982, for example, the cost of servicing the debt incurred by African states rose from $2 billion to $8 billion. When in 1982 Mexico announced that it could not meet its debt obligations, many other developing nations followed it into default, including Angola, Cameroon, Congo, Ivory Coast, Gabon, Mozambique, Niger, Nigeria, Tanzania, The Gambia, and Zambia. Global financial stability appeared at risk.

The International Monetary Fund (IMF) – formed along with the World Bank after World War II in order to ensure that the economic and financial chaos that followed the Great Depression would not be repeated – felt compelled to act to restore confidence in the threatened financial markets across the globe. In order to provide funds to defaulting countries so that they could repay their massive debts to the world's banks it established the

Structural Adjustment Facility. This served to put poor countries even deeper in debt. By establishing conditions on its assistance it made extraordinary interventions into the economies of supposedly sovereign nations, inducing many commentators to speak of structural adjustment as nothing short of neo-colonialism. For in return for help in paying off their debts recipients of IMF monies had to agree to introduce free-market practices – liberalizing trade, privatizing state-owned industries, and slashing the number of civil service jobs. Structural adjustment policies had devastating effects on people everywhere they were imposed, immiserating millions of Africans. One critic noted that they amounted to the recolonization of African states, with "smart white boys" from the IMF being sent in to tell Africans how to manage their affairs.[15]

The continuation of white rule in southern Africa

In southern Africa one colony did not fit the broad process of decolonization that we have outlined here. As African economies struggled in the 1960s and 1970s it remained economically successful, in large part owing to its close association with the South African apartheid regime. This colony was Southern Rhodesia, populated by a hardy white population that rarely took kindly to outside interference in its affairs. As Northern Rhodesia and Nyasaland won their independence the white minority government of Ian Smith likewise pressed for Rhodesia's liberation from British rule. From the perspective of the British government in London, however, there could be no independence before Africans' legal and electoral rights had been secured in some sort of system that guaranteed majority rule and adherence to the principle of one person, one vote. Smith and his followers balked at this condition, loath to hand power over to African leaders whom they regarded as the stalking horses of communism. In 1964 and 1965 the Labour government of Harold Wilson tried to both resolve the impasse and to impose increasingly harsh strictures on the Rhodesian government. By late 1965, fed up, the Rhodesians would take no more.

On November 11, Armistice Day, Prime Minister Smith, a former British fighter pilot, took to the airwaves to make a unique and dramatic declaration of independence. "We may be a small country," he told his audience,

> but we are a determined people. . . . We Rhodesians have rejected the doctrinaire philosophy of appeasement and surrender. The decision which we have taken today is a refusal by Rhodesians to sell their birthright. And, even if we were to surrender, does anyone believe that Rhodesia would be the last target of the Communists in the Afro-Asian block? We have struck a blow for the preservation of justice, civilization, and Christianity; and in the spirit of this belief we have this day assumed our sovereign independence. God bless you all.[16]

Ian Smith's Unilateral Declaration of Independence, or UDI as it quickly became known, stunned Wilson and his ministers. They had believed they could negotiate a firm timetable to black majority rule but the lanky farmer-turned-politician refused to consider it. Smith and his supporters claimed that Rhodesia would not only defend its white minority population against "uncivilized" and "savage" Africans, it would also stand as a vital holdout against a Soviet-inspired takeover of its government.

Britain responded to UDI by imposing sanctions against Rhodesia but the rogue nation – never formally recognized by any other country – negotiated them easily with assistance provided by South Africa. South Africa had declared itself a republic in 1961, ending its British dominion status and withdrawing from the commonwealth. Following the Sharpeville massacre (see Chapter 6) the country had become something of an international pariah. In 1964 the International Olympic Committee banned South Africa from participating in the Olympics, though international rugby and cricket organizations took longer to ban it from competition. South Africans regarded Rhodesia as a natural ally. Staunchly anti-communist and firmly under the control of white minority rule, the two nations formed a bulwark against the development of socialism and communism in Portuguese Angola and Mozambique. (South Africa, indeed, worked diligently to destabilize the two countries during the 1970s after they became independent from Portugal.) South Africa's government had made liberal use of the Suppression of Communism Act of 1950 to ban or restrict the movement of anyone who had apparent "communist" leanings. The extensive use of the legislation enabled the nation to blame its racial problems on communism. The country's anti-communist stance also provided Britain and the United States the cover they needed to delay (and in the case of Britain, altogether avoid) imposing sanctions on South Africa during the years of apartheid.

In response to UDI Africans in Rhodesia intensified an incipient guerrilla campaign against the Rhodesian government. The guerrilla forces developed out of the two prominent African political parties in the colony, the largely Shona Zimbabwe African National Union (ZANU) headed first by Ndbaningi Sithole and later by Robert Mugabe, and the Ndebele-dominated Zimbabwe African People's Union (ZAPU) of Joshua Nkomo. Each had their own militant wings – ZANLA and ZIPRA, respectively – that competed against and clashed with one another on occasion. ZANLA based its operations in Mozambique, where it was friendly with the insurgent force and later Marxist government of FRELIMO (which itself was engaged in a battle against the South African-supported RENAMO). ZIPRA established its base in Lusaka under the protection of Kenneth Kaunda. The "Rhodesian Bush War," as it became known, was a long-drawn-out affair. The government's forces – half black and half white – were well-trained and highly capable but they could not prevail over a movement that enjoyed the mass of African support.

From the perspective of Shona in the villages the Rhodesian Bush War constituted more than a secular guerrilla war of weapons, ammunition, and tactics. They linked the conflict to preexisting belief systems, meaning that spirit mediums played a determinative role in organizing the struggle. Mediums were special people who could become possessed by *mhondoro* – ancestral spirits – and in such a state represent the voices of long-dead and highly respected Shona men and women, ancestors who had successfully led their people long before Europeans had arrived in Rhodesia. Spirit mediums blessed the cause of the youthful guerrilla fighters, who stood in stark contrast to the colonial chiefs appointed by the white government. As the Bush War progressed, Shona people increasingly ignored their chiefs, believing that the mediums should determine how their communities would be run. The mediums' connection to the ancestors enabled them to provide spiritual protection over the guerrilla warriors, which in turn earned the warriors tremendous respect in their communities. Shona villagers believed that the spirit mediums had formally sanctioned the warriors' actions and they joined the movement in increasing numbers.

Gradually South Africa's support for Rhodesia waned, the guerrilla forces increased in size, and the Rhodesian economy began to collapse. Under these pressures Smith negotiated, agreeing to open the government to Africans. The country known as Zimbabwe Rhodesia, under the leadership of Bishop Abel Muzorewa, held elections in 1980. Robert Mugabe's party won handily. Once in power Mugabe, like many other leaders of independent African states, quickly transitioned Zimbabwe to one-party rule under ZANU-PF.

Decolonization in Britain

When Harold Macmillan delivered his "wind of change" speech in Cape Town in 1960 many Britons cheered his signal that Britain would no longer support the Nationalist government against UN resolutions decrying its apartheid policies. A good deal of media and public opinion rallied in support of what amounted to the prime minister's denunciation of the racist regime. In South Africa, ironically, the speech helped to increase the power of the white supremacist government; whites in other settler colonies had no doubt that it meant that Britain had betrayed its obligations to its "kith and kin" who lived in places like Rhodesia and Kenya. In response to the conviction that the British empire was abrogating its responsibilities to sustain a "British way of life" in Africa, an influential far-right leaning opposition to Conservative rule in Westminster formed in the metropole. A new political lobby called the Monday Club appeared, so called for the day of the week it held its meetings. Made up of a number of prominent politicians and statesmen, club members saw in the decline of empire generally – and the backing away from white settler communities in Africa in particular – an assault on all they held dear. This movement formed the elite political core of what would, in the later 1960s and 1970s, emerge as the New Right in Britain.

The Monday Club championed the rights of white settlers in Africa, first those in Nyasaland, Northern Rhodesia, and Southern Rhodesia who fiercely resisted the dismantling of the Central African Federation, and then, more vociferously, Rhodesians after UDI in 1965. With the backing of powerful media and business interests, Monday Club members who sat in parliament fought every attempt to undermine Smith's government. They forced the biggest split in the Conservative party in more than 20 years over the issue of imposing oil sanctions on Rhodesia. Smith hit upon precisely the fears and anxieties of large numbers of Britons at home and in settler colonies when he asserted in 1966, "if Winston Churchill were alive today, I believe he would probably emigrate to Rhodesia – because I believe that all those admirable qualities and characteristics of the British that we believed in, loved and preached to our children, no longer exist in Britain."[17]

The lament of a lost British ethos was not restricted to white settlers in Africa. At home from the late 1950s onward a great many public intellectuals questioned what had happened to their country in the wake of World War II and especially with the loss of empire. "What's wrong with Britain?" they asked in books, articles, speeches, and interviews. A kind of national malaise emerged in response to Britons' recognition of their weakness on the world stage. Where once their nation had dominated the globe now it performed as a decidedly second fiddle to a much greater power. Imperial decline, many Britons intimated, stood at the heart of all the troubles – economic, political, and cultural – their country faced.

For ordinary Britons the end of empire manifested itself in the appearance of significant numbers of former colonial subjects "at home." In the 1940s no more than 1000 people of color entered the country each year. (Britons had long lumped all such categories of people together, using the term "black" to describe all of them regardless of their actual color.) By the mid-1950s that figure had risen to 20,000 per year. In 1961, the year before Britain placed restrictions on numbers of immigrants, 100,000 black people arrived. In 1951 the numbers of blacks in Britain totaled perhaps 74,500. By 1959 it had grown to 336,000 and reached 500,000 by 1962. These figures set off alarm bells among politicians and government officials, who saw in the flow of black migrants a threat to the identity and social stability of Great Britain. Despite the fact that Britain needed workers to keep the small post-war boom going in the 1950s, and despite the fact that the sluggish birth rate had created fears about population decline, migrants of color from Britain's former and current colonies did not receive a warm welcome, even from official sources. As the Royal Commission on Population put it in its report in 1949, "immigration on a large scale into a fully established society like ours could only be welcomed without reserve if the immigrants were of good human stock and were not prevented by their religion or race from intermarrying with the host population and becoming merged with it."[18]

As this statement and many other pronouncements, official and unofficial, suggest, Britons' anxieties about black migration often appeared as fears of black sexuality and miscegenation. Winston Churchill opposed immigration from the colonies because whites and blacks would engage in sex and intermarry. "We would have a magpie society," he warned, calling up the mixture of colors characterizing the bird, and "that would never do." One sociologist asserted in 1960 that "Africans and West Indians do manifest an exuberance and lack of restraint which is the very reverse of English reserve and self control," while an official of the Conservative party declared in 1963 that "most of them have vile habits. If only they behaved like us it would be all right." A sociological study on West Indian immigrants to Brixton in the 1950s – entitled *Dark Strangers* – delineated the traits, as whites saw them, that differentiated black Britons from white Britons: "primitiveness, savagery, violence, sexuality, general lack of control, sloth, irresponsibility – all these are part of the image." These descriptions and terms could have been lifted right out of any racist eighteenth- or nineteenth-century tract on the nature of Britain's subject peoples.[19]

In the 1940s, 1950s, and early 1960s debates about immigration centered on criminal behavior on the part of blacks in Britain. They focused on what police and civil authorities believed was blacks' disproportionate participation in criminal activities that were sexual in nature and that usually involved white women. Newspapers, and in 1954, the home secretary, reported on the existence of a large class of black men living off the earnings of white prostitutes, pimping for them in numbers far in excess of their proportion to the population as a whole. In 1958 Tory MP Sir Cyril Osborne declared that "the tendency of those crimes to occur among coloured people is a hundred times more per person, than among white people in the London area."[20] Fears of sexuality and miscegenation dominated discussions of the roles played by immigrants and their children in the life of the nation.

Violence carried out by white Britons against people of color sometimes followed what whites perceived as black men transgressing the boundaries that should have set them apart from white women. In August 1958, for instance, whites in Nottingham rioted after "a Jamaican" began a conversation with a white woman in a pub. Between 1500 and 4000 whites took to the streets and burned and looted. A month later, a four-day riot in Notting Hill in West London broke out in protest of blacks settling there. These riots gave the issue of immigration a national prominence it had not enjoyed before, prompting televised debates, editorials in the press, sermons from the pulpits, and opinion polls seeking to gauge Britons' thinking. A Gallup poll taken just after the rioting revealed that 80 percent of the poll's respondents favored controlling immigration of people of color. In July 1962 the Conservative government obliged them, passing into law the Commonwealth Immigration Bill, which restricted the immigration of people of color, though not whites, from commonwealth countries and the colonies of Great Britain.

Distress over the presence of people of color often found voice as a lament about a breakdown in "law and order," collapsing popular anxieties about postwar society into fears about crime and delinquency. By the late 1960s these fears about a somewhat distant and even abstract criminality on the part of blacks combined with unease about personal safety to produce a slightly different racial discourse. Conservatives and traditionalists decried the apparent loss of a British "way of life" as a result of the loss of empire and the immigration of former colonial subjects to their country. In 1968 Enoch Powell, Conservative MP for Ulster, declared the settlement of blacks in Britain to be a threat to the nation's very existence. In his so-called "Rivers of Blood" speech, he foresaw, "like the Roman . . . 'the River Tiber foaming with much blood'" if immigration was not banned outright and the "re-emigration" of former colonial subjects back to their countries of origin not put into effect. He framed his images of violence around a story about an elderly white woman under siege from blacks who had "invaded" her neighborhood. "Eight years ago in a respectable street in Wolverhampton," he recounted, "a house was sold to a negro. Now only one white (a woman old-age pensioner) lives there." Powell suggested an image of "negroes" breeding like rabbits until they had overwhelmed the white population. "With growing fear, she saw one house after another taken over. The quiet street became a place of noise and confusion. Regretfully, her white tenants moved out." Without their protection, Powell intimated, the pensioner found herself at the mercy of her new neighbors. "The day after the last [white tenant] left, she was awakened at 7:00 a.m. by two negroes who wanted to use her phone to contact their employer. When she refused, as she would have refused any stranger at such an hour, she was abused and feared she would have been attacked but for the chain on her door."

This tale utilized elements from the 1950s that emphasized the encroachment upon whites' private spaces by black people and the intimations of miscegenation and hypersexuality among blacks, and mixed them in with new fears about violence and personal safety. Isolated, alone, and unwilling to let rooms in her house out to immigrants, the white woman "is becoming afraid to go out. Windows are broken. She finds excreta pushed through her letterbox. When she goes to the shops, she is followed by children, charming, wide-grinning piccaninnies. They cannot speak English, but one word they know. 'Racialist,' they chant." In this account, in which the British nation is represented by an elderly, frail white woman vulnerable to the sexual and physical threats of black men, Powell conveyed the ominous message that if blacks in Britain were given the same freedoms from discrimination that white Britons enjoyed, then those very freedoms and the British way of life they represented would be destroyed in a traumatic blood-letting.[21]

By the 1970s what were once the racist rantings of a fringe politician became core beliefs held by many Britons and manifested themselves in the ideology of the New Right. Its grassroots support derived from Britons who saw in the immigration of large numbers of people of color from former colonies a threat to the life they had known. Crime in the forms of robbery, "mugging," and urban riots came to the fore in discourses about black settlement, race relations, and social disorder. Black people, and black men in particular, came to stand for illegality, a decidedly "unBritish" trait, conservatives told themselves, despite the fact that government reports showed that "immigrant crime rates were, if anything, a little lower than those for the indigenous population." In any case, union militancy, Ulster politics, and soccer "hooliganism" had been producing a great deal of violence among white Britons for years. For many conservatives, people of color represented the forces responsible for Britain's decline, for the social instability brought on by unemployment and recession, despite all evidence to the contrary. "The nation has been and is still being, eroded and hollowed out from within by implantation of unassimilated and unassimilable populations . . . alien wedges in the heartland of the state," asserted Powell in 1976. By this time, his message of racial intolerance and of black people as the source of danger to British society had been embraced by a majority of Britons and would soon help to produce the electoral victory of the Conservative party in 1979, with Margaret Thatcher at its head. As Alfred Sherman, a prominent right-wing theorist, put it in September of that year on the eve of Thatcher's election as prime minister,

> the imposition of mass immigration from backward alien cultures is just one symptom of this self-destructive urge reflected in the assault on patriotism, the family – both as a conjugal and economic unit – the Christian religion in public life and schools, traditional morality, in matters of sex, honesty, public display, and respect for the law – in short, all that is English and wholesome.[22]

Many Britons had difficulty accepting the end of empire. It symbolized much more than the loss of colonies or even the decline of British power on the world stage. It spoke of a loss of national values, of a "Britishness" defined by long-standing ideas about duty, loyalty, stoicism – that "stiff upper lip" – selflessness, and gentlemanly conduct. The social revolutions of the 1960s threw up new demands pertaining to sexuality, feminism, and popular culture that seemed to overthrow all that previous generations of Britons had known and esteemed. Immigration from Britain's former colonies introduced what many perceived to be an alien, un-British presence. All this was too much to bear for many, many people. They brought Thatcher and her Conservative party to power in 1979.

Thatcher sought to return Britain to a position of world prominence. As she and other conservatives saw it restoring Britain to greatness required first an ideological battle under which all other struggles were subsumed. She maintained the need to resolve the political problems facing the country before the economic ones could be tackled. Thatcher resolved to deal with the "political" problem by introducing what one critic has called "authoritarian populism," a regime characterized by the exercise of the disciplinary powers of the state against what were regarded as disruptive elements in society who had no respect for law and order.[23] At a time when the number of unemployed had reached two million, widespread concerns about law and order enabled Thatcher's government to expand the powers of the police, of the law, and of agencies of surveillance to control and suppress activities and behaviors it deemed dangerous to the state – activities and behaviors construed as "alien," "unBritish," and committed by "outsiders." One such tool was the use of mass "stop and search" powers by the police against black men and women; in Brixton in April 1981 this provoked a major riot. The June debate over a new Nationality Bill demonstrated just how readily white Britons displaced onto racial "others" the consequences of economic problems that seemed to have no solution. MP Ivor Stanbrook declared, "we are in the grip of forces which, because of the large influx of immigrants into Britain, we now seem unable to control. Racial violence is occurring with increasing frequency. The British people are sick at heart about it all." In July 1981 riots involving young people of all races and ethnicities broke out in a number of cities across the nation, prompting *The Financial Times* to declare an "Outbreak of an Alien Disease" in its headline, attributing to the presence of immigrants and their children protests produced by poverty, unemployment, and heavy-handed police measures.[24]

Figure 7.2 Police arrest a young black man at the Notting Hill Carnival riots, 1977. Men and women of West Indian and African origin found themselves increasingly harassed by the police, who had come to equate color with crime.

Economic difficulties and dislocations continued throughout 1981 and into 1982, creating much dissatisfaction in the country with the Conservative party, which, it appeared in early 1982, was in danger of losing its majority in the upcoming 1983 election. Thatcher's popularity had plummeted in the fall of 1981 while that of the newly created alliance between the Social Democratic and Liberal parties soared. In March of 1982 the government of Argentina, acting on its claim that the Malvinas islands – what the British claimed as the Falklands, containing 1800 people of British "stock" and 600,000 sheep – belonged to Argentina, invaded them, throwing Britons at home into a frenzy of jingoistic, neo-imperialist patriotism. It prompted the British government to declare war; and, with victory in the "Falklands War" secured in June 1982, reestablished the popularity of Thatcher and the Conservative party at record levels.

"Great Britain is great again," exulted Thatcher, collapsing victory over the Argentines into that over the unions and her reversal of Labour's efforts in previous decades to nationalize industry. "We have ceased to be a nation in retreat. We have instead a new-found confidence – born in the economic battles at home and tested and found true 8,000 miles away." As one perceptive critic noted of the enthusiasm surrounding the sending of the fleet to re-take the Falklands from the "Argies," "if the Falkland Islanders were British citizens with black or brown skins, spoke with strange accents or worshipped different Gods it is doubtful whether the Royal Navy and Marines would today be fighting for their liberation." Indeed, he pointed out, "most Britons today identify more easily with those of the same stock 8000 miles away . . . than they do with West Indian or Asian immigrants living next door."[25]

The victory over the Argentines gave white Britons something to feel good about; it seemed to mark an end to the humiliation they experienced with the loss of Britain's colonies and its preeminent position in the world. A new mood of decisiveness and strength, which Thatcher identified as the aspects of her ruling style that made her so popular with Britons at a time when economic conditions had only gotten worse, not better, seems to have reflected a nostalgia for imperialism. Britain seemed once again a manly nation in control of its destiny, one that was "not prepared to be pushed around." Its imperial incursion overseas had made it possible for Britons to "rediscover . . . ourselves" and to "recover . . . our self-respect. Britain found herself again in the South Atlantic and will not look back from the victory she has won."[26]

By the end of the 1970s even the most optimistic of observers found little cause for celebration in Africa. Political upheaval and economic disaster seemed to stalk the continent. Even when the fledgling African nations were relatively stable they were subject to the whims of European markets and political happenings, which often compounded their difficulties. There was a deep sense of disappointment that the promises and excitement of the early 1960s seemed to have faded into struggle. Africa's politicians found themselves returning to western banks and financial institutions again and again to try to provide for their ever-expanding populations, and the west seemed to exert as powerful an influence 20 years after the end of colonialism as it did before.

For Britons the decline of the empire was cause for tremendous outpourings of uncertainly and concern. Their own economic struggles were a significant part of this and right-wing politicians were unafraid to play on popular fears of black crime and miscegenation in Britain to win support from their constituents. Race riots were common across the country, as white and black Britons struggled to come to terms with the new multiracial society that they inhabited. This rather gloomy outlook, however, would be transformed over the next few decades as British society moved toward becoming one of the most diverse and open in the west.

Notes

1 Alhaji Sir Abubakar Tafawa Balewa, "Independence Day," accessed December 16, 2014, www.blackpast.org/1960-sir-abubakar-tafawa-balewa-independence-day.
2 Margery Perham, *The Colonial Reckoning* (London: Collins, 1961), 198.
3 "Nigerian High Society Celebrates Independence," *The Guardian*, October 3, 1960.
4 Robert Rotberg, *The Rise of Nationalism in Central Africa: The Making of Malawi and Zambia, 1873–1964* (Cambridge, MA: Harvard University Press, 1965), 303.
5 Andy DeRoche, "Non-Alignment on the Racial Frontier: Zambia and the USA, 1964–68," *Cold War History* 7 (2007), 230.
6 Susan Williams, *Who Killed Hammarskjöld? The UN, the Cold War and White Supremacy in Africa* (New York: Columbia University Press, 2011), 36–37.
7 Quoted in Williams, *Who Killed Hammarskjöld?*, 51.
8 Quoted in Williams, *Who Killed Hammarskjöld?*, 137.
9 Martin Meredith, *The Fate of Africa: From the Hopes of Freedom to the Heart of Despair: A History of Fifty Years of Independence* (New York: Public Affairs, 2005), 183.
10 Meredith, *Fate of Africa*, 184.
11 Charles Hornsby, *Kenya: A History Since Independence* (London: I.B. Tauris, 2013), 109.
12 Oginga Odinga, *Not Yet Uhuru: The Autobiography of Oginga Odinga* (London: Heinemann Educational Books, 1967), 269.
13 Harry Johnston, "The Uganda Protectorate, Ruwenzori, and the Semliki Forest," *The Geographical Journal* 19 (1902), 21.
14 Quoted in Phares Mutibwa, *Uganda Since Independence: A Story of Unfulfilled Hopes* (London: Hurst, 1992), 93.
15 Quoted in Barbara Bush, *Imperialism, Race and Resistance: Africa and Britain, 1919–1945* (London: Routledge, 1999), 273.
16 Ian Smith, "Announcement of Unilateral Declaration of Independence," November 11, 1965, accessed September 30, 2014, www.fordham.edu/halsall/mod/1965Rhodesia-UDI.html.
17 Quoted in Stuart Ward, "Whirlwind, Hurricane, Howling Tempest: The Wind of Change and the British World," in *The Wind of Change: Harold Macmillan and British Decolonization*, eds. Sarah Stockwell and L.J. Butler (Basingstoke, UK: Palgrave Macmillan, 2013), 59.

18 Quoted in Chris Waters, "'Dark Strangers' in Our Midst: Discourses of Race and Nation in Britain, 1947–1963," *Journal of British Studies* 36 (1997): 207–38.
19 Zig Layton-Henry, *The Politics of Immigration: Immigration, "Race" and "Race" Relations in Post-War Britain* (Oxford: Blackwell Publishers, 1992), 31; Bill Schwarz, "Black Metropolis, White England," in *Modern Times: Reflections on a Century of English Modernity*, eds. Mica Nava and Alan O'Shea (London: Routledge, 1996), 196; Waters, "Dark Strangers."
20 Quoted in Paul Gilroy, *"There Ain't No Black in the Union Jack": The Cultural Politics of Race and Nation* (Chicago, IL: University of Chicago Press, 1991), 81.
21 J. Enoch Powell, *Freedom and Reality* (New Rochelle, NY: Arlington House, 1969), 287–88.
22 Quoted in Gilroy, *"Ain't No Black,"* 43; John Solomos, Bob Findlay, Simon Jones, and Paul Gilroy, "The Organic Crisis of British Capitalism and Race: The Experience of the Seventies," in *The Empire Strikes Back: Race and Racism in 70s Britain* (London: Hutchinson in association with the Centre for Contemporary Cultural Studies, University of Birmingham, 1982), 27.
23 See Stuart Hall, *The Hard Road to Renewal: Thatcherism and the Crisis of the Left* (London: Verso, 1988), Chapters 8–9.
24 Solomos, Findlay, Jones, and Gilroy, "Organic Crisis," 29, 31.
25 Quoted in Gilroy, *"Ain't No Black,"* 51–52.
26 Quoted in Susan Kingsley Kent, *Gender and Power in Britain, 1640–1990* (London: Routledge, 1999), 349.

Bibliography

Berry, Sara. *No Condition Is Permanent: The Social Dynamics of Agrarian Change in Sub-Saharan Africa*. Madison: University of Wisconsin Press, 1993.

Bush, Barbara. *Imperialism, Race and Resistance: Africa and Britain, 1919–1945*. London: Routledge, 1999.

Cooper, Frederick. *Africa Since 1940: The Past of the Present*, 2nd edn. Cambridge: Cambridge University Press, 2002.

DeRoche, Andy. "Non-Alignment on the Racial Frontier: Zambia and the USA, 1964–68." *Cold War History* 7 (2007): 227–50.

Falola, Toyin, and Matthew Heaton. *A History of Nigeria*. Cambridge: Cambridge University Press, 2008.

Gilroy, Paul. *"There Ain't No Black in the Union Jack": The Cultural Politics of Race and Nation*. Chicago, IL: University of Chicago Press, 1991.

Hall, Stuart. *The Hard Road to Renewal: Thatcherism and the Crisis of the Left*. London: Verso, 1988.

Hornsby, Charles. *Kenya: A History Since Independence*. London: I.B. Tauris, 2013.

Johnston, Harry. "The Uganda Protectorate, Ruwenzori, and the Semliki Forest." *The Geographical Journal* 19 (1902): 1–39.

Kent, Susan Kingsley. *Gender and Power in Britain, 1640–1990*. London: Routledge, 1999.

Lan, David. *Guns and Rain: Guerrillas & Spirit Mediums in Zimbabwe*. London: James Currey, 1985.

Layton-Henry, Zig. *The Politics of Immigration: Immigration, "Race" and "Race" Relations in Post-War Britain*. Oxford: Blackwell Publishers, 1992.

Meredith, Martin. *The Fate of Africa: From the Hopes of Freedom to the Heart of Despair: A History of Fifty Years of Independence*. New York: Public Affairs, 2005.

Mutibwa, Phares. *Uganda Since Independence: A Story of Unfulfilled Hopes*. London: Hurst, 1992.
Namikas, Lise. *Battleground Africa: Cold War in the Congo, 1960–1965*. Stanford, CA: Stanford University Press, 2013.
"Nigerian High Society Celebrates Independence." *The Guardian*. October 3, 1960.
Odinga, Oginga. *Not Yet Uhuru: The Autobiography of Oginga Odinga*. London: Heinemann Educational Books, 1967.
Parsons, Timothy. *The 1964 Army Mutinies and the Making of Modern East Africa*. Westport, CT: Praeger, 2003.
Perham, Margery. *The Colonial Reckoning*. London: Collins, 1961.
Powell, J. Enoch. *Freedom and Reality*. New Rochelle, NY: Arlington House, 1969.
Schwarz, Bill. "Black Metropolis, White England." In *Modern Times: Reflections on a Century of English Modernity*, edited by Mica Nava and Alan O'Shea, 176–207. London: Routledge, 1996.
Schwarz, Bill. *Memories of Empire*, Vol. I: *The White Man's World*. London: Oxford University Press, 2011.
Smith, Ian. "Announcement of Unilateral Declaration of Independence." November 11, 1965. Accessed September 30, 2014, www.fordham.edu/halsall/mod/1965 Rhodesia-UDI.html.
Solomos, John, Bob Findlay, Simon Jones, and Paul Gilroy. "The Organic Crisis of British Capitalism and Race: The Experience of the Seventies." In *The Empire Strikes Back: Race and Racism in 70s Britain*. London: Hutchinson in association with the Centre for Contemporary Cultural Studies, University of Birmingham, 1982.
Ward, Stuart. *British Culture and the End of Empire*. Manchester: Manchester University Press, 2001.
Ward, Stuart. "Whirlwind, Hurricane, Howling Tempest: The Wind of Change and the British World." In *The Wind of Change: Harold Macmillan and British Decolonization*, edited by Sarah Stockwell and L.J. Butler, 48–69. Basingstoke, UK: Palgrave Macmillan, 2013.
Waters, Chris. "'Dark Strangers' in Our Midst: Discourses of Race and Nation in Britain, 1947–1963." *Journal of British Studies* 36 (1997): 207–38.
Williams, Susan. *Who Killed Hammarskjöld? The UN, the Cold War and White Supremacy in Africa*. New York: Columbia University Press, 2011.

Epilogue

The legacy of colonialism

On April 7, 2011, four elderly Kenyans stood shoulder-to-shoulder in front of the High Court of Justice on The Strand in London. Each held a placard. "We stand with the Mau Mau," read Wambuga wa Nyingi's; "Justice now for the Mau Mau victims of torture," demanded Jane Muthoni Mara's sign; "Human rights for all," proclaimed the one held by Paolo Nzili, while Gitu wa Kahengeri's insisted that the government "Pay up for the British gulag in Kenya." The demonstrators had sued the British government for the treatment they had suffered during the Mau Mau war of the 1950s in colonial detention camps. Nyingi had been badly beaten and disfigured during nine years of imprisonment; Mara repeatedly raped and otherwise sexually abused; and Nzili castrated. "I felt completely destroyed and without hope [in the camps]," the 85-year-old man told reporters.[1] The government acknowledged that torture and abuse had taken place but it declined to accept responsibility. That responsibility had passed to the Kenyan government at the time of independence, it contended.

But the High Court ruled otherwise. The plaintiffs, it decided in 2011, had demonstrated that they had "arguable cases in law" and could go forward with their claims. The government appealed, arguing that far too much time had passed since the events had taken place and that it could not adequately defend itself in such circumstances, given the difficulty in obtaining the witnesses and the records it would need. In October 2012 the High Court once again found against the government and ordered that the case proceed. This time the Mau Mau veterans were not present to hear the judgment but from Nairobi they expressed how "absolutely delighted" they were when they learned of the court's landmark decision. Their delight increased exponentially when, in June 2013, Britain's foreign secretary, William Hague, announced in parliament that the government had decided to settle the claims of some 5000 Mau Mau fighters who, the government recognized, had been "subject to torture and other forms of ill treatment at the hands of the colonial administration" while held in detention camps. "We understand the pain and grievance felt by those who were involved in the events of the Emergency in Kenya," Hague told members of parliament, and "the British government sincerely regrets that these abuses took place, and that they marred Kenya's progress towards independence." Britain agreed to pay out nearly £20 million and help build a memorial in Nairobi commemorating the suffering and injustices undergone by Kenyans at the hands of imperial Britain. In settling the claims of the Mau Mau plaintiffs the government refused to accept any legal liability, arguing that the case did not establish "a precedent in relation to any other former British colonial administration."[2] Others saw things differently; legal commentators have suggested that Britons should expect a number of similar cases to come forward.

The Mau Mau court case serves as an extraordinarily useful exemplar of the complex legacy of British colonialism in Africa. All parties involved, Africans and Britons alike, can find in the decade-long case and its settlement an instructive, affirmative, or cautionary tale. The issues it raises include the legacies of empire; the contemporary significance of colonialism in former British colonies; the uses to which historical memory is put; and the changed demographics of a once nearly all-white mother country.

The court case proved immensely controversial in Britain. Former members of the colonial service viewed it as a witch hunt that ignored the violence committed by Mau Mau fighters against European settlers and "loyal" Kenyans. Supporters of empire insisted that it was an aberration in a system

Figure 8.1 Mau Mau veterans protest outside the residence of the British prime minister, April 2011

that – in the main – benefitted Africans. This approach received backing in the academic world by some prominent scholars, notably Niall Ferguson. Ferguson suggested that the negative aspects of colonialism were outweighed by the positives: the introduction of the English language, British common law, the Protestant religion, and the English system of individual land tenure, amongst others. He and other apologists for empire cite the economic, political, and social breakdown that took place in many African countries in the 1970s in support of their position.

The fact that difficulties occurred after the end of formal colonialism does not mean that colonialism played no role in them. As we saw in the last chapter, economic disasters following the oil embargoes wreaked havoc on the political systems and societies of the former colonies, which did not possess the infrastructure, the personnel, the investment, or the diversity of manufacturing and commerce to withstand massive inflation and recession. Poor leadership in a variety of nations certainly contributed to the problems Africans faced, as fledgling democracies fell to authoritarian rule and dictators in places like Nigeria, Ghana, Uganda, Zimbabwe, Sudan, and Somalia lined their pockets and those of their supporters at the expense of their countrymen and -women. Many of these states failed to provide even basic services for their citizens, and as the economic and financial crises worsened over the 1980s dictators could no longer even keep their cronies and clients satisfied with bribes and official corruption. Their positions became increasingly precarious, prompting rivals to stage coups against governments and states to move against other states. Instability within states and across regions characterized the period from 1973.

A few statistics provide a stark picture of the difficulties African nations faced. Gross national product (GNP) per person in Africa grew by some 2.4 percent a year between 1950 and 1975, and between 1966 and 1976 it grew by 20 percent. But in the next ten years it fell by 20 percent, wiping out all of the gains of the previous years. Sub-Saharan Africans earn, on average, $1 a day, making them the poorest people in the world. To compound these difficulties, the number of people on the continent living in poverty doubled in the years between 1981 and 2002, so that fully half of the world's poor live in sub-Saharan Africa today. Roughly one in seven children in Africa die before they reach the age of five, most often to diseases such as malaria and diarrhea that health authorities, were they available, could prevent and treat. The failure of governments to meet the needs of their people also means that adult literacy rates, which had been rising, have fallen below levels achieved in the years before 1980. If we drill down into the aggregate figures we see that the numbers measuring women's access to education fall behind those of men.

The failures of new African states following decolonization is frequently put down to the inherent incapability of Africans to govern themselves and plays into the rhetoric about backward peoples that characterized so much of Britain's justification for imperialism and colonialism (even if it is expressed more politely today). But those conditions created under colonial rule are precisely the ones that have made it extraordinarily difficult for Africans to succeed since the end of British rule on the continent. British colonies possessed no geographic, historical, ethnic, political, economic, social, or cultural coherence, rendering their successor states artificial entities with little prospect of generating a cohesive national unity. On independence days across Africa, Kikuyu or Fulani were suddenly meant to become "Kenyans" or "Nigerians." Statehood and civil authority had nothing organic to connect them. Moreover, the new African governments inherited the export-oriented extractive economies created by British imperialists, along with the distorted transportation systems that serviced that extraction.

These inheritances rendered new African states weak and vulnerable, and the lack of a sufficiently large, educated political class exacerbated the problems. These leaders and their authoritarian and corrupt governments were tolerated and indeed actively supported by Cold War belligerents from east and west to further their own agendas. In many cases aid to African countries was siphoned directly into the coffers of dishonest, brutal, and even murderous leaders and used to exploit their nations and feather their own nests. Expensive loans compounded the problem by the early 1980s, and governments often ended up paying back far more in interest than they had ever borrowed.

The legacies of colonialism are particularly prominent in cultural aspects of life in Africa today. Children and their parents clamor to learn English, the language of the colonizer – and also the language vital to succeeding in almost any career. Perched on the pediments that surround Nairobi's high-rise buildings, for instance, Kenyans with a little schooling struggle slowly through the *Nation*, one of Kenya's English-language daily newspapers, rather than be seen reading the Swahili *Taifa Leo* and be viewed as "backward" or unintelligent. Intellectuals and writers such as Ngugi wa Thiong'o lament this phenomenon: why, asks Ngugi provocatively in *Decolonizing the Mind*, do we forbid Kenyan children from attending school in traditional dress and expect them to wear the blazers and uniforms of Britain? Thinkers like Ngugi view Kenya's political decolonization and independence in 1963 as only the first step in a process that has yet to fully unfold; Kenyans are still waiting for economic and cultural decolonization, he would argue. He and others have heavily criticized those elites who, they assert, have maintained the ordering of the colonial state and simply replaced white faces with black.

What of the role colonialism continues to play in Africa today? Here the example of Zimbabwe is highly instructive. President Robert Mugabe blames colonialism and neo-colonialism for his country's slide into economic recession in 2008. Zimbabwe may well be the colony where the hand of colonialism fell most heavily, as white settlers maintained control of the state until 1980 (see Chapter 7). The colony never enjoyed the more moderate "indirect rule" that had existed in colonies like Tanganyika or Gold Coast.

For much of the 1980s and 1990s newly independent Zimbabwe was the darling of the development community and a source for tremendous optimism among observers of Africa. It stood as a beacon in southern Africa: South Africa was still in the grip of an increasingly violent apartheid system and Mozambique and Angola were beset with civil war. Under black majority rule Zimbabwe maintained its position as the "breadbasket" of the region; the tourism and mining industries grew steadily; and Zimbabweans enjoyed prosperity brought by a nation free from the sanctions imposed on the Smith regime. The Gukurahundi massacres of Ndebele in the southwest of the country during the mid-1980s were overlooked by Britain and the rest of the international community, for Zimbabwe was "supposed" to succeed. In a gesture reflecting the cordial relations between Britain and Zimbabwe, Queen Elizabeth II knighted Mugabe during his state visit in 1994.

By the late 1990s, however, optimism had waned. Drought, corruption, poor economic policy, and Mugabe's decision to join a war in Congo combined to cause food shortages, popular discontent, and economic instability. The roots of dissatisfaction lay with Zimbabwe's white-owned farms. At the time of the country's political independence in 1980 the positions of privilege that white farmers had enjoyed continued as before. The problem was one that confronted a variety of African nations at independence, Kenya among them: wiping away settlers' legal title to land would make companies wary of investing in Zimbabwe. Settlers, moreover, had the resources and expertise to remain successful and continue sustaining Zimbabwe's economy. By the late 1990s Mugabe was under pressure to do something about the white-owned land, much of which came from veterans of the Rhodesian Bush War (or "Second Chimurenga") who argued that they had sacrificed much in the conflict but had received no reward for their efforts.

As war veterans – many of whom were too young to have actually fought in the war – increasingly demanded more from Mugabe, relations with Britain soured. Mugabe bought off the veterans temporarily with one-time cash payments but he needed a more lasting solution. He told British government officials that they were responsible for funding a program to buy out white farmers. The land question had long been a bone of contention. In the late 1970s it had almost derailed negotiations between Britain and Zimbabwe over the transition to independence. Finally, though, both sides had agreed upon the principle of "willing buyer, willing seller," a policy that protected white farmers from farm seizures. Britain and Zimbabwe agreed to share the responsibility for providing funds to buy out white farmers when they chose to leave, which many did in the 1980s.

But now, in the late 1990s and early 2000s, Tony Blair's Labour government refused to accept responsibility for what Mugabe described as problems caused by colonialism. As Clare Short, the foreign secretary, wrote to the Zimbabwean government, "we do not accept that Britain has a special responsibility to meet the costs of land purchase in Zimbabwe . . . We are a new government from diverse backgrounds without links to former colonial interests. My own origins are Irish, and as you know, we were colonised, not colonisers."[3] Britain's refusal enraged Mugabe. He regarded Cecil Rhodes' disbursement of tens of millions of acres as directly responsible for Zimbabwe's travails, a point he raised frequently and loudly. Upon the loss of British support he pressed forward with land redistribution, an action that caused investors to pull out of the country; their exodus sped up following the passage of "indigenisation" laws that required all companies to demonstrate at least 50 percent Zimbabwean ownership. White farmers deserted in droves, their farms given over to Mugabe's cronies and those to whom he owed favors. Few enterprises remained productive. The Zimbabwean dollar began a freefall that ended in its disuse in favor of the US dollar and South African rand, with inflation officially measured in mid-2008 at a peak of 231 billion percent.

Mugabe blamed the British for interfering in his country, both during the colonial era but also for decades afterward. His charges gained traction from the support given by Blair's government to Mugabe's perennial opponent, Morgan Tsvangirai, the leader of the Movement for Democratic Change. Mugabe depicted his rival as an agent of Tony Blair, who was himself frequently attacked with homophobic slurs. In an effort to tie his opposition to Britain to events that occurred under colonial rule, Mugabe's information minister, Jonathan Moyo, called raids and confiscations of white farms the "Third Chimurenga." Other claims were more outrageous: in 2008, Moyo laid the blame for a cholera outbreak that derived from poor housing conditions and sanitation on Britain. "This is a serious biological-chemical weapon," he charged, "a genocidal onslaught on the people of Zimbabwe by the British [who are] still fighting to recolonise Zimbabwe and using their allies."[4] Within Zimbabwe Mugabe's assault on neo-colonialism and the British effectively deflected attention away from his shortcomings and the failures of his government. The government's nearly total control over the Zimbabwean media made it possible for Mugabe's charges to seem plausible in the minds of his people.

The Mau Mau court case reminds us to think carefully about the nuances of colonialism and their often-simplified depictions in the present day. Few journalists reporting on the Mau Mau case viewed the struggle as anything but a "black versus white" conflict; in fact, as we saw in Chapter 6, it was arguably more a civil war among Kikuyu people. The war has left a bitter legacy in many communities in central Kenya that should not be forgotten in the face of the British aspects of the conflict. But many of these more subtle distinctions have been forgotten as people try to rewrite history to fit their present interests and perceptions.

This effort to manipulate the memory of the colonial period is nothing new. As early as the 1960s people tried to write Mau Mau out of history. For Kenya's first president, Jomo Kenyatta (and indeed for the British), Mau Mau was something to be forgotten. It represented the struggle of poor, oppressed Africans against wealthy elites, white *and* black, something that did not mesh well with his small loyalist ruling class. Kenyatta feared nothing so much as a second outbreak of Mau Mau. It was also a potential stumbling block in the process of nation-building: a Kikuyu "struggle for freedom" was hardly useful material in building the new Republic of Kenya. So Kenyatta, by and large, "forgot" Mau Mau. His close confidant Waruhiu Itote – "General China" – took a different tack, recording Mau Mau for posterity as a nationalist movement fought by all peoples of Kenya; in so doing he ignored much of the reality of the war itself. Mau Mau continues to play a role in Kenyan politics today as Kikuyu nationalists press for a larger slice of the Kenyan pie based on the sacrifices their people made during the 1950s. History is thus often used as a tool to address present circumstances.

Mau Mau should also remind us to avoid sweeping stereotypes about empire. This is especially true when thinking about the men and (some) women who comprised the colonial service. The Mau Mau court case was driven – and had been for a decade before its final verdict – by John Nottingham, a former district officer stationed in central and eastern Kenya during the 1950s. Nottingham had resigned from his posting because of the ill treatment he saw Africans receiving; he chose to become a Kenyan citizen at independence. Men like Nottingham believed sincerely and firmly that the work they were doing in the colonies benefitted Africans. Nottingham remembered some of his colleagues' horrified reactions when they heard of the atrocities committed by British officials during Mau Mau. Arthur Young, for instance, who became police commissioner in Kenya in March 1954, was "knocked for 6" when news of a brutality scandal came out. Tom Askwith, the official in charge of the detention camps, was, Nottingham insists, a man who genuinely believed in the merits of rehabilitation but was unable to successfully achieve his vision, being steamrollered by his less savory colleagues.[5] Some colonial administrators gave countless years of their lives at minimal pay to serve in the colonies. Many, certainly, exhibited the racism of the time and some were misguided in their efforts, a criticism that might just as easily be laid at the door of many non-governmental organization workers today. But those who went too far – the Meinertzhagens, or Gavaghans, in the Kenya case – should not be taken to represent all those others who believed in the worth of their efforts. Plenty of Africans would testify to the efficacy of their work. Others would certainly agree, but perhaps express that they wish Africa could have been left to develop on its own.

Finally, we should not lose sight of the fact that the progress of the Mau Mau court case led the British government to openly and forthrightly acknowledge that the British colonial administration had acted wrongly and maliciously in Kenya during the emergency. Although it refused to accept legal accountability for the abuses that occurred during its colonial past, the government recognized in parliament that British imperialism had done harm to those subject to it, and it expressed its regret that abuse and ill treatment had occurred. This is no small thing, especially for a Conservative government removed by only three decades from the 1982 invasion of the Falkland Islands by an earlier Conservative prime minister. We saw in the last chapter how the jingoism of a newly energized imperialism was articulated – Great Britain was great again, it had recovered its self-respect in a colonial war, it would never again be pushed around by upstarts who challenged its right to act imperially. Now, in 2013, a different sensibility about Britain's imperial history prevailed. What had happened between then and now, between 1980 and 2013, to produce so different a response from a Conservative government?

In a word, multiculturalism. The immigration of former colonial subjects – Indians, Pakistanis, West Indians, and Africans – that had alarmed so many in the 1960s, 1970s, and 1980s had reached a critical mass by 2000, despite the restrictions placed on immigration by various acts passed in 1962, 1971, and 1981. After 1980 the majority of those migrants to Britain classified as "black" in the census came from Africa – mainly Nigeria, Ghana, Uganda, Kenya, Zimbabwe, and South Africa. In 2001, according to the census of that year, 1.15 million "blacks" resided in the United Kingdom, constituting some 2 percent of the total British population. The 2011 census counted 1.9 million "blacks," who made up 3 percent of the total population of 63 million Britons. When other non-white people are added, including those who list themselves as mixed race, the total number of people of color in Britain rises to constitute 13 percent of the population. The trend toward a broadly diverse society will only continue – in 2005, 35 percent of the children born in England and Wales were non-white.

The influx of people from former British colonies and the increasing number of British-born people of color has dramatically altered the complexion of British society, literally and figuratively. The large urban centers boast vibrant multicultural populations whose economic contributions have made them a force to be reckoned with. (This is not to discount the fact that non-white unemployment rates in Britain surpass those of white Britons, or to suggest that racial disparities and racial discrimination do not exist. They most certainly do.) Black and Asian politicians have emerged to take seats on county and borough councils and in parliament. In 1992, six black members of parliament represented various London constituencies; by 1997 their numbers had grown to nine; today, 28 blacks and people of Asian origin sit in the House of Commons. They hold seats in the House of Lords, occupy some of the highest positions in the labor movement, chair the boards of numerous corporations, and run some of the most vital British industries. Politicians of all stripes cannot ignore their new constituents – though, to be sure, far-right groups use them to espouse a "white Britain" policy – and have had to adjust their positions accordingly. Foreign Minister Hague's 2013 announcement to the House of Commons that Britain would pay reparations for the damage it had done as a colonial power amounts to only one – however spectacular – manifestation of the new reality that is multicultural Britain.

There is great irony here. In this book we have considered the complexities of the interactions between Africans and Britons over a 300-year period. This historical analysis leads us to view the Mau Mau settlement as yet another example of the relations between Africans and Britons in which people, ideas, conversations, and debates have traveled from Africa to Britain and from Britain to Africa. As we have seen, they were – and are – complex, nuanced, often difficult to quantify, and infinitely more fascinating as a result. In the Mau Mau settlement we have a perfect example of this phenomenon: an episode driven by Africans that has compelled Britons to consider and question the legacy of their empire today.

Fifty years after the end of the British empire in Africa there are good reasons to believe that the continent is emerging from its difficulties. Even by western standards of gauging "progress" – gross national product, economic growth, per capita income, and the like – we see modest improvement. No other developing area of the world offers as high a return on investment these days as does Africa. Out of the ten fastest growing economies in the world, seven of them are African; many are expanding at a rate of 5 percent per year. Western-educated, Zambian economist Dambisa Moyo attributes the positive trend at least in part to the structural adjustment policies insisted upon by the IMF and World Bank in the 1980s. Stringent market-based policies, she argues, have curbed inflation and provided more transparent, responsible, and steady management of economic and financial resources. These practices have in turn made private investors more confident about investing in African ventures. The drop in HIV/AIDS cases in places like Kenya, Moyo notes, along with the introduction of more democratic elections in many African countries, augers well for the future.

But a different set of practices and ways of measuring them, argues Dayo Olopade, a Nigerian journalist born in the United States, offers us an even more optimistic forecast for the future of what she calls "the Bright Continent." Rather than assessing the situation in Africa by means of formal, western-oriented metrics, she asks us to look at the behaviors and actions of ordinary Africans. For instance, if we were to take the low gross domestic product (GDP) per person in Nigeria at face value, we would assume that Nigerians were too poor to afford cell phones. But in fact more than 60 million Nigerians have cell phone service. "Obviously something doesn't add up," comments a private equity investor, who sees past the formal measures of analyzing economies and has been able to take great advantage of the opportunities for investing in sub-Saharan African business opportunities.[6]

Like Moyo, Olopade sees western aid as playing a decidedly negative role in African affairs, distorting economies, permitting authoritarian leaders to enrich themselves at the expense of their citizens, and inclining governments to such corruption and incompetence that they end up not being able to function at all. But Olopade adds that African communities and individuals have, by their own initiative and utilizing the resources available to them, made their lives better precisely because their governments have failed them.

She calls this phenomenon *kanju* – a Yoruba word that conjurs up "the specific creativity born from African difficulty. . . . an extraordinary capacity for making do." *Kanju* practices and developments have arisen across Africa because governments have been so irresponsible and have let down their citizens to such a degree that everyone understands "you are on your own." Families and communities, not states, are acting to better their living conditions and if they have to break the rules to do so, so be it. The ineffective state, Olopade observes wryly, has "created millions of libertarians."[7] (Unfortunately, this can have tragic unintended consequences. Mistrust of government and foreign assistance has meant that some villagers in West Africa prevented – sometimes by violence – health workers from entering their communities to treat outbreaks of Ebola in 2014. Responding effectively to the scope and scale of the Ebola catastrophe extends beyond most local communities' capabilities.)

One of the most successful examples of *kanju* appears in Kenya and is related to the extraordinary cell phone and internet boom that has hit Africa in the past ten years. Some 80 percent of Africans lack banking services. They do not have a secure place to put their money nor do they have the opportunity to borrow. In 2007 Safaricom introduced M-Pesa to remedy and take advantage of this failure of government to provide basic financial services. In its kiosks across Kenya – 37,000 of them now – cell phone users armed only with an ID, a PIN number, and their phone number can deposit cash – *pesa*, in Swahili – into their mobile phone accounts. They can, similarly, take out cash from any kiosk so that M-Pesa serves as a kind of ATM. The system goes further than merely receiving and dispensing cash, however: it allows individuals and families to build assets safely and securely and to make those assets available to members of their communities hundreds of miles away. Some 65 percent of Kenyan households now utilize M-Pesa, undertaking transactions worth $20 million a day (over $7 billion per year. By comparison, Kenya's GDP in 2013 was $44.1 billion).[8] Hidden from the view of standard western methods of economic analysis, M-Pesa has opened up possibilities that simply did not exist before.

Olopade finds much to be bullish about in the informal sectors of African life where family and community networks rule supreme and she celebrates the working around and breaking of rules that Africans must engage in to make their ways through life. The African middle class, comprised of men and women who have steady work, who have been able to purchase some property, educate their children, and gain access to health care, is flourishing and growing by the day. But she knows well that Africans don't wish to and should not have to resort to the kinds of *kanju* operations that enable them to survive. In the absence of effectual state institutions, private enterprise has had to fill the gap. Networks of individuals, families, and communities have created the material and financial infrastructure and the health and educational services that are making Africa into a continent that attracts private investment and promotes growth. Olopade agrees entirely

Figure 8.2 A Kenyan man uses his cell phone to effect a banking transaction in Nairobi, April 2013

with what Moyo says must happen if Africa is to prosper: create conditions in which private investment and growth will thrive. She finds those conditions in places that Moyo simply doesn't look, given her perspective as a western-trained economist.

In 2011 Myles Osborne journeyed 10,000 miles overland from Mbabane in Swaziland to Marrakesh in Morocco. He spent several months on trucks, buses, camels, bicycles, and one 152-carriage coal train that runs from the depths of the Sahara out to the Mauritanian coast. He first traveled east, through Mozambique, and then back to the west through Zimbabwe, Zambia, and the Democratic Republic of Congo (DRC) before heading due north through Congo-Brazzaville, Gabon, and Cameroon. A short ferry ride into Nigeria's Calabar brought the journey back on land: west to Benin, then north into Burkina Faso, through Mali, Mauritania, and finally up the desolate coast of Western Sahara into Morocco and his destination, Marrakesh. Instead of returning with horrific stories of dangerous border crossings, violent crime, and rampant bribery, he offers memories of a quite different nature: a quiet cup of tea with an immigration officer at the DRC border; a warm reception and place to sleep from a stranger in Ouagadougou, the capital of Burkina Faso; and a grand total of one $4 bribe paid in Gabon near the Cameroon border at Batam at 3 AM.

The journey reveals two inescapable truths about modern Africa. First, we must recognize that much of what we think we know about Africa is determined by what the media tells us. We hear nothing, for example, about middle-class Africans going to work or arguing with their spouses or kids about any number of issues, just as westerners do. Nor do we hear about Africa's success stories. Take Botswana, an example of extraordinary political, economic, and social stability. Blessed with a relatively small population – and aided by the discovery of a huge cache of diamonds just as the British vacated their former colony – the "upper-middle income" Botswana had an adjusted gross national income per capita of $14,650 in 2012, placing it above Mexico and Brazil. Botswana enjoys a strong record of democracy, human rights, and a low level of corruption. But these elements don't fit into the "doomed and backward" Africa stories of the last 100 years, the kind of stories members of the public expect to read when they click on "Africa" on their news websites. Nor are they the subject of much popular non-fiction treating Africa, in which editors demand tales of violence, exoticism, or wild animals. As Binyavanga Wainaina puts it in a famous satirical essay, "Never have a picture of a well-adjusted African on the cover of your book, or in it, unless that African has won the Nobel Prize. An AK-47, prominent ribs, naked breasts: use these."[9]

Second, the journey highlights the reality of Africa today. African governments are accountable in ways that they have never been before. The days of the dictator and of rampant government corruption are numbered, though both still exist in certain places. In Nairobi or Accra thousands of drivers heading into the cities each morning listen to young radio hosts poking fun at their politicians, something that could never have happened in years past. The internet age has played a role in this transformation; young people take to Facebook and Twitter to discuss their leaders and make plans to protest their actions.

These kinds of realities lead us to believe that for perhaps the first time since the 1960s Africa is close to shaking off the weights of colonialism and poor leadership that have plagued the past half-century of the continent's development. We may look back on the Mau Mau settlement as a sort of watershed moment, an event that divides a half-century of independent Africa's difficult history from a new era in which the continent claims its place as a political, economic, cultural, and moral powerhouse.

Notes

1 "Mau Mau Uprising: Kenyans Win UK Torture Ruling," *BBC News*, October 5, 2012, accessed September 17, 2014, www.bbc.com/news/uk-19843719.

2 William Hague, "Statement to Parliament on Settlement of Mau Mau Claims," June 6, 2013, accessed September 17, 2014, www.gov.uk/government/news/statement-to-parliament-on-settlement-of-mau-mau-claims.

3 Richard Bourne, *Catastrophe: What Went Wrong in Zimbabwe?* (London: Zed Books, 2011), 145.

4 "Zimbabwe Blames Cholera on Britain," *Al Jazeera*, December 13, 2008, accessed May 14, 2014, www.aljazeera.com/news/africa/2008/12/20081212112525295564.html.

5 John Nottingham, personal communication, 2012.
6 Quoted in Dayo Olopade, *The Bright Continent: Breaking Rules and Making Change in Modern Africa* (Boston, MA: Houghton Mifflin Harcourt, 2014), 123.
7 Olopade, *Bright Continent*, 20, 31, 41, 50.
8 World Bank, "Kenya," accessed October 1, 2014, http://data.worldbank.org/country/kenya.
9 Binyavanga Wainaina, "How to Write About Africa," *Granta* 92 (2005): 1–4.

Bibliography

Bourne, Richard. *Catastrophe: What Went Wrong in Zimbabwe?* London: Zed Books, 2011.

Clough, Marshall. "Mau Mau and the Contest for Memory." In *Mau Mau and Nationhood: Arms, Authority & Narration*, edited by E. S. Atieno Odhiambo and John Lonsdale, 251–67. Oxford: James Currey, 2003.

Cole, Jennifer. *Forget Colonialism? Sacrifice and the Art of Memory in Madagascar*. Berkeley: University of California Press, 2001.

Ferguson, Niall. *Empire: How Britain Made the Modern World*. London: Penguin, 2003.

Hague, William. "Statement to Parliament on Settlement of Mau Mau Claims." June 6, 2013. Accessed September 17, 2014, www.gov.uk/government/news/statement-to-parliament-on-settlement-of-mau-mau-claims.

"Mau Mau Uprising: Kenyans Win UK Torture Ruling." *BBC News*. October 5, 2012. Accessed September 17, 2014, www.bbc.com/news/uk-19843719.

Moyo, Dambisa. *Why Aid is Not Working and How There is a Better Way for Africa*. London: Allen Lane, 2009.

Olopade, Dayo. *The Bright Continent: Breaking Rules and Making Change in Modern Africa*. Boston, MA: Houghton Mifflin Harcourt, 2014.

Thiong'o, Ngugi wa. *Decolonising the Mind: The Politics of Language in African Literature*. London: James Currey, 1986.

Wainaina, Binyavanga. "How to Write About Africa." *Granta* 92 (2005): 1–4.

World Bank. "Kenya." Accessed October 1, 2014, http://data.worldbank.org/country/kenya.

Index